AF333163

Du Bois on Education

Du Bois on Education

EDITED BY EUGENE F. PROVENZO JR.

ALTAMIRA
PRESS

A Division of
ROWMAN & LITTLEFIELD PUBLISHERS, INC.
Walnut Creek • Lanham • New York • Oxford

ALTAMIRA PRESS
A Division of Rowman & Littlefield Publishers, Inc.
1630 North Main Street, #367
Walnut Creek, CA 94596
www.altamirapress.com

Rowman & Littlefield Publishers, Inc.
A Member of the Rowman & Littlefield Publishing Group
4720 Boston Way
Lanham, MD 20706

12 Hid's Copse Road
Cumnor Hill, Oxford OX2 9JJ, England

Copyright © 2002 by AltaMira Press

All rights reserved. No part of this publication may be reproduced,
stored in a retrieval system, or transmitted in any form or by any
means, electronic, mechanical, photocopying, recording, or otherwise,
without the prior permission of the publisher.

British Library Cataloguing in Publication Information Available

Library of Congress Cataloging-in-Publication Data

Du Bois on education / edited by Eugene F. Provenzo, Jr.
     p. cm.
     Includes bibliographical references (p. 307) and index.
     ISBN 0-7591-0199-X (cloth)—ISBN 0-7591-0200-7 (paper)
     1. Du Bois, W. E. B. (William Edward Burghardt), 1868–1963—Views on
Education. 2. Education—Philosophy. 3. African Americans—Education. I. Provenzo,
Eugene F.

     LB875.D83 D833 2002
     370'.896'073—dc21   2002003241

Printed in the United States of America

♾™ The paper used in this publication meets the minimum requirements of American
National Standard for Information Sciences—Permanence of Paper for Printed Library
Materials, ANSI/NISO Z39.48–1992.

For Warren Button
in recognition of his contributions to the field of Educational Studies and his
patience and tolerance with a young scholar.

Contents

Preface   ix

Introduction   1

Part One: Du Bois's Experience as a Student and Teacher   19

  1. A Negro Schoolmaster in the New South   21

  2. A Negro Student at Harvard at the End of the Nineteenth Century   31

Part Two: Du Bois on Education and Social Power   49

  3. Of the Training of Black Men   51

  4. The Training of Negroes for Social Power   65

  5. The Talented Tenth   75

Part Three: Du Bois on Elementary and Secondary Education   93

  6. The Freedman's Bureau   95

  7. Heredity and the Public Schools   111

  8. Negro Education   123

  9. Does the Negro Need Separate Schools?   133

  10. How Negroes Have Taken Advantage of Educational   145
      Opportunities Offered by Friends

  11. Two Hundred Years of Segregated Schools   157

Part Four: Du Bois, Washington and the Hampton Model   161

  12. Of Mr. Booker T. Washington and Others   163

  13. Hampton   175

  14. Education and Work   179

Part Five: Du Bois and Higher Education — 199

15. Careers Open to College-Bred Negroes — 201

16. Atlanta University — 215

17. Gifts and Education — 233

18. Negroes in College — 235

19. The Negro College — 243

20. The Future of Wilberforce University — 253

21. The Future and Function of the Private Negro College — 277

Part Six: Du Bois, Education and Literature — 287

22. The New Education — 289

Bibliography — 307

Index — 319

About the Editor — 329

Preface

In many ways, I began working on this book during the winter of 1968. At that time, I was a senior in high school at a small private school in upstate New York. It was at the height of the Viet Nam War. Martin Luther King would be assassinated the following April. The same morning I graduated from high school, Sirhan Sirhan shot Robert F. Kennedy.

During the winter of 1968 I had picked up a copy of W. E. B. Du Bois's *The Souls of Black Folks* at a local drug store. I didn't have much money at the time and remember buying the book, in part, because it was cheap and looked interesting. I had a term paper to write for an American history course and thought that it might be exciting to research something to do with black history. I knew almost nothing about Du Bois. I had no idea that he was the first African-American to complete a Ph.D. at Harvard, that he was one of the leaders of the Niagara movement, a founder of the National Association for the Advancement of Colored People (NAACP), an editor for the magazine *The Crisis*, a novelist and children's author, and a leading figure in the international Pan-African movement.

Reading that book was the beginning of an education that continues today. I had been isolated by my Italian, English and Central European immigrant culture from the black experience. At the time, despite my family's liberal sympathies and concerns, and those of my teachers at school, I had no understanding of the complexity or the denigration of the black experience in the United States. Certainly I had read about slavery in my history classes and knew about George Washington Carver and Booker T. Washington, but figures like Du Bois were excluded from my textbooks.

Although my school was proud of its liberal/democratic tradition, there were no black or other minority students. To my knowledge, none had ever attended the school. I lived in a totally segregated neighborhood. My only regular contact with a black family was through a close friend of my mother's. Her name was Irene Howard. She had met my mother when they were working on their elementary teaching degrees. Her husband, Robert, had worked his way through the fire department in Buffalo, becoming its first black Captain and eventually its first black Chief. They lived with their daughter, Jeannie, in a middle-class and racially segregated neighborhood in the city. As far as I know, no blacks lived in suburban Buffalo at that time. Sometime during the summer of

1961 or 1962, I remember the Howards coming to dinner one Sunday evening. A nervous neighbor asked me several days later if my parents were planning to sell the house.

As I read *The Souls of Black Folks*, I was introduced to a totally new intellectual and cultural universe that I had no reason to know existed up until that time. I met a gifted black intellectual and thinker talking about issues at the beginning of the twentieth century that still had extra-ordinary meaning and power in my own era. I realized, without hesitation, the power of Du Bois and his writing. Through his work I was transported to the poverty of black belt Georgia. I was made aware that Booker T. Washington's ideas and the Tuskegee model were by no means universally accepted. I followed a young college student's steps through Tennessee as he sought out a rural school to teach in during the summer recess; I listened to the sad reflections of a man who had lost his first-born son; and for the first time, I came across what undoubtedly remains Du Bois's most profound and succinct reflection: "The problem of the twentieth century is the problem of the color-line,—the relation of the darker to the lighter races of men in Asia and Africa, in America and the islands of the sea."

In college I read his *Autobiography* and later *Dusk of Dawn*. At first I thought of Du Bois only as an activist and polemicist—a founder of the National Association for the Advancement of Colored People and the editor of the magazine *The Crisis*. In graduate school I discovered *The Suppression of the African Slave Trade* and realized that I was dealing with a pioneering and innovative historian. I suppose, although the memory is not completely clear, that it was not until I was well into my professional career that I began to discover Du Bois the pioneering sociologist. In retrospect, this oversight—perhaps better described as pure ignorance on my part—seems incredible. Through the study of sociology—through the careful and scientific enumeration of the conditions of black Americans—he felt the greatest potential existed to address the American problem of race.

In 1978 Dan S. Green and Edwin D. Driver edited a pioneering collection of Du Bois's work on sociology, *W. E. B. DuBois: On Sociology and the Black Community*. Green and Driver's work was important for a number of reasons. To begin with, it made available to sociologists and other scholars a wide selection of Du Bois's works, which were out of print and difficult to obtain. In addition, the collection and its introduction established Du Bois's extraordinarily important contribution to the field of American Sociology.

As I read Du Bois's sociological work, going back to government reports, studies like *The Philadelphia Negro*, the reports of the Atlanta

Conferences and finally, the sociological study of the Georgia Negro he and his students did as part of the exhibit of the Negro Race for the 1900 World's Fair in Paris, I also realized for the first time the extent to which Du Bois was a major educational writer and theorist. Remarkably, this was an aspect of Du Bois's work that has been largely overlooked. With the exception of Du Bois's debate with Booker T. Washington about the Tuskegee model, a collection of essays on higher education edited by Herbert Aptheker in 1973, a few doctoral dissertations, and an excellent recent article by Derrick R. Alridge that deals with his educational writings largely from the perspective of the 1930s, little work has been done on Du Bois as an educational thinker and writer.

I am attempting to correct this situation in this book and to extend our understanding of Du Bois and his contribution to the field of education. Like Green and Driver's work, it is an attempt to bring to the attention of scholars and more general readers a neglected but critically important aspect of Du Bois's work.

In addition to this preface, an introductory essay provides an overview of Du Bois and of the significance of his educational writings. Five selections from Du Bois's educational writings follow: the first recounts Du Bois's own educational experience, not only as a student, but as a young teacher; the second set of selections focuses on his general essays on the relationship between education and social power; the third on his critiques and studies of elementary and secondary education; and the fourth and final selections are drawn from his writings on higher education. A general research bibliography, together with a comprehensive bibliography of Du Bois's educational writings, concludes the book.

It should be noted that throughout the introduction and introductory sections of this book I use the term *Negro* in reference to African-Americans, as well as the term *black*. My choice to use one term in place of the other is largely determined by its context—i.e., when Du Bois makes references to the "Negro" or the "Negro Problem," then I tend to use the term (in this case, *Negro*) in a way that reflects or is consistent with Du Bois's use. Often choosing the right term to use was a challenge, and the selection made less than ideal.

Miami, Florida
October 2001

Acknowledgments

I would like to thank the many individuals and institutions that have contributed to the development of this work. The staff of the Moorland-Spingaren Research Center at Howard University; the staff of the Schomberg Research Center, City Libraries of New York; the Library of Congress; and, in particular, the Interlibrary Loan division at the Otto G. Richter Library, University of Miami, have all been extremely helpful. Special thanks go to Gary N. McCloskey, O.S.A., and Spencer Crew and Lonnie Bunch of the Smithsonian Institution. Very special thanks go to Victoria Carcamo—work-study student extraordinaire—who helped in scanning and proofing many of the essays and articles included in this volume. Catherin Curry provided technical help that was invaluable in the completion of the project. As always, Alan Whitney helped with computers. Finally, my thanks go to Asterie Baker Provenzo—fellow scholar, editor, friend and wife.

The material excerpted in this volume from the works of W. E. B. Du Bois is reprinted with the permission of David Graham Du Bois.

Introduction

William Edward Burghardt Du Bois (1868-1963) is not typically thought of as an educational writer. Compared to other areas of his scholarship, relatively little attention has been paid to his work in the field of education. This is a remarkable oversight. Like Derrick P. Alridge, I believe that "Du Bois was one of the most significant educational thinkers of the twentieth century and that his many works and educational views have much relevance to the social, economic, and political realities of contemporary African-American life" (Alridge 1999, 359).

This book tries to correct this situation by compiling Du Bois's major educational writings and placing them in a critical and historical context. The works that are included in this volume cover a period of approximately sixty years. They reflect the extraordinary vitality and complexity of Du Bois as an educational thinker and social activist.

William Edward Burghardt Du Bois was born in Great Barrington, Massachusetts, on February 23, 1868, and died in Accra, Ghana, in 1963. He showed great promise early in his education. After graduating from high school in Great Barrington in 1884, he attended Fisk University in Nashville, Tennessee, completing his B.A. there in 1888. In the fall of that same year, he entered Harvard University as a junior, and graduated *cum laude* from Harvard in 1890.

From 1892 to 1894, Du Bois attended graduate school at the Frederic Wilhelm University in Berlin, where he studied history and economics. He came back to the United States in 1894 to pursue doctoral studies at Harvard. In 1895 he became the first African-American to receive a Ph.D. from Harvard University.

His doctoral thesis, *The Suppression of the African Slave Trade in America*, remains the definitive work on the subject. It is the first volume in Harvard's Historical Series. At Harvard and in Berlin, Du Bois studied with luminaries ranging from Max Weber to George Santayana and William James.

In 1894 he became a professor of Latin and Greek at Wilberforce University in Ohio where he met his first wife, Nina Gomer. In 1896 he married Gomer and assumed a position as an instructor of sociology at the University of Pennsylvania. It was at the University of Pennsylvania that he conducted his monumental work *The Philadelphia Negro*. From 1897 to 1910, Du Bois worked as a professor at Atlanta University, where he took responsibility for organizing the school's conference on Negro issues. Du Bois made it into what is widely considered the most important sociological research project on black culture and society to emerge from the late nineteenth and early twentieth centuries in the United States (Du Bois 1903).

In 1910 Du Bois left Atlanta University to take a position as the Director of Publications and Research at the newly organized National Association for the Advancement of Colored People (NAACP). He continued to work at the NAACP until 1934, when disagreements over editorial policies lead him to resign his position. At that time, he returned as a professor to Atlanta University.

By the late 1940s, Du Bois found himself increasingly alienated from American culture and politics. Considering himself a "socialist" throughout most of his life, he became increasingly radicalized. In April of 1950 he founded and was elected the Chairman of the Peace Information Center. The purpose of the group is to disseminate information about the international peace movement and more specifically to prohibit the use of atomic weapons on a worldwide basis. Du Bois quickly came under attack as part of the anti-Communist campaign in the United States. On February 9, 1951, he was indicted under the Foreign Agents Registration Act of 1938 for his work with the Peace Information Center. Tried as "an agent of a foreign principal," he was eventually acquitted.

By the time he reached his early nineties, Du Bois believed that capitalism could not reform itself and was doomed to destruction, and that Communism was the only way of life that he wished to be part of. In 1961, at the age of ninety-three, he joined the Communist Party. With his second wife, Shirley Graham, whom he had married in 1951, Du Bois accepted the invitation of Kwame Nkrumah to come to Ghana and work on an "Encyclopedia Africana."

Du Bois remained in Ghana the rest of his life, becoming a Ghanian citizen. He died in Accra on August 27, 1963, at the age of ninety-five, just hours before the great Civil Rights march in Washington, D.C. At the beginning of the march, before Martin Luther King Jr. made his famous "I Have a Dream" speech and following a song by Odetta, Roy Wilkins, the Executive Secretary of the NAACP announced the passing of Du Bois, explaining that

> Regardless of the fact that in his later years Dr. Du Bois chose another path, it is incontrovertible that at the dawn of the twentieth century his was the voice calling you to gather here today in this cause. (Quoted by Lewis 1993, 2)

There is an obvious irony—one that Du Bois would almost certainly have appreciated—that he should leave the earth just hours before perhaps the most important symbolic event in the history of the Civil Rights movement began. With his death one era was coming to an end and a new one was beginning.

W. E. B. Du Bois as Educator

Cornel West has pointed out that W. E. B. Du Bois was first and foremost "a black New England Victorian seduced by the Enlightenment ethos and enchanted with the American Dream" (West 1999, 1967). His views on education were certainly shaped by his experience as a young boy growing up in Great Barrington, Massachusetts.

Du Bois describes in his autobiography *Dusk of Dawn*, how the black community in which he lived consisted of "perhaps twenty-five, certainly not more than fifty, colored folk in a population of five thousand" (Du Bois 1986, 560). His education took place in integrated schools, where he described how he was presented as a student with a simple curriculum involving: "reading, writing, spelling and arithmetic; grammar geography and history. We learned the alphabet; we were drilled rigorously on the multiplication tables and we drew accurate maps. We could spell correctly and read clearly" (Du Bois 1986, 562).

In high school, Du Bois recalled experiencing some social and racial discrimination, although less than the Irish in his community. Discrimination was mostly based on social and economic class, although he did recall in a number of autobiographical accounts how a young girl, new to Great Barrington, rejected his exchange of a valentine card because of his color (Du Bois 1986, 563).

Du Bois was encouraged by his high school principal, Frank Hosmer, to take the college preparatory course. On graduating, he found himself wanting to go to Harvard University not because he really knew anything about the school, but, as he explained, because "it was the greatest and oldest college and therefore I thought it was the one I must attend" (Du Bois 1986, 568).

Du Bois's early education in Great Barrington undoubtedly shaped his adult views on the role and importance of education. Raised by a single parent on the edge of poverty, school became the primary means of personal advancement for Du Bois. Free public education allowed him the means by which to compete for the scholarships that eventually sent him on to college at Fisk and Harvard.

While Du Bois saw education as a means of social, he also saw it as key to the process of disempowering individuals. Well ahead of other figures in the field of sociology and education, Du Bois understood that education was a two-edged sword, which could be used either to liberate or subjugate specific social and cultural groups. In his 1903 essay, "The Training of Negroes for Social Power," for example, he wrote that many people in the United States are interested in training the Negro "as a subject caste, as men to be thought for, but not to think; to be led, but not to lead themselves" (page 66 of this book).

Du Bois makes clear that the "Negro problem" was largely a result of the racial caste system and that ignorance, crime and poverty in black culture could only be overcome if African-Americans, as a people, were given responsibility for their own lives. Du Bois defined "the Negro problem" as being not just a problem of illiteracy, but instead: "a deeper ignorance of the world and its ways, of the thought and experience of men; an ignorance of self and the possibilities of human souls" (page 67 of this book). For Du Bois, this "deeper ignorance" could

> be gotten rid of only by training; and primarily such training must take the form of that sort of social leadership which we call education. To apply such leadership to themselves, and to profit by it, means that negroes would have among themselves men of careful training and broad culture, as teachers and teachers of teachers.... It is, therefore, of crying necessity among negroes that the heads of their educational system—the teachers in the normal schools, the heads of high schools, the principals of public systems, should be unusually well trained men; men trained not simply in common school branches, not simply in the technique of school management and normal methods, but trained beyond this, broadly and carefully, into the meaning of the age whose civilization it is their peculiar duty to interpret to the youth of a new race, to the minds of untrained people. Such educational leaders should be prepared by long and rigorous courses of study similar to those which the world over have been designed to strengthen the intellectual

powers, fortify character, and facilitate the transmission from age to age of the stores of the world's knowledge. (page 67 of this book)

Du Bois believed that only a selected few, "not the majority of men," were capable of this "higher training."

This is the essence of Du Bois's idea of "the talented tenth." Articulated in detail in an article in the second chapter of the 1903 book *The Negro Problem*, entitled "The Talented Tenth," Du Bois argued that

> The Negro race, like all races, is going to be saved by its exceptional men. The problem of education, then, among Negroes must first of all deal with the Talented Tenth; it is the problem of developing the Best of this race that they may guide the Mass away from the contamination and death of the Worst, in their own and other races. (page 76 of this book)

Du Bois saw this process as one that was both complex and difficult. He was convinced that culture and civilization for the Negro would only be realized by the masses through the example of a talented leadership.

This leadership would be trained in the country's colleges and universities:

> The best and most capable of their youth must be schooled in the colleges and universities of the land. We will not quarrel as to just what the university of the Negro should teach or how it should teach it—I willingly admit that each soul and each race-soul needs its own peculiar curriculum. But this is true: A university is a human invention for the transmission of knowledge and culture from generation to generation, through the training of quick minds and pure hearts, and for this work no other human invention will suffice, not even trade and industrial schools. (pages 80-81 of this book)

Du Bois did not think that there should be a single model of education for the Negro. Likewise, he argued that education was much more than just schools. For him education was "that whole system of human training within and without the school house walls, which molds and develops men" (page 86 of this book).

Education was dependent on family and group life, the training found in one's home and daily life and in one's social class. Significantly, despite his famous debate with Booker T. Washington about the importance of industrial education in the education of blacks, Du Bois did not necessarily oppose its appropriate use. As he explained:

I believe that next to the founding of Negro colleges the most valuable addition to Negro education since the war, has been industrial training for black boys. Nevertheless, I insist that the object of all true education is not to make men carpenters, it is to make carpenters men; there are two means of making the carpenter a man, each equally important: the first is to give the group and community in which he works, liberally trained teachers and leaders to teach him and his family what life means; the second is to give him sufficient intelligence and technical skill to make him an efficient workman; the first object demands the Negro college and college-bred men—not a quantity of such colleges, but a few of excellent quality; not too many college-bred men, but enough to leaven the lump, to inspire the masses, to raise the Talented Tenth to leadership; the second object demands a good system of common schools, well-taught, conveniently located and properly equipped. (page 88 of this book)

Education was essential in Du Bois's mind because it was the principal means available for black empowerment. Along with the ballot, it would defend the Negro from a "second slavery."

Du Bois advocated the concept of a meritocracy. His views were clearly elitist. They were not, however, undemocratic and provide an important counterpoint to the "Hampton Model" of education advocated by Samuel Chapman Armstrong and his protégé, Booker T. Washington.

The Hampton Model

The most prominent model of education for African-Americans to emerge out the second half of the nineteenth century was the creation of Samuel Chapman Armstrong and Booker T. Washington. Known as the Hampton Model, this system, unlike the Freedman schools established in the wake of the Civil War, did not challenge traditional social power. Instead, its accomodationist approach established an inferior set of expectations for blacks in higher education—ones which largely contradicted Du Bois's ideas of an elite educated black leadership class or "Talented Tenth."

Traditionally, Hampton has been described as a trade or technical/industrial school. In fact, as the educational historian James Anderson has pointed out, it was founded and maintained as a normal school for the training of teachers. During its first twenty years, according to Anderson, approximately 84 per cent of its 723 graduates became teachers. Hampton did not offer a trade certificate until 1895. In 1900 only 45 of its 656 students were enrolled in the trade school program and only 4 students were listed as majoring in agriculture (Anderson 1988, 33-34).

Hampton did not grant a bachelor's degree as part of its program. Admission was not dependent on the completion of a secondary school degree. As a normal school, Hampton took students who had completed an elementary school program and gave them two years of coursework that provided them with the training necessary to become elementary school teachers. While training in manual and shop skills was provided to both male and female students at Hampton, and later at Tuskegee, as part of its "industrial" model, its actual purpose was not, according to Anderson, to develop skilled workers in these areas, but instead to inculcate into these future teachers the importance of hard work and the "dignity of labor." In turn, it was assumed that when black graduates took positions as teachers throughout the South, they would communicate these values to the children whom they taught (Anderson 1988, 34).

Hampton provided the template for Tuskegee. Booker T. Washington, its founding principal, was born a slave on April 5, 1856, on a plantation in Franklin County, Virginia. From 1872 to 1875, he attended Hampton. Following his graduation he taught school for two years in Malden, West Virginia, and then studied at Wayland Seminary, in Washington, D.C. In 1879 he returned to Hampton as an instructor. Washington eventually worked as Chapman's secretary, and through his sponsorship in 1881 became the head of a state sponsored industrial training school for blacks in Tuskegee, Alabama.

In many regards, Washington was a remarkable figure. Poorly educated compared to Du Bois, he was an extraordinarily astute politician. Using Tuskegee as his political base, by the middle of the 1890s he had become the most prominent black leader in America. Much of his influence was a result of his ability to get along with conservative Southern leaders and Northern white philanthropists. Nowhere is this clearer than his famous 1895 Cotton States Exposition speech in Atlanta, Georgia, in which he renounced the demand for immediate social equality for blacks. As he argued, while the future of blacks and whites were inevitably linked, "in all things that are purely social we can be separate as the fingers, yet one as the hand in all things essential to human progress."

Washington's speech, which came to be known as the "Atlanta Compromise," established him as the principal spokesman of the black community, despite the fact that it was perceived as highly problematic by many blacks. James Anderson has perceptively argued that the Hampton-Tuskegee philosophy, upon which the speech was based, was not in fact a great compromise. Instead, according to him, "it was the logical extension of an ideology that rejected black political power while recognizing that the South's agricultural economy rested on the backs of black agricultural workers" (Anderson 1988, 44).

Contrary to what many people believe, the rise of industrial education in the 1880s—i.e., the Hampton-Tuskegee model—did not represent the dominant form of education in black normal schools and colleges throughout the country. While there was an acceptance throughout many of the black normal schools and liberal arts schools of the usefulness of manual training for certain students, this curriculum was not seen as a means of developing a viable black leadership (Anderson 1988, 66-67).

Missionary leaders such as Thomas J. Morgan and William Hayes Ward argued that the Hampton-Tuskegee model undermined the democratic rights of Southern black students by assuming that they were destined for subordinate working roles in the Southern economy. In an 1895 article in the *Independent*, Ward noted that "the primary motivation of the white men in the South who urge most strongly the industrial education of the Negroes, is the conviction in their minds that all the Negro needs to know is how to work. This proceeds upon the assumption that the race is doomed to servitude" (Anderson 1988, 68). Ward urged the establishment of technical departments and schools "to develop among them architects, artists, engineers, master mechanics, superintendents of mines, overseers of mills," and so on (Anderson 1988, 69).

While black educational leaders may have rejected the Hampton-Tuskegee model, American political, business and philanthropic leaders including Ulysees S. Grant, Ruther B. Hayes, James A. Garfield, Theodore Roosevelt, William Howard Taft, Woodrow Wilson, Andrew Carnegie, John D. Rockefeller Jr., Julius Rosenwald, George Eastman, Charles Eliot, Jabez L. M. Curry and Clark Howell viewed the model as desirable (Anderson 1988, 72). Washington's rise to prominence as a result of the Atlanta Compromise speech evidently breathed new life into the model.

Du Bois did not immediately engage Washington in a debate over the Hampton-Tuskegee model or the Atlanta Compromise speech. Evidence suggests that he did not want to alienate Washington—then the most powerful black leader in America. In addition, it seems that Du Bois was interested in leaving the door open to some form of compromise.

Whatever the case, Du Bois abandoned virtually any possibility of working with Washington and the "Tusekegee Machine" with the publication of his 1903 work *The Souls of Black Folks. The Souls of*

Black Folks includes a wide range of essays, many of which had been previously published in magazines and journals. Many dealt with education.

The most important chapter included in *The Souls of Black Folks* is the essay by Du Bois entitled "Of Mr. Booker T. Washington and Others." Specifically, Du Bois argues that as a result of Washington's policies three things occurred: (1) the disfranchisement of the Negro; (2) the legal creation of a distinct status of civil inferiority for the Negro; and (3) the steady withdrawal of aid from institutions for the higher training of the Negro. According to Du Bois:

> These movements are not, to be sure, direct results of Mr. Washington's teachings; but his propaganda has, without a shadow of doubt, helped their speedier accomplishment. The question then comes: Is it possible, and probable, that nine millions of men can make effective progress in economic lines if they are deprived of political rights, made a servile caste, and allowed only the most meager chance for developing their exceptional men? If history and reason give any distinct answer to these questions, it is an emphatic No. (pages 168-169 of this book)

Du Bois saw Washington's actions as being essentially contradictory. While he was supposedly striving to create Negro artisans, businessmen and property owners, he did so while allowing them to be deprived of the right of suffrage. He "insists on thrift and self-respect," explained Du Bois, but accepts the assignment of an inferior status to blacks, which Du Bois saw as sapping "the manhood" of the race. Finally, Washington advocated common school and industrial training for blacks, but discouraged the development of black higher education, even though this was the source of teachers for the schools.

Those opposing Washington and his policies, according to Du Bois, asked for three things: (1) The right to vote; (2) Civic equality; and (3) The education of youth according to ability (page 169 of this book). Du Bois saw the results of Washington's policies as having

> tended to make the whites, North and South, shift the burden of the Negro problem to the Negro's shoulders and stand aside as critical and rather pessimistic spectators; when in fact the burden belongs to the nation, and the hands of none of us are clean if we bend not our energies to righting these great wrongs. (page 172 of this book)

Du Bois called on the "black men of America" to oppose Washington. He concluded the chapter by arguing:

By every civilized and peaceful method we must strive for the rights which the world accords to men, clinging unwaveringly to those great words which the sons of the Fathers would fain forget: "We hold these truths to be self-evident: That all men are created equal; that they are endowed by their Creator with certain unalienable rights; that among these are life, liberty, and the pursuit of happiness." (page 173 of this book)

Du Bois and Higher Education

Du Bois's scathing criticism of Washington in *The Souls of Black Folks* represented the greatest challenge the "Tuskegee Machine" had faced. By the beginning of the First World War, as a result of Du Bois's efforts, and those of other black leaders, Washington's model had been overturned. What Du Bois had done was demand the political and social empowerment of American blacks.

Education, and in particular higher education, was key to realizing his goal. Earlier, I introduced Du Bois's idea of the "Talented Tenth." The question arises as to what role higher education would play in the creation of an elite leadership group? How have these views evolved over the course of time?

Du Bois's views on higher education have been collected together by Herbert Aptheker in *The Education of Black People: Ten Critiques 1906-1960* (1973). This book, which is essentially a compilation of essays on higher education by Du Bois, is based on an unpublished manuscript, "Seven Critiques of Negro Education, 1908-1938," which Du Bois, then Chairman of the Sociology Department at Atlanta University, had submitted to the University of North Carolina Press. The project was a collection of essays dealing with higher education, spanning a period of thirty years. Many were addresses given at colleges and universities.

Taken as a whole, the essays included in *The Education of Black People*—several of which are included in this volume—provide a valuable overview of Du Bois's views on higher education. Throughout them Du Bois emphasized the idea of "the college as the true founding stone of all education, and not as some would have it, the kindergarten" (Aptheker 1973, 3).

In the first of the essays in the Aptheker collection, nearly thirty-five years after the fact, Du Bois described himself as causing an "outrage" in 1906 at Hampton Institute with his speech on "The Hampton Idea." Essentially, Du Bois continued the theme from his essay on the "Talented Tenth" that "we must give to our youth as training designed above all to make them men of power, of thought, of trained and cultivated taste; men who know wither civilization is tending and what its means" (Aptheker 1973, 14).

Du Bois continued his attack on the Hampton model when he spoke at Fisk University in 1908—twenty years after his graduation. In the 1906-07 catalogue, Fisk advertised a new department of "Applied Science." The General Education Board provided money for the program. An associate professor of agriculture and an associate professor of mechanical arts were added to the faculty. Associated "industrial art" courses were soon added to the curriculum. Du Bois recalled many years later how he felt that:

> On the face of it, the proposed department did not look genuine. First of all it was going to teach agriculture without a farm and on the limestone rocks of the city of Nashville. In the second place only two teachers were detailed for all this work, and they were teaching not simply college students but high school students and even elementary students. There was no machinery or adequate laboratory. (Aptheker 1973, 18)

For Du Bois, the industrial curriculum at Fisk seemed "a Surrender and a Lie" (Aptheker 1973, 18). While he argued that there were many benefits to be gained from the vocational training of black children, industrial training could not be allowed to take the place of college education for blacks (Aptheker 1973, 28). Du Bois called for Fisk to refocus its attention on a true collegiate curriculum, rather than a poorly conceived and funded industrial model of education. As he explained:

> The vocational training of children is one of the greatest and most promising movements of modern days. But the place for that kind of training is not in the college department of Fisk University. To do this would be to use a surgeon's knife for chopping wood. The world needs wood but it needs axes for cutting it. There are good and deserving schools for trade teaching. There are but two or three colleges. These colleges are devoted to higher training and they must not be diverted from it. (Aptheker 1973, 28)

In this, and other critiques of industrial education and the Hampton model, Du Bois emphasized the idea of the cultivation of "the Talented Tenth" and the "College-bred Negro." In 1910 he spoke in Brookline, Massachusetts, before potential white benefactors to Atlanta University. In his speech, "The College-bred Community," he articulated the notion of the college—and more specifically, the Negro college—as "a center where knowledge of the past connects with the idea of the future" (Aptheker 1973, 38).

Every community, according to Du Bois, whether black or white, needed to have its contingent of college-educated individuals. Their training would provide the "foundation" of black culture. For him, the black colleges and universities would create the necessary social and cultural perspective and insight required to advance the culture.

Du Bois and the Student Revolt at Fisk

Du Bois had largely withdrawn from higher education issues when he left Atlanta University in 1910 to head up publications and research at the NAACP. Beginning in 1924, he emerged as a critical leader in the protest for greater student rights among black college students during the 1920s. In particular, Du Bois attacked what was taking place at his alma mater Fisk University.

In June 1923, Du Bois was invited by Fisk's Alumni Association to speak at his daughter Yolande's graduation the following year. The head of the Alumni Association left the choice of a topic open to Du Bois (Lewis 2000, 132). Du Bois spoke on June 1, 1924. His speech was a direct attack on Fisk's increasingly restrictive educational program, and more specifically on the policies of the school's white president, Fayette A. McKenzie.

The repercussions from his speech were immediate. The school's president resigned. The industrial education program, which Du Bois objected to, was withdrawn—not without consequences. Local support from the leadership in Nashville, as well as Northern philanthropic support, was withdrawn, leading Du Bois to speculate many years later that his speech had, at least in part, contributed to the school's decline (Aptheker 1973, 30).

Du Bois's criticism of Fisk in 1924 was not so much focused on curricular issues, but instead on the personal policies and administration of the school's president. President McKenzie began his career in education working as a teacher with Shoshone Indians in Wyoming. At Fisk he conducted a successful million-dollar campaign for the school's endowment. The Rockefeller family's General Education Board (GEB) provided an initial $500,000, and an additional $250,000 came from the Carnegie Corporation. The remaining $250,000 was raised from friends and alumni (Lewis 2000, 133).

McKenzie was an autocrat and racist. He forbid fraternities and sororities on campus, abolished student government, eliminated the school's newspaper (the *Herald*), expelled students for infractions without due process, made chapel compulsory, and banned smoking and drinking, as well as dating. Conservative dress codes were put into place, and men and women were not even allowed to walk together across campus (Lewis 2000, 133).

Faculty hiring and promotion was based on loyalty to McKenzie. Under McKenzie, Fisk had become an increasingly accomodationist institution serving the needs of Northern philanthropists and the local white Nashville community. Racial separation was required at public events sponsored by the university. Thus, at a Nashville concert to launch the European tour of the men's glee club, separate ticket windows were set up for blacks and whites. The faculty was seated in racially segregated seats. Paul Cravath, a prominent New York lawyer who served on Fisk's board of trustees, declared at a fund-raiser in Cleveland (to which no alumni were invited) that "complete [racial] separation" was the "only solution to the Negro problem" (quoted by Lewis 2000, 134).

Du Bois saw Fisk and its administration as being fundamentally dishonest. In his 1924 alumni address, he explained:

> Fisk University is not taking an honest position with regard to the Southern situation. It has deliberately embraced a propaganda which discredits all of the hard work which the forward looking fighters for Negro freedom have been doing. It continually teaches its students and constituency that this liberal white South is in the ascendancy and that it is ruling; and that the only thing required of the black man is acquiescence and submission.... Fisk University is choking freedom. Self knowledge is being hindered by refusal of all initiative to the students. Fisk is not teaching the truth about the race problem. (Apthetker 1973, 49, 51)

As a result of editorials and articles inspired by the situation at Fisk, considerable national attention was given to the question of the role of Negro colleges in American society and the rights of the students who attended them.

From his office at the NAACP in New York, Du Bois took the remarkable step of publishing the *Fisk Herald*. In addition, he published articles critical of Fisk, including "The Dilemma of the Negro" in the *The American Mercury* and a brief essay in the February 1925 issue of *The Crisis*, "Gifts and Education." In this piece, Du Bois lamented the fact that "the only hope for Negro education lies in the gift of the [white] rich" (page 233 of this book). Funding for schools needed to come from taxes and not be dependant on the charity of groups such as the General Education Board. As Du Bois complained:

It is a shame that our dependence on the rich for donations to absolutely necessary causes makes intelligent, free and self-respecting manhood and frank, open and honest criticism increasingly difficult among us. If someone starts to tell the truth or disclose incompetency or rebel at injustice, a chorus of "Sh!" arises from the whole black race. "Sh!" You're opposing the General Education Board! "Hush!" You're making enemies in the Rockefeller Foundation! "Keep still!" or the Phelps Stokes Fund will get you. "Stop!" or the rich Mr. This and the affluent Mrs. That will dam the flow of funds to Fisk or Talladega, to hospital or home. (pages 233-234 of this book)

As was the case with President Merrill sixteen years earlier, Du Bois's speech led to the eventual dismissal of President McKenzie.

By the beginning of the Great Depression, Du Bois's ideas about higher education seemed to have shifted. Increasingly, he began to talk about black colleges and universities as centers for cultural formation, anticipating in many regards the emergence of Black and African-American Studies. However, for him, the entire Negro college or university would have as its purpose the pursuit of black problems and issues.

In 1933, Du Bois spoke again at Fisk University. As black colleges changed from religious/missionary institutions to secular schools, it was increasingly argued that the mission of these schools as "Negro" institutions was less and less important. Du Bois argued instead that "the American Negro problem is and must be the center of the Negro university" (Aptheker 1973, 92). Du Bois saw the university as a command post for interpreting the Negro and his place in the culture. Its role as a center for organizing ideas and, ultimately, action that would advance the black race was crucial.

Du Bois's Ideas about Education in His Final Years

Du Bois was by no means concerned just with higher education in the 1920s and 1930s. At the elementary and secondary level, for example, he argued that segregating black and white children from one another in school was to virtually guarantee "their separation through life" (quoted by Franklin 1976, 112). Du Bois was also enough of a pragmatist to realize that racial prejudice was so strong in many parts of the country that the integration of the schools was practically impossible.

In "The Tragedy of Jim Crow," which appeared in the July 1923 issue of *The Crisis*, Du Bois argued that segregation in the schools was "the greatest possible menace to democracy" and to the advancement of black people in the United States (Franklin 1976, 113). Despite this fact,

Du Bois believed that a "Negro school," even with its lack of resources and offerings, was an infinitely better place for black children to be than in a place where "social climbers" could "make our boys and girls doormats to be spit and trampled upon" (quoted by Franklin 1976, 113).

As he explained in a major article in the *Journal of Negro Education* published in 1935, "Does the Negro Need Separate Schools?"

> ...the Negro needs neither segregated schools nor mixed schools. What he needs is Education. What he must remember is that there is no magic either in mixed schools or in segregated schools. A mixed school with poor and unsympathetic teachers, with hostile public opinion, and no teaching or truth concerning black folk, is bad. A segregated school with ignorant placeholders, inadequate equipment, poor salaries and wretched housing, is equally bad. Other things being equal, the mixed school is the broader, more natural basis for the education of all youth. It gives wider contacts; it inspires greater self-confidence; and suppresses the inferiority complex. Bother other things are seldom equal, and in that case, Sympathy, Knowledge, and the Truth, outweigh all that the mixed school can offer. (Du Bois 1936, 335)

While favoring the idea of desegregation in education, Du Bois only supported such programs if they were founded on the basis of true equality for the races.

Du Bois was ever the innovator and attempted to not just affect the policy of Negro schools, but also the content of their curriculum. On an informal level in 1920, he began publishing a children's magazine, *The Brownies' Book*. He did so because of his belief that black children were introduced, in their textbooks, to the world too much in terms of white culture and society. As he announced in the October 1991 issue of *The Crisis*, the Negro child finds that "All through school life his textbooks contain much about white people and little about his own race" (quoted by Lewis 2000, 33).

The Brownies ceased publication with its twenty-fourth issue in December 1921. It was remarkably ahead of its time, anticipating the idea of modern multicultural education and the need to make African-Americans, as well as the more general population, aware of the contributions of black culture to American history and society (Lewis 2000, 34). Du Bois also developed textbooks dealing with African culture during the 1930s—books which he felt would provide black Americans with a broader idea of how their struggle for personal freedom and dignity was connected to a much larger Pan-African struggle.

Derrick P. Alridge has pointed out that when Du Bois began his work as a researcher in the mid-1890s, he held a utopian belief that scientific research in the social sciences would "dismiss and debunk views of Negro inferiority." By the 1930s, according to Alridge, Du Bois realized that other means would have to be employed to overcome the irrational racism of the majority white population.

> During the 1930s, Negroes were on the lowest rung of the social ladder. At the core of their situation was many whites' belief that Negroes were innately inferior. Many whites associated Negroes' dark skin, woolly hair, and other "Negroid" features with servile caste, low intelligence, backward culture, and lack of morals. A prevailing view among some whites during the 1930s was that Negroes were hundreds or thousands of years developmentally behind the white race. Many whites feared that unrestricted social movement between Negroes and themselves would lead to miscegenation between the races and inevitably to a "dilution" of Nordic blood. Such views perpetuated Jim Crowism and made segregation a way of life, particularly in the South. (Alridge 1999)

By this time, Du Bois realized that there would be no easy or "scientifically" reasoned reconciliation between black and white cultures. Temperamentally, Du Bois was a scholar and scientific thinker and recognized that what was needed was a "hardheaded, pragmatic, and culturally grounded educational perspective" that would provide blacks with genuine social, economic and political power in America (Alridge 1999). Alridge notes that in the final years of his life, Du Bois had evolved a highly practical model of education for the American Negro.

> This new "post-1930" Du Bois was a complex hybrid of many different philosophical views that included Afro-centric, Marxist, black nationalist, pragmatist, and progressive views. Through this multidimensional lens, he saw that democracy for Negroes would not be obtained through Dewey's sole reliance on pragmatism, but instead by Negroes first building strong Negro-based social, economic, and political institutions in America. (Alridge 1999)

Clearly Du Bois's educational philosophy had been shaped and redefined by his historical experience.

Du Bois and Contemporary Education

Alridge has developed an extremely interesting model of black education based on the work of Du Bois. It includes six basic principles: (1) African-American-centered education, (2) communal education, (3) broad-based education, (4) group leadership education, (5) Pan-

Africanist education, and (6) global education (Alridge 1999). It is interesting to reflect that forty years after his death Du Bois's ideas remain vital and meaningful to not only African-Americans, but also to American culture in general. In a certain sense, the model Alridge outlines is a recapitulation of Du Bois's evolution as a educational theorist and writer.

In the pages that follow, one can find the most important words and ideas of W. E. B. Du Bois on education. In a certain sense, they speak completely for themselves. They also reflect a man caught in the complexities of race and European and American civilization. As he explained in his autobiography *Dusk of Dawn*:

> In the folds of this European civilization I was born and shall die, imprisoned, conditioned, depressed, exalted and inspired. Integrally a part of it and yet much more significant, one of its rejected parts; one who has expressed in life and action and made vocal to many, a single whirlpool of social entanglement and inner psychological paradox, which always seem to me more significant for the meaning of the world today than other similar and related problems. (555)

Du Bois's ideas on education clearly continue to remain vital and tell us much about the "meaning of the world today." Like Alridge, I believe that there is a unity to be found in Du Bois's educational writings. While not specifically a philosopher of education like John Dewey, or a conscious "sociologist of education," I believe that Du Bois nonetheless represents one of the most important and interesting educational thinkers of the past century. It is hoped that this volume will bring the full breadth and scope of his writing to the attention of readers, and that increasingly his ideas on education and their meaning for culture will be more thoroughly understood and appreciated.

PART ONE

Du Bois's Experience as a
Student and Teacher

CHAPTER ONE

A Negro Schoolmaster in the New South

This article, published in the January 1899 *Atlantic Monthly*, is among the earliest pieces by Du Bois to reach a national audience. It was later included as chapter 4, "Of the Meaning of Progress," in *The Souls of Black Folks.*

In the article, Du Bois recounts his experiences teaching in a rural Tennessee school during two summer vacations in 1886 and 1887. Rather than return home following his sophomore year at Fisk University, Du Bois walked about fifty miles east from Nashville on the Lebanon Pike until he reached Lebanon, the county seat of Wilson County. There he attended the Lebanon Teacher Institute. Following a week of study, he passed the necessary exam and was awarded a certificate to teach first grade on June 27, 1886, by the county superintendent, R. C. McMillan.

Du Bois's experience in rural Tennessee is important for a number of reasons. To begin with, it was his first significant encounter with poor blacks in the South. As he later explained, through these experiences he "touched the very shadow of slavery." Summarizing his experience in rural Tennessee, Du Bois explained in *Dusk of Dawn*:

> I determined to know something of the Negro in the country districts; to go out and teach during the summer vacation. I was not compelled to do this, for my scholarship was sufficient to support me, but that was not the point. I had heard about the country in the South as the real seat of slavery. I wanted to know it. I walked out into east Tennessee ten or more miles a day until at last in a little valley near Alexandria I found a place where there had been a Negro public school only once since the Civil War; and there for two successive terms during the summer I taught at $28 and $38 a month. (576)

According to David Levering Lewis, Alexandria, Tennessee, would remain in Du Bois's "memory bank for a lifetime, influencing a prose to which he was beginning to give a mythic spin, his conception of what he would later call the black proletariat, and most profoundly, his gestating, romantic ideas about African-American 'racial traits'" (Lewis 1993, 68).

In addition, Du Bois confronted at a personal level a type of discrimination unlike anything he had experienced in his relatively protected upbringing in New England, or during his first two years at Fisk. As he recounts in *Dusk of Dawn*, his experience in rural Tennessee was "an enthralling experience:"

> I met new and intricate and unconscious discrimination. I was pleasantly surprised when the white school superintendent, on whom I had made a business call, invited me to stay for dinner; and he would have been astonished if he had dreamed that I had expected to eat at the table with him and not after he was through. (576)

Du Bois also encountered the poverty of the black rural South for the first time. He recalled his experience as a teacher in Alexandria:

> All the appointments of my school were primitive; a windowless log cabin, hastily manufactured benches; no blackboard; almost no books; long, long distances to walk. And on the other hand, I heard the sorrow songs sung with primitive beauty and grandeur. I saw the hard, ugly drudgery of country life and the writhing of landless ignorant peasants. I saw the race problem at its lowest terms. (576)

Finally, it was during his time in Alexandria that Du Bois had his first sexual encounter—a fact not documented until over sixty years later. In his *Autobiography*, Du Bois recounted that during his first or second summer working as a teacher he lost his virginity. He was "literally raped by the woman who was my landlady" (280).

The woman with whom Du Bois had his first sexual encounter was the mother of Josie Dowell, the young girl who had told Du Bois about the possibility of finding a country school near Alexandria. Du Bois had been extremely close to his mother who had raised him by herself. She had died in 1885, just before he entered Fisk. David Levering Lewis speculates on the Freudian and Oedipal overtones of his sexual relationship with Mrs. Dowell, and how it might have influenced his attitude toward sex throughout the rest of his life (Lewis 1995, 71-72). Whatever the case, his two summers spent in rural Tennessee as a teacher were clearly a watershed for him, both personally and in terms of his social awareness of the experience of being black in America.

Once upon a time I taught school in the hills of Tennessee, where the broad dark vale of the Mississippi begins to roll and crumple to greet the Alleghanies. I was a Fisk student then, and all Fisk men think that Tennessee—beyond the Veil—is theirs alone, and in vacation time they sally forth in lusty bands to meet the country school commissioners. Young and Happy, I too went, and I shall not soon forget that summer, ten years ago.

First, there was a teachers' Institute at the county-seat; and there distinguished guests of the superintendent taught the teachers fractions and spelling and other mysteries,—white teachers in the morning, Negroes at night. A picnic now and then, and a supper, and the rough world was softened by laughter and song. I remember how—But I wander.

There came a day when all the teachers left the Institute, and began the hunt for schools. I learn from hearsay (for my mother was mortally afraid of firearms) that the hunting of ducks and bears and men is wonderfully interesting, but I am sure that the man who has never hunted a country school has something to learn of the pleasures of the chase. I see now the white, hot roads lazily rise and fall and wind before me under the burning July sun; I feel the deep weariness of heart and limb, as ten, eight, six miles stretch relentlessly ahead; I feel my heart sink heavily as I hear again and again, "Got a teacher? Yes." So I walked on and on,—horses were too expensive,—until I had wandered beyond railways, beyond stage lines, to a land of "varmints" and rattlesnakes, where the coming of a stranger was an event, and men lived and died in the shadow of one blue hill.

Sprinkled over hill and dale lay cabins and farmhouses, shut out from the world by the forests and the rolling hills toward the east. There I found at last a little school. Josie told me of it; she was a thin, homely girl of twenty, with a dark brown face and thick, hard hair. I had crossed the stream at Watertown, and rested under the great willows; then I had gone to the little cabin in the lot where Josie was resting on her way to town. The gaunt farmer made me welcome, and Josie, hearing my errand, told me anxiously that they wanted a school over the hill; that but once since the war had a teacher been there; that she herself longed to learn,—and thus she ran on, talking fast and loud, with much earnestness and energy.

Next morning I crossed the tall round hill, lingered to look at the blue and yellow mountains stretching toward the Carolinas; then I plunged into the wood, and came out at Josie's home. It was a dull frame cottage with four rooms, perched just below the brow of the hill, amid peach trees. The father was a quiet, simple soul, calmly ignorant, with no touch of vulgarity. The mother was different,—strong, bustling, and energetic, with a quick, restless tongue, and an ambition to live "like folks." There was a crowd of children. Two boys had gone away. There remained two growing girls; a shy midget of eight; John, tall, awkward, and eighteen; Jim, younger, quicker, and better looking; and two babies of indefinite age. Then there was Josie herself. She seemed to be the centre of the family: always busy at service or at home, or berry-picking; a little nervous and inclined to scold, like her mother, yet faithful, too, like her father. She had about her certain fineness, the shadow of an unconscious moral heroism that would willingly give all of life to make life broader, deeper and fuller for her and hers. I saw much of this family afterward, and grew to love them for their honest efforts to be decent and comfortable, and for their knowledge of their own ignorance. There was with them no affectation. The mother would scold the father for being so "easy"; Josie would roundly rate the boys for carelessness; and all knew that it was a hard thing to dig a living out of a rocky sidehill.

I secured the school. I remember the day I rode horseback out to the commissioner's house, with a pleasant young white fellow, who wanted the white school. The road ran down the bed of a stream; the sun laughed and the water jingled, and we rode on. "Come in," said the commissioner,—"come in. Have a seat. Yes, that certificate will do. Stay to dinner. What do you want a month?" Oh, thought I, this is lucky; but even then fell the awful shadow of the Veil, for they ate first, then I— alone.

The schoolhouse was a log hut, where Colonel Wheeler used to shelter his corn. It sat in a lot behind a rail fence and thorn bushes, near the sweetest of spring. There was an entrance where a door once was, and within, a massive rickety fireplace; great chinks between the logs served as windows. Furniture was scarce. A pale blackboard crouched in the corner. My desk was made of three boards, reinforced at critical points, and my chair, borrowed from the landlady, had to be returned every night. Seats for the children,—these puzzled me much. I was haunted by a New England vision of neat little desks and chairs, but, alas, the reality was rough plank benches without backs, and at times without legs. They had the one virtue of making naps dangerous,— possibly fatal, for the floor was not to be trusted.

It was a hot morning late in July when the school opened. I trembled when I heard the patter of little feet down the dusty road, and saw the growing row of dark solemn faces and bright eager eyes facing me. First came Josie and her brothers and sisters. The longing to know, to be a student in the great school at Nashville, hovered like a star above this child woman amid her work and worry, and she studied doggedly. There were the Dowells from their farm over toward Alexandria: Fanny, with her smooth black face and wondering eyes; Martha, brown and dull; the pretty girl wife of a brother, and the younger brood. There were the Burkes, two brown and yellow lads, and tine haughty-eyed girl. Fat Reuben's little chubby girl came, with golden face and old gold hair, faithful and solemn. 'Thenie was on hand early,—a jolly, ugly, good-hearted girl, who slyly dipped snuff and looked after her little bowlegged brother. When her mother could spare her, 'Tildy came,—a midnight beauty, with starry eyes and tapering limbs; and her brother, correspondingly homely. And then the big boys: the hulking Lawrences; the lazy Neills, unfathered sons of mother and daughter; Hickman, with a stoop in his shoulders; and the rest.

There they sat, nearly thirty of them, on the rough benches, their faces shading from a pale cream to a deep brown, the little feet bare and swinging, the eyes full of expectation, with here and there a twinkle of mischief, and the hands grasping Webster's blue-back spelling-book. I loved my school, and the fine faith the children had in the wisdom of their teacher was truly marvelous. We read and spelled together, wrote a little, picked flowers, sang, and listened to stories of the world beyond the hill. At times the school would dwindle away, and I would start out. I would visit Mun Eddings, who lived in two very dirty rooms, and ask why little Lugene, whose flaming face seemed ever ablaze with the dark red hair uncombed, was absent all last week, or why I missed so often the inimitable rags of Mack and Ed. Then the father, who worked Colonel Wheeler's farm on shares, would tell me how the crops needed the boys; and the thin, slovenly mother, whose face was pretty when washed, assured me that Lugene must mind the baby. "But we'll start them again next week." When the Lawrences stopped, I knew that the doubt of the old folks about book-learning had conquered again, and so, toiling up the hill, and getting as far into the cabin as possible, I put Cicero pro Archia Poeta in the simplest English with local applications, and usually convinced them—for a week or so.

On Friday nights I often went home with some of the children; sometimes to Doc Burke's farm. He was a great, loud, thin Black, ever working, and trying to buy the seventy-five acres of hill and dale where he lived; but people said that he would surely fail, and the "white folks would get it all." His wife was a magnificent Amazon, with saffron face and shining hair, uncorseted and barefooted, and the children were strong and beautiful. They lived in a one-and-a-half-room cabin in the hollow of the farm, near the spring. The front room was full of great fat white beds, scrupulously neat; and there were bad chromos on the walls, and a tired centre-table. In the tiny back kitchen I was often invited to "take out and help" myself to fried chicken and wheat biscuit, "meat" and corn pone, string beans and berries. At first I used to be a little alarmed at the approach of bedtime in the one lone bedroom, but embarrassment was very deftly avoided. First, all the children nodded and slept, and were stowed away in one great pile of goose feathers; next, the mother and the father discreetly slipped away to the kitchen while I went to bed; then, blowing out the dim light, they retired in the dark. In the morning all were up and away before I thought of awakening. Across the road, where fat Reuben lived, they all went outdoors while the teacher retired, because they did not boast the luxury of a kitchen.

I liked to stay with the Dowells, for they had four rooms and plenty of good country fare. Uncle Bird had a small, rough farm, all woods and hills, miles from the big road; but he was full of tales,—he preached now and then,—and with his children, berries, horses, and wheat he was happy and prosperous. Often, to keep the peace, I must go where life was less lovely; for instance, 'Tildy's mother was incorrigibly dirty, Reuben's larder was limited seriously, and herds of untamed bedbugs wandered over the Eddingses' beds. Best of all I loved to go to Josie's, and sit on the porch, eating peaches, while the mother bustled and talked: how Josie had bought the sewing-machine; how Josie worked at service in winter, but that four dollars a month was "mighty little" wages; how Josie longed to go away to school, but that it "looked like" they never could get far enough ahead to let her; how the crops failed and the well was yet unfinished; and, finally, how "mean" some of the white folks were.

For two summers I lived in this little world; it was dull and humdrum. The girls looked at the hill in wistful longing, and the boys fretted, and haunted Alexandria. Alexandria was "town,"—a straggling, lazy village of houses, churches, and shops, and an aristocracy of Toms, Dicks, and Captains. Cuddled on the hill to the north was the village of the colored folks, who lived in three or four room unpainted cottages, some neat and homelike, and some dirty. The dwellings were scattered rather aimlessly, but they centred about the twin temples of the hamlet, the Methodist and the Hard-Shell Baptist churches. These, in turn, leaned gingerly on a sad-colored schoolhouse. Hither my little world wended its crooked way on Sunday to meet other worlds, and gossip, and wonder, and make the weekly sacrifice with frenzied priest at the altar of the "old-time religion." Then the soft melody and mighty cadences of Negro song fluttered and thundered.

I have called my tiny community a world, and so its isolation made it; and yet there was among us but a half-awakened common consciousness, sprung from common joy and grief, at burial, birth, or wedding; from a common hardship in poverty, poor land, and low wages; and, above all, from the sight of the Veil that hung between us and Opportunity. All this caused us to think some thoughts together; but these, when ripe for speech, were spoken in various languages. Those whose eyes thirty and more years before had seen "the glory of the coming of the Lord" saw in every present hindrance or help a dark fatalism bound to bring all things right in His own good time. The mass of those to whom slavery was a dim recollection of childhood found the world a puzzling thing: it asked little of them, and they answered with little, and yet it ridiculed their offering. Such a paradox they could not understand, and therefore sank into listless indifference, or shiftlessness, or reckless bravado. There were, however, some such as Josie, Jim, and Ben,—they to whom War, Hell, and Slavery were but childhood tales, whose young appetites had been whetted to an edge by school and story and half-awakened thought. Ill could they be content, born without and beyond the World. And their weak wings beat against their barriers,— barriers of caste, of youth, of life; at last, in dangerous moments, against everything that opposed even a whim.

The ten years that follow youth, the years when first the realization comes that life is leading somewhere,—these were the years that passed after I left my little school. When they were past, I came by chance once more to the walls of Fisk University, to the halls of the chapel of melody. As I lingered there in the joy and pain of meeting old school friends, there swept over me a sudden longing to pass again beyond the blue hill, and to see the homes and the school of other days, and to learn how life had gone with my school-children; and I went.

Josie was dead, and the gray-haired mother said simply, "We've had a heap of trouble since you've been away." I had feared for Jim. With a cultured parentage and a social caste to uphold him, he might have made a venturesome merchant or a West Point cadet. But here he was, angry with life and reckless; and when Farmer Durham charged him with stealing wheat, the old man had to ride fast to escape the stones which the furious fool hurled after him. They told Jim to run away; but he would not run, and the constable came that afternoon. It grieved Josie, and great awkward John walked nine miles every day to see his little brother through the bars of Lebanon jail. At last the two came back together in the dark night. The mother cooked supper, and Josie emptied her purse, and the boys stole away. Josie grew thin and silent, yet worked the more. The hill became steep for the quiet old father, and with the boys away there was little to do in the valley. Josie helped them sell the old farm, and they moved nearer town. Brother Dennis, the carpenter, built a new house with six rooms; Josie toiled a year in Nashville, and brought back ninety dollars to furnish the house and change it to a home.

When the spring came, and the birds twittered, and the stream ran proud and full, little sister Lizzie, bold and thoughtless, flushed with the passion of youth, bestowed herself on the tempter, and brought home a nameless child. Josie shivered, and worked on, with the vision of schooldays all fled, with a face wan and tired,—worked until, on a summer's day, some one married another; then Josie crept to her mother like a hurt child, and slept—and sleeps.

I paused to scent the breeze as I entered the valley. The Lawrences have gone; father and son forever, and the other son lazily digs in the earth to live. A new young widow rents out their cabin to fat Reuben. Reuben is a Baptist preacher now, but I fear as lazy as ever, though his cabin has three rooms; and little Ella has grown into a bouncing woman, and is ploughing corn on the hot hillside. There are babies a plenty, and one half-witted girl. Across the valley is a house I did not know before, and there I found, rocking one baby and expecting another, one of my schoolgirls, a daughter of Uncle Bird Dowell. She looked somewhat worried with her new duties, but soon bristled into pride over her neat cabin, and the tale of her thrifty husband, the horse and cow, and farm they were planning to buy.

My log schoolhouse was gone. In its place stood Progress, and Progress, I understand, is necessarily ugly. The crazy foundation stones still marked the former site of my poor little cabin, and not far away, on six weary boulders, perched a jaunty board house, perhaps twenty by thirty feet, with three windows and a door that locked. Some of the window glass was broken, and part of an old iron stove lay mournfully under the house. I peeped through the window half reverently, and found things that were more familiar. The blackboard had grown by about two feet, and the seats were still without backs. The county owns the lot now, I hear, and every year there is a session of school. As I sat by the spring and looked on the Old and the New I felt glad, very glad, and yet—

After two long drinks I started on. There was the great double log house on the corner. I remembered the broken, blighted family that used to live there. The strong, hard face of the mother, with its wilderness of hair, rose before me. She had driven her husband away, and while I taught school a strange man lived there, big and jovial, and people talked. I felt sure that Ben and 'Tildy would come to naught from such a home. But this is an odd world; for Ben is a busy farmer in Smith County, "doing well, too," they say, and he had cared for little 'Tildy until last spring, when a lover married her. A hard life the lad had led, toiling for meat, and laughed at because he was homely and crooked.

There was Sam Carlon, an impudent old skinflint, who had definite notions about niggers, and hired Ben a summer and would not pay him. Then the hungry boy gathered his sacks together, and in broad daylight went into Carlon's corn; and when the hard-fisted farmer set upon him, the angry boy flew at him like a beast. Doc Burke saved a murder and a lynching that day.

The story reminded me again of the Burkes, and an impatience seized me to know who won in the battle, Doc or the seventy-five acres. For it is a hard thing to make a farm out of nothing, even in fifteen years. So I hurried on, thinking of the Burkes. They used to have a certain magnificent barbarism about them that I liked. They were never vulgar, never immoral, but rather rough and primitive, with an unconventionality that spent itself in loud guffaws, slaps on the back, and naps in the corner. I hurried by the cottage of the misborn Neill boys. It was empty, and they were grown into fat, lazy farm hands. I saw the home of the Hickmans, but Albert, with his stooping shoulders, had passed from the world. Then I came to the Burkes' gate and peered through; the inclosure looked rough and untrimmed, and yet there were the same fences around the old farm save to the left, where lay twenty five other acres. And lo! the cabin in the hollow had climbed the hill and swollen to a half-finished six-room cottage.

The Burkes held a hundred acres, but they were still in debt. Indeed, the gaunt father who toiled night and day would scarcely be happy out of debt, being so used to it. Some day he must stop, for his massive frame is showing decline. The mother wore shoes, but the lionlike physique of other days was broken. The children had grown up. Rob, the image of his father, was loud and rough with laughter. Birdie, my school baby of six, had grown to a picture of maiden beauty, tall and tawny. "Edgar is gone," said the mother, with head half bowed,—"gone to work in Nashville; he and his father couldn't agree."

Little Doc, the boy born since the time of my school, took me horseback down the creek next morning toward Farmer Dowell's. The road and the stream were battling for mastery, and the stream had the better of it. We splashed and waded, and the merry boy, perched behind me, chattered and laughed. He showed me where Simon Thomspon had bought a bit of ground and a home; but his daughter Lana, a plump, brown, slow girl, was not there. She had married as man and a farm twenty miles away. We wound on down the stream till we came to a gate that I did not recognize, but the boy insisted that it was "Uncle Bird's." The farm was fat with the growing crop. In that little valley was a strange stillness as I rode up; for death and marriage had stolen youth, and left age and childhood there. We sat and talked that night, after the chores were done. Uncle Bird was grayer, and his eyes did not see so well, but he was still jovial. We talked of acres bought,—one hundred and twenty-five,—of the new guest, chamber added, of Martha's marrying. Then we talked of death: Fanny and Fred were gone; a shadow hung over the other daughter, and when it lifted she was to go to Nashville to school. At last we spoke of the neighbors, and as night fell Uncle Bird told me how, on a night like that, 'Thenie came wandering back to her home over yonder, to escape the blows of her husband. And next morning she died in the home that her little bow-legged brother, working and saving, had bought for their widowed mother.

My journey was done, and behind me lay hill and dale, and Life and Death. How shall man measure Progress there where the dark-faced Josie lies? How many heartfuls of sorrow shall balance a bushel of wheat? How hard a thing is life to the lowly, and yet how human and real! And all this life and love and strife and failure,—is it the twilight of nightfall or the flush of some faint-dawning day?

Thus sadly musing, I rode to Nashville in the Jim Crow car.

CHAPTER TWO

A Negro Student at Harvard at the End of the Nineteenth Century

Although Du Bois attended Fisk for his undergraduate degree, he had always wanted to attend Harvard University. He was always prevented from applying by a lack of funds and an inadequate academic preparation. On completion of his degree at Fisk in June 1888, Du Bois applied to Harvard and was admitted with standing as a junior.

> I was happy at Harvard, but for unusual reasons. One of these unusual circumstances was my acceptance of racial segregation. Had I gone from Great Barrington high school directly to Harvard I would have sought companionship with my white fellows and been disappointed and embittered by a discovery of social limitations to which I had not been used. But I came by way of Fisk and the South and there I had accepted and embraced eagerly the companionship of my own color. (Du Bois 1940, 1986, 579)

Du Bois recalled how in general he asked

> nothing of Harvard but the tutelage of teachers and the freedom of the library. I was quite voluntarily and willingly outside its social life. I knew nothing of and cared nothing for fraternities and clubs. Most of those which dominated the Harvard life of my day were unknown to me even by name. I asked no fellowship of my fellow students. I found friends and most interesting and inspiring friends among the colored folk of Boston and surrounding places. (Du Bois 1940,1986,579)

There was a remarkable collection of intellects at Harvard when Du Bois was there:

> There were William James, the psychologist, Palmer in ethics, Royce and Santayana in philosophy, Shaler in geology and Hart in history. There were Francis Child, Charles Eliot Norton, Justin Winsor and John Trowbridge; Goodwin, Taussig and Kittridge. The president was the cold, precise but exceedingly just Charles William Eliot, while Oliver Wendell Holmes and James Russell Lowell were still alive and emeriti. (Du Bois 1940, 1986, 581)

Du Bois recalled in *Dusk of Dawn*, as well as in the essay that follows, how he was often a guest at the home of William James. In general, Du Bois was happy at Harvard. While there his academic interests shifted from philosophy and history to economics and social problems (584). Instinctively, Du Bois was pursuing the field of sociology while the field was actually in the process of defining itself.

Du Bois graduated from Harvard with his bachelor's degree in 1890. He was one of five commencement speakers, taking as his subject Jefferson Davis. His analysis went beyond looking at Davis as an individual. Instead, it focused on the civilization and culture he reflected.

From 1890 through 1892, Du Bois was given a fellowship in the graduate school at Harvard where he studied history, political science and "what would have been sociology if Harvard had yet recognized such a field" (Du Bois 1940, 1986, 585). In 1891 he was awarded a master degree. Throughout his two years in graduate school, Du Bois worked on what would be his thesis, "The Suppression of the African Slave Trade."

While conducting his graduate studies, Du Bois came across and article in which ex-President Rutherford B. Hayes, who was heading the Slater Fund for the education of Negroes, stated that if there was "any young colored man in the South we find to have a talent for art or literature or any special aptitude for study, we are willing to give him money from the education funds to send him to Europe or give him an advanced education" (Du Bois 1940, 1986, 585).

Du Bois contacted Hayes and was told that the newspaper quotation was incorrect—that the fund had no such plans for scholarships of the type described. Collecting recommendations from people at Harvard and elsewhere, Du Bois persisted. Eventually, because of his talent and perseverance, he was awarded $750, half as a grant and half as a repayable loan. There was the possibility that it would be renewed for the second year.

Du Bois sailed for Europe in the summer of 1892. He stayed two years and was profoundly affected by his experience. While there, he described how: "something of the possibility of beauty and elegance permeated my soul. I gained a respect for manners. I had been before, above all, in a hurry. I wanted a world, hard, smooth and swift, and had no time for rounded corners and ornament, for unhurried thought and slow contemplation" (Du Bois 1940, 1986, 587). In the fall, Du Bois registered at the University of Berlin. After a year of study, he renewed his fellowship for a second year, and then returned to the United States. Du Bois presented himself for the award of his Ph.D. by Harvard on his return from Germany in 1895—the first black ever awarded the degree.

Harvard University in 1888 was a great institution of learning. It was 238 years old and on its governing board were Alexander Agassiz, Phillips Brooks, Henry Cabot Lodge and Charles Francis Adams; and a John Quincy Adams, but not the ex-President. Charles William Eliot, a gentleman by training and a scholar by broad study and travel, was president. Among its teachers emeriti were Oliver Wendell Holmes and James Russell Lowell. Among the active teachers were Francis Child, Charles Eliot Norton, Justin Winsor and John Trowbridge; Frank Taussig, Nathaniel Shaler, George Palmer, William James, Francis Peabody, Josiah Royce, Barrett Wendell, Edward Channing and Albert Bushnell Hart. In 1890 arrived a young instructor, George Santayana. Seldom, if ever, has any American university had such a galaxy of great men and fine teachers as Harvard in the decade between 1885 and 1895.

To make my own attitude toward the Harvard of that day clear, it must be remembered that I went to Harvard as a Negro, not simply by birth, but recognizing myself as a member of a segregated caste whose situation I accepted. But I was determined to work from within that caste to find my way out.

The Harvard of which most white students conceived I knew little. I had not even heard of Phi Beta Kappa, and of such important social organizations as the Hasty Pudding Club, I knew nothing. I was in Harvard for education and not for high marks, except as marks would insure my staying. I did not pick out "snap" courses. I was there to enlarge my grasp of the meaning of the universe. We had had, for instance, no chemical laboratory at Fisk; our mathematics courses were limited. Above all I wanted to study philosophy! I wanted to get hold of the bases of knowledge, and explore foundations and beginnings. I chose, therefore, Palmer's course in ethics, but since Palmer was on sabbatical that year, William James replaced him, and I became a devoted follower of James at the time he was developing his pragmatic philosophy. Fortunately I did not fall into the mistake of regarding Harvard as the beginning rather than the continuing of my college training. I did not find better teachers at Harvard, but teachers better known, who had had wider facilities for gaining knowledge and lived in a broader atmosphere for approaching truth.

I hoped to pursue philosophy as my life career, with teaching for support. With this program I studied at Harvard from the fall of 1888 to 1890, as undergraduate. I took a varied course in chemistry, geology, social science and philosophy. My salvation here was the type of teacher I met rather than the content of the courses. William James guided me out of the sterilities of scholastic philosophy to realist pragmatism; from Peabody's social reform with a religious tinge I turned to Albert Bushnell Hart to study history with documentary research; and from Taussig, with his reactionary British economics of the Ricardo school, I approached what was later to become sociology. Meantime Karl Marx was mentioned, but only incidentally and as one whose doubtful theories had long since been refuted. Socialism was dismissed as unimportant, as a dream of philanthropy or as a will-o-wisp of hotheads: When I arrived at Harvard, the question of board and lodging was of first importance. Naturally, I could not afford a room in the college Yard in the old and venerable buildings which housed most of the well-to-do students under the magnificent elms. Neither did I think of looking for lodgings among white families, where numbers of the ordinary students lived. I tried to find a colored home, and finally at 20 Flagg Street I came upon the neat home of a colored woman from Nova Scotia, a descendant of those black Jamaican Maroons whom Britain had deported after solemnly promising them peace if they would surrender. For a very reasonable sum I rented the second story front room and for four years this was my home. I wrote of this abode at the time:

> My room is, for a college man's abode, very ordinary indeed. It is quite pleasantly situated—second floor, front, with a bay window and one other window.... As you enter you will perceive the bed in the opposite corner, small and decorated with floral designs calculated to puzzle a botanist.... On the left hand is a bureau with a mirror of doubtful accuracy. In front of the bay window is a stand with three shelves of books, and on the left of the bureau is an improvised bookcase made of unpainted boards and uprights, containing most of my library of which I am growing quite proud. Over the heat register, near the door, is a mantel with a plaster of Paris pug-dog and a calendar, and the usual array of odds and ends.... On the wall are a few quite ordinary pictures. In this commonplace den I am quite content.

Following the attitudes which I had adopted in the South, I sought no friendships among my white fellow students, nor even acquaintanceships. Of course I wanted friends, but I could not seek them. My class was large—some three hundred students. I doubt if I knew a dozen of them. I did not seek them, and naturally they did not seek me. I made no attempt to contribute to the college periodicals since the editors were not interested in my major interests. But I did have a good singing voice and loved music, so I entered the competition for the Glee Club. I ought to have known that Harvard could not *afford* to have a Negro on its Glee Club traveling about the country. Quite naturally I was rejected.

I was happy at Harvard, but for unusual reasons. One of these was my acceptance of racial segregation. Had I gone from Great Barrington high school directly to Harvard, I would have sought companionship with my white fellows and been disappointed and embittered by a discovery of social limitations to which I had not been used. But I came by way of Fisk and the South and there I had accepted color caste and embraced eagerly the companionship of those of my own color. This was of course no final solution. Eventually, in mass assault, led by culture, we Negroes were going to break down the boundaries of race; but at present we were banded together in a great crusade, and happily so. Indeed, I suspect that the prospect of ultimate full human intercourse, without reservations and annoying distinctions, made me all too willing to consort with my own and to disdain and forget as far as was possible that outer, whiter world.

In general, I asked nothing of Harvard but the tutelage of teachers and the freedom of the laboratory and library. I was quite voluntarily and willingly outside its social life. I sought only such contacts with white teachers as lay directly in the line of my work. I joined certain clubs, like the Philosophical Club; I was a member of the Foxcroft dining club because it was cheap. James and one or two other teachers had me at their homes at meal and reception. I escorted colored girls to various gatherings, and as pretty ones as I could find to the vesper exercises, and later to the class day and commencement social functions. Naturally we attracted attention and the Crimson noted my girl friends. Sometimes the shadow of insult fell, as when at one reception a white woman seemed determined to mistake me for a waiter.

In general, I was encased in a completely colored world, self-sufficient and provincial, and ignoring just as far as possible the white world that conditioned it. This was self-protective coloration, with perhaps an inferiority complex, but with belief in the ability and future of black folk.

My friends and companions were drawn mainly from the colored students of Harvard and neighboring institutions, and the colored folk of Boston and surrounding towns. With them I led a happy and inspiring life. There were among them many educated and well-to-do folk, many young people studying or planning to study, many charming young women. We met and ate, danced and argued, and planned a new world.

Towards whites I was not arrogant; I was simply not obsequious, and to a white Harvard student of my day a Negro student who did not seek recognition was trying to be more than a Negro. The same Harvard man had much the same attitude toward Jews and Irishmen.

I was, however, exceptional among Negroes at Harvard in my ideas on voluntary race segregation. They for the most part saw salvation only in integration at the earliest moment and on almost any terms in white culture; I was firm in my criticism of white folk and in my dream of a self-sufficient Negro culture even in America.

This cutting of myself off from my white fellows, or being cut off, did not mean unhappiness or resentment. I was in my early manhood, unusually full of high spirits and humor. I thoroughly enjoyed life. I was conscious of understanding and power, and conceited enough still to imagine, as in high school, that they who did not know me were the losers, not I. On the other hand, I do not think that my white classmates found me personally objectionable. I was clean, not well-dressed but decently clothed. Manners I regarded as more or less superfluous and deliberately cultivated a certain brusquerie. Personal adornment I regarded as pleasant but not important. I was in Harvard, but not of it, and realized all the irony of my singing "Fair Harvard." I sang it because I liked the music, and not from any pride in the pilgrims.

With my colored friends I carried on lively social intercourse, but necessarily one which involved little expenditure of money. I called at their homes and ate at their tables. We danced at private parties. We went on excursions down the Bay. Once, with a group of colored students gathered from surrounding institutions, we gave Aristophanes' *The Birds* in a Boston colored church. The rendition was good, but not outstanding, not quite appreciated by the colored audience, but well worth doing. Even though it worked me near to death, I was proud of it.

Thus the group of professional men, students, white collar workers and upper servants, whose common bond was color of skin in themselves or in their fathers, together with a common history and current experience of discrimination, formed a unit that like many tens of thousands of like units across the nation had or were getting to have a common culture pattern which made them an interlocking mass, so that increasingly a colored person in Boston was more neighbor to a colored person in Chicago than to a white person across the street.

Mrs. [Josephine St. Pierre] Ruffin of Charles Street, Boston, and her daughter Birdie were often hostesses to this colored group. She was widow of the first colored judge appointed in Massachusetts, an aristocratic lady, with olive skin and high piled masses of white hair. Once a Boston white lady said to Mrs. Ruffin ingratiatingly: "I have always been interested in your race." Mrs. Ruffin flared: "Which race?" She began a national organization of colored women and published the *Courant*, a type of small colored weekly paper which was then spreading over the nation. In this I published many of my Harvard daily themes.

Naturally in this close group there grew up among the young people friendships ending in marriages. I myself, outgrowing the youthful attractions of Fisk, began serious dreams of love and marriage. There were, however, still my study plans to hold me back and there were curious other reasons. For instance, it happened that two of the girls whom I particularly liked had what was to me then the insuperable handicap of looking like whites, while they had enough black ancestry to make them "Negroes" in America. I could not let the world even imagine that I had married a white wife. Yet these girls were intelligent and companionable. One went to Vassar College, which then refused entrance to Negroes. Years later when I went there to lecture I remember disagreeing violently with a teacher who thought the girl ought not to have "deceived" the college by graduating before it knew of her Negro descent! Another favorite of mine was Deenie Pindell. She was a fine forthright woman, blonde, blue-eyed and fragile. In the end I had no chance to choose her, for she married Monroe Trotter.

Trotter was the son of a well-to-do colored father and entered Harvard in my first year in the Graduate School. He was thick-set, yellow, with close-cut dark hair. He was stubborn and strait-laced and an influential member of his class. He organized the first Total Abstinence Club in the Yard. I came to know him and joined the company when he and other colored students took in a trip to Amherst to see our friends [George] Forbes and [William H.] Lewis graduate in the class with Calvin Coolidge.

Lewis afterward entered the Harvard Law School and became the celebrated center rush of the Harvard football team. He married the beautiful Bessie Baker, who had been with us on that Amherst trip. Forbes, a brilliant, cynical dark man, later joined with Trotter in publishing the *Guardian*, the first Negro paper to attack Booker T. Washington openly. Washington's friends retorted by sending Trotter to jail when he dared to heckle Washington in a public Boston meeting on his political views. I was not present nor privy to this occurrence, but the unfairness of the jail sentence led me eventually to form the Niagara movement, which later became the NAACP.

Thus I lived near to life, love and tragedy; and when I met Maud Cuney, I became doubly interested. She was a tall, imperious brunette with gold-bronze skin, brilliant eyes and coils of black hair, daughter of the Collector of Customs at Galveston, Texas. She had come to study music and was a skilled performer. When the New England Conservatory of Music tried to "Jim Crow" her in the dormitory, we students rushed to her defense and we won. I fell deeply in love with her, and we were engaged.

Thus it is clear how in the general social intercourse on the campus I consciously missed nothing. Some white students made themselves known to me and a few, a very few, became lifelong friends. Most of my classmates I knew neither by sight nor name. Among them many made their mark in life: Norman Hapgood, Robert Herrick, Herbert Croly, George Dorsey, Homer Folks, Augustus Hand, James Brown Scott, and others. I knew none of these intimately. For the most part I do not doubt that I was voted a somewhat selfish and self-centered "grind" with a chip on my shoulder and a sharp tongue.

Only once or twice did I come to the surface of college life. First I found by careful calculation that I needed the cash of one of the Boylston prizes in oratory to piece out my year's expenses. I got it through winning a second oratorical prize. The occasion was noteworthy by the fact that another black student, Clement Morgan, got first prize at the same contest.

With the increase at Harvard of students who had grown up outside New England, there arose at this time a certain resentment at the way New England students were dominating and conducting college affairs. The class marshal on commencement day was always a Saltonstall, a Cabot, a Lowell, or from some such New England family. The crew and most of the heads of other athletic teams were selected from similarly limited social groups. The class poet, class orator, and other commencement officials invariably were selected because of family and not for merit. It so happened that when the officials of the class of 1890 were being selected in early spring, a plot ripened. Personally, I knew nothing of it and was not greatly interested. But in Boston and in the Harvard Yard the result of the elections was of tremendous significance, for this conspiratorial clique selected Clement Morgan as class orator. New England and indeed the whole country reverberated.

Morgan was a black man. He had been working in a barber shop in St. Louis at the time when he ought to have been in school. With the encouragement and help of a colored teacher, whom he later married, he came to Boston and entered the Latin School. This meant that when he finally entered Harvard, he entered as freshman in the orthodox way and was well acquainted with his classmates. He was fairly well received, considering his color. He was a pleasant unassuming person and one of the best speakers of clearly enunciated English on the campus. In his junior year he had earned the first Boylston prize for oratory in the same contest where I won second prize. It was, then, logical for him to become class orator, and yet this was against all the traditions of America. There were editorials in the leading newspapers, and the South especially raged and sneered at the audience of "black washerwomen" who would replace Boston society at the next Harvard commencement.

Morgan's success was contagious, and that year and the next in several leading Northern colleges colored students became the class orators. Ex-President Hayes, as I shall relate later, sneered at this fact. While, as I have said, I had nothing to do with the plot, and was not even present at the election which chose Morgan, I was greatly pleased at this breaking of the color line. Morgan and I became fast friends and spent a summer giving readings along the North Shore to defray our college costs.

Harvard of this day was a great opportunity for a young man and a young American Negro and I realized it. I formed habits of work rather different from those of most of the other students. I burned no midnight oil. I did my studying in the daytime and had my day parceled out almost to the minute. I spent a great deal of time in the library and did my assignments with thoroughness and with prevision of the kind of work I wanted to do later. From the beginning my relations with most of the teachers at Harvard were pleasant. They were on the whole glad to receive a serious student, to whom extracurricular activities were not of paramount importance, and one who in a general way knew what he wanted.

Harvard had in the social sciences no such leadership of thought and breadth of learning as in philosophy, literature and physical science. She was then groping and is still groping toward a scientific treatment of human action. She was facing at the end of the century a tremendous economic era. In the United States, finance was succeeding in monopolizing transportation and raw materials like sugar, coal and oil. The power of the trust and combine was so great that the Sherman Act was passed in 1890. On the other hand, the tariff, at the demand of manufacturers, continued to rise in height from the McKinley to the indefensible Wilson tariff, making that domination easier. The understanding between the Industrial North and the New South was being perfected and, beginning in 1890, a series of disfranchising laws was enacted by the Southern states that was destined in the next sixteen years to make voting by Southern Negroes practically impossible. A financial crisis shook the land in 1893 and popular discontent showed itself in the Populist movement and Coxey's Army. The whole question of the burden of taxation began to be discussed.

These things we discussed with some clearness and factual understanding at Harvard. The tendency was toward English free trade and against the American tariff policy. We reverenced [David] Ricardo and wasted long hours on the "Wages-fund." I remember [Frank] Taussig's course supporting dying Ricardean economics. Wages came from what employers had left for labor after they had subtracted their own reward. Suppose that this profit was too small to attract the employer, what would the poor worker do but starve! The trusts and monopolies were viewed frankly as dangerous enemies of democracies, but at the same time as inevitable methods of industry. We were strong for the gold standard and fearful of silver. On the other hand, the attitude of Harvard toward labor was on the whole contemptuous and condemnatory. Strikes like that of the anarchists in Chicago and the railway strikes of 1886, the terrible Homestead strike of 1892 and Coxey's Army of 1894 were pictured as ignorant lawlessness, lurching against conditions largely inevitable.

Karl Marx was mentioned only to point out how thoroughly his theses had been disproven; of the theory itself almost nothing was said. Henry George was given but tolerant notice. The anarchists of Spain, the Nihilists of Russia, the British miners—all these were viewed not as part of political and economic development but as sporadic evil. This was natural. Harvard was the child of its era. The intellectual freedom and flowering of the late eighteenth and early nineteenth centuries were yielding to the deadening economic pressure which would make Harvard rich but reactionary. This defender of wealth and capital, already half ashamed of Sumner and Phillips, was willing finally to replace an Eliot with a manufacturer and a nervous warmonger. The social community that mobbed Garrison easily electrocuted Sacco and Vanzetti.

It was not until I was long out of college and had finished my first studies of economics and politics that I realized the fundamental influence man's efforts to earn a living had upon all his other efforts. The politics which we studied in college were conventional, especially when it came to describing and elucidating the current scene in Europe. The Queen's Jubilee in June, 1887, while I was still at Fisk, set the pattern of our thinking. The little old woman at Windsor became a magnificent symbol of Empire. Here was England with her flag draped around the world, ruling more black folk than white and leading the colored peoples of the earth to Christian baptism, and, as we assumed, to civilization and eventual self-rule. In 1885, [Henry] Stanley, the traveling American reporter, became a hero and symbol of white world leadership in Africa.

The wild, fierce fight of the Mahdi and the driving of the English out of the Sudan for thirteen years did not reveal their inner truth to me. I heard only of the martyrdom of the drunken Bible-reader and free-booter, Chinese Gordon.

After the Congo Free State was established, the Berlin Conference of 1885 was reported to be an act of civilization against the slave trade and liquor. French, English and Germans pushed on in Africa, but I did not question the interpretation which pictured this as the advance of civilization and the benevolent tutelage of barbarians. I read of the confirmation of the Triple Alliance in 1891. Later I saw the celebration of the renewed Triple Alliance on the Tempelhofer Feld, with the new young Emperor Wilhelm II, who, fresh from his dismissal of Bismarck, led the splendid pageantry; and, finally, the year I left Germany, Nicholas II became Czar of all the Russias. In all this I had not yet linked the political development of Europe with the race problem in America.

I was repeatedly a guest in the home of William James; he was my friend and guide to clear thinking; as a member of the Philosophical Club I talked with Royce and Palmer; I remember vividly once standing beside Mrs. Royce at a small reception. We ceased conversation for a moment and both glanced across the room. Professor Royce was opposite talking excitedly. He was an extraordinary sight: a little body, indifferently clothed; a big red-thatched head and blazing blue eyes. Mrs. Royce put my thoughts into words: "Funny-looking man, isn't he?" I nearly fainted! Yet I knew how she worshipped him.

I sat in an upper room and read Kant's *Critique* with Santayana; Shaler invited a Southerner, who objected to sitting beside me, to leave his class; he said he wasn't doing very well, anyway. I became one of Hart's favorite pupils and was afterwards guided by him through my graduate course and started on my work in Germany. Most of my courses of study went well. It was in English that I came nearest my Waterloo at Harvard. I had unwittingly arrived at Harvard in the midst of a violent controversy about poor English among students. A number of fastidious scholars like Barrett Wendell, the great pundit of Harvard English, had come to the campus about this time; moreover, New England itself was getting sensitive over Western slang and Southern drawls and general ignorance of grammar. Freshmen at this time could elect nearly all their courses except English; that was compulsory, with daily themes, theses, and tough examinations. But I was at the point in my intellectual development when the content rather than the form of my writing was to me of prime importance. Words and ideas surged in my mind and spilled out with disregard of exact accuracy in grammar, taste in word or restraint in style. I knew the Negro problem and this was more important to me than literary form. I knew grammar fairly well, and I had a pretty wide vocabulary; but I was bitter, angry and intemperate in my first thesis. Naturally my English instructors had no idea of nor interest in the way in which Southern attacks on the Negro were scratching me on the raw flesh. Tillman was raging like a beast in the Senate, and literary clubs, especially those of rich and well-dressed women, engaged his services eagerly and listened avidly. Senator Morgan of Alabama had just published a scathing attack on "niggers" in a leading magazine, when my first Harvard thesis was due. I let go at him with no holds barred. My long and blazing effort came back marked "E"—not passed!

It was the first time in my scholastic career that I had encountered such a failure. I was aghast, but I was not a fool. I did not doubt but that my instructors were fair in judging my English technically even if they did not understand the Negro problem. I went to work at my English and by the end of that term had raised it to a "C". I realized that while style is subordinate to content, and that no real literature can be composed simply of meticulous and fastidious phrases, nevertheless solid content with literary style carries a message further than poor grammar and muddled syntax. I elected the best course on the campus for English composition—English 12.

I have before me a theme which I submitted on October 3, 1890, to Barrett Wendell. I wrote:

> Spurred by my circumstances, I have always been given to systematically planning my future, not indeed without many mistakes and frequent alterations, but always with what I now conceive to have been a strangely early and deep appreciation of the fact that to live is a serious thing. I determined while in high school to go to college— partly because other men did, partly because I foresaw that such discipline would best fit me for life.... I believe, foolishly perhaps, but sincerely, that I have something to say to the world, and I have taken English 12 in order to say it well.

Barrett Wendell liked that last sentence. Out of fifty essays, he picked this out to read to the class.

Commencement was approaching, when, one day, I found myself at midnight on one of the swaggering streetcars that used to roll out from Boston on its way to Cambridge. It was in the spring of 1890, and quite accidentally I was sitting by a classmate who would graduate with me in June. As I dimly remember, he was a nice-looking young man; well-dressed, almost dapper, charming in manner. Probably he was rich or at least well-to-do, and doubtless belonged to an exclusive fraternity, although that did not interest me. Indeed I have even forgotten his name. But one thing I shall never forget and that was his rather regretful admission (which slipped out as we gossiped) that he had no idea as to what his life work would be, because, as he added, "There's nothing in which I am particularly interested!"

I was more than astonished—I was almost outraged to meet any human being of the mature age of twenty-one who did not have his life all planned before him, at least in general outline, and who was not supremely, if not desperately, interested in what he planned to do.

In June 1890, I received my bachelor's degree from Harvard *cum laude* in philosophy. I was one of the five graduating students selected to speak at commencement. My subject was "Jefferson Davis." I chose it with the deliberate intent of facing Harvard and the nation with a discussion of slavery as illustrated in the person of the president of the Confederate States of America. Naturally, my effort made a sensation. I said, among other things:

> I wish to consider not the man, but the type of civilization which his life represented: its foundation is the idea of the strong man—Individualism coupled with the rule of might—and it is this idea that has made the logic of even modern history, the cool logic of the Club. It made of a naturally brave and generous man, Jefferson Davis, one who advanced civilization by murdering Indians; then a hero of a national disgrace, called by courtesy the Mexican War; and finally, as the crowning absurdity, the peculiar champion of a people fighting to be free in order that another people should not be free. Whenever this idea has for a moment escaped from the individual realm, it has found an even more secure foothold in the policy and philosophy of the State. The strong man and his mighty Right Arm has become the Strong Nation with its armies. However, under whatever guise a Jefferson Davis may appear as man, as race, or as a nation, his life can only logically mean this: the advance of a part of the world at the expense of the whole; the overwhelming sense of the I, and the consequent forgetting of the Thou. It has thus happened that advance in civilization has always been handicapped by shortsighted national selfishness. The vital principle of division of labor has been stifled not only in industry, but also in civilization; so as to render it well-nigh impossible for a new race to introduce a new idea into the world except by means of the cudgel. To say that a nation is in the way of civilization is a contradiction in terms, and a system of human culture whose principle is the rise of one race on the ruins of another is a farce and a lie. Yet this is the type of civilization which Jefferson Davis represented: it represents a field for stalwart manhood and heroic character, and at the same time for moral obtuseness and refined brutality. These striking

contradictions of character always arise when a people seemingly become convinced that the object of the world is not civilization, but Teutonic civilization.

A Harvard professor wrote to *Kate Field's Washington,* then a leading periodical:

> Du Bois, the colored orator of the commencement stage, made a ten-strike. It is agreed upon by all the people I have seen that he was the star of the occasion. His paper was on "Jefferson Davis," and you would have been surprised to hear a colored man deal with him so generously. Such phrases as a "great man," a "keen thinker," a "strong leader," and others akin occurred in the address. One of the trustees of the University told me yesterday that the paper was considered masterly in every way. Du Bois is from Great Barrington, Massachusetts, and doubtless has some white blood in his veins. He, too, has been in my classes the past year. If he did not head the class, he came pretty near the head, for he is an excellent scholar in every way, and altogether the best black man that has come to Cambridge.

Bishop Potter of New York wrote in the *Boston Herald:*

> When at the last commencement of Harvard University, I saw a young colored man appear... and heard his brilliant and eloquent address, I said to myself: "Here is what an historic race can do if they have a clear field, a high purpose, and a resolute will."

Already I had now received more education than most young white men, having been almost continuously in school from the age of six to twenty-two. But I did not yet feel prepared. I felt that to cope with the new and extraordinary situations then developing in the United States and the world I needed to go further and that as a matter of fact I had just well begun my training in knowledge of social conditions.

I reveled in the keen analysis of William James, Josiah Royce and young George Santayana. But it was James with his pragmatism and Albert Bushnell Hart with his research method who turned me back from the lovely but sterile land of philosophic speculation to the social sciences as the field for gathering and interpreting that body of fact which would apply to my program for the Negro. As an undergraduate, I had talked frankly with William James about teaching philosophy, my major subject. He discouraged me, but not by any means because of my record in his classes. He used to give me "A's" and even "A-plus," but as he said candidly, there is "not much chance of anyone earning a living as a philosopher." He was repeating just what Chase of Fisk had said a few years previously.

I knew by this time that practically my sole chance of earning a living combined with study was to teach, and after my work with Hart in United States history I conceived the idea of applying philosophy to an historical interpretation of race relations. In other words, I was trying to take my first steps toward sociology as the science of human action. It goes without saying that no such field of study was then recognized at Harvard or came to be recognized for twenty years after. But I began with some research in Negro history and finally at the suggestion of Hart, I chose the suppression of the African slave trade to America as my doctor's thesis. Then came the question as to whether I could continue study in the graduate school. I had no resources in wealth or friends. I applied for a fellowship in the graduate school of Harvard, was appointed Henry Bromfield Rogers fellow for a year and later the appointment was renewed; so that from 1890 to 1892 I was a fellow in Harvard University, studying history and political science and what would have been sociology if Harvard had yet recognized such a field.

I finished the first draft of my thesis and delivered an outline of it at the seminars of American history and political economy December 7, 1891. I received my master's degree in the spring. I was thereupon elected to the American Historical Society and asked to speak in Washington at their meeting in December, 1891. The *New York Independent* noted this among the "three best papers presented," and continued:

> The article upon the "enforcement of the Slave Laws" was written and read by a black man. It was thrilling when one could, for a moment turn his thoughts from listening to think that scarcely thirty years have elapsed since the war that freed his race, and here was an audience of white men listening to a black man—listening, moreover, to a careful, cool, philosophical history of the laws which had not prevented the enslavement of his race. The voice, the diction, the manner of the speaker were faultless. As one looked at him, one could not help saying, "Let us not worry about the future of our country in the matter of race distinctions."

I had begun with a bibliography of Nat Turner and ended with a history of the suppression of the African slave trade to America; neither would need to be done again, at least in my day. Thus in my quest for basic knowledge with which to help guide the American Negro, I came to the study of sociology, by way of philosophy and history rather than by physics and biology. After hesitating between history and economics,

I chose history. On the other hand, psychology, hovering then on the threshold of experiment under [Hugo] Muensterberg, soon took a new orientation which I could understand from the beginning.

Already I had made up my mind that what I needed was further training in Europe. The German universities were at the top of their reputation. Any American scholar who wanted preferment went to Germany for study. The faculties of Johns Hopkins and the new University of Chicago were beginning to be filled with German Ph.D.'s, and even Harvard, where Kuno Frank had long taught, had imported Muensterberg. British universities did not recognize American degrees and French universities made no special effort to encourage American graduates. I wanted then to study in Germany. I was determined that any failure on my part to become a recognized American scholar must not be based on lack of modern training.

I was confident. So far I had met no failure. I willed and lo! I was walking beneath the elms of Harvard—the name of allurement, the college of my youngest, wildest visions! I needed money; scholarships and prizes fell into my lap—not all I wanted or strove for, but all I needed to keep me in school. Commencement came, and standing before governor, president, and grave gowned men, I told them certain truths, waving my arms and breathing fast! They applauded with what may have seemed to many as uncalled-for fervor, but I walked home on pink clouds of glory! I asked for a fellowship and got it. I announced my plan of studying in Germany, but Harvard had no more fellowships for me. A friend, however, told me of the Slater Fund and that the board was looking for colored men worth educating.

No thought of modest hesitation occurred to me. I rushed at the chance. It was one of those tricks of fortune which always seem partly due to chance. In 1882, the Slater Fund for the education of Negroes had been established and the board in 1890 was headed by ex-President R. B. Hayes. Ex-President Hayes went down to Johns Hopkins University, which admitted no Negro students, and told a "darkey" joke in a frank talk about the plans of the fund. The *Boston Herald* of November 2, 1890 quoted him as saying: "If there is any young colored man in the South whom we find to have a talent for art or literature or any special aptitude for study, we are willing to give him money from the educational funds to send him to Europe or give him advanced education." He added that so far they had been able to find only "orators." This seemed to me a nasty fling at my black classmate, Morgan, who had been Harvard class orator a few months earlier.

The Hayes statement was brought to my attention at a card party one evening; it not only made me good and angry but inspired me to write ex-President Hayes and ask for a scholarship. I received a pleasant reply saying that the newspaper quotation was incorrect; that his board had some such program in the past but had no present plans for such scholarships. I responded referring him to my teachers and to others who knew me, and intimating that his change of plan did not seem to me fair nor honest. He wrote again in apologetic mood and said that he was sorry the plan had been given up, that he recognized that I was a candidate who might otherwise have been given attention. I then sat down and wrote Mr. Hayes this letter:

May 25, 1891

Your favor of the 2nd, is at hand. I thank you for your kind wishes. You will pardon me if I add a few words of explanation as to my application. The outcome of the matter is as I expected it would be. The announcement that any agency of the American people was willing to give a Negro a thoroughly liberal education and that it had been looking in vain for men to educate was to say the least rather startling. When the newspaper clipping was handed me in a company of friends, my first impulse was to make in some public way a categorical statement denying that such an offer had ever been made known to colored students. I saw this would be injudicious and fruitless, and I therefore determined on the plan of applying myself. I did so and have been refused along with a "number of cases" beside mine.

As to my case, I personally care little. I am perfectly capable of fighting alone for an education if the trustees do not see fit to help me. On the other hand the injury you have—unwittingly I trust—done the race I represent, and are not ashamed of, is almost irreparable. You went before a number of keenly observant men who looked upon you as an authority in the matter, and told them in substance that the Negroes of the United States either couldn't or wouldn't embrace a most liberal opportunity for advancement. That statement went all over the country. When now finally you receive three or four applications for the fulfillment of that offer, the offer is suddenly withdrawn, while the impression still remains.

If the offer was an experiment, you ought to have had at least one case before withdrawing it; if you have given aid before (and I mean here toward liberal education—not toward training plowmen) then your statement at Johns Hopkins was partial. From the above facts I think you owe an apology to the Negro people. We are ready to furnish competent men for every European scholarship furnished us off paper. But we can't educate ourselves on nothing and we can't have the moral courage to try, if in the midst of our work our friends turn public sentiment against us by making statements which injure us and which they cannot stand by.

That you have been looking for men to liberally educate in the past may be so but it is certainly strange so few have heard it. It was never mentioned during my three years stay at Fisk University. President Price of Livingstone [then a leading Negro spokesman] has told me that he never heard of it, and students from various other Southern schools have expressed great surprise at the offer. The fact is that when I was wanting to come to Harvard, while yet in the South, I wrote to Dr. Haygood [Atticus G. Haygood, a leader of Southern white liberals], for a loan merely, and he never even answered my letter. I find men willing to help me thro' cheap theological schools. I find men willing to help me use my hands before I have got my brains in working order. I have an abundance of good wishes on hand, but I never found a man willing to help me get a Harvard Ph.D.

Hayes was stirred. He promised to take up the matter the next year with the board. Thereupon, the next year I proceeded to write the board: "At the close of the last academic year at Harvard, I received the degree of Master of Arts, and was reappointed to my fellowship for the year 1891-92. I have spent most of the year in the preparation of my doctor's thesis on the Suppression of the Slave Trade in America. I prepared a preliminary paper on this subject and read it before the American Historical Association at its annual meeting at Washington during the Christmas holidays.... Properly to finish my education, careful training in a European university for at least a year is, in my mind and the minds of my professors, absolutely indispensable." I thereupon asked respectfully "aid to study at least a year abroad under the direction of the graduate department of Harvard or other reputable auspices" and if this was not practicable, "that the board loan me a sufficient sum for this purpose." I did not of course believe that this would get me an appointment, but I did think that possibly through the influence of people who thus came to know about my work, I might somehow borrow or beg enough to get to Europe.

I rained recommendations upon Mr. Hayes. The Slater Fund Board surrendered, and I was given a fellowship of $750 to study a year abroad, with the promise that it might possibly be renewed for a second year. To salve their souls, however, this grant was made half as gift and half as repayable loan with 5 per cent interest. I remember rushing down to New York and talking with ex-President Hayes in the old Astor House, and emerging walking on air. I saw an especially delectable shirt in a shop window. I went in and asked about it. It cost three dollars, which was about four times as much as I had ever paid for a shirt in my life; but I bought it.

PART TWO

Du Bois on Education and Social Power

CHAPTER THREE

Of the Training of Black Men

The following article was first published in 1902 in the *Atlantic Monthly.* It was later included in a slightly different form as chapter 6 of *The Souls of Black Folks.* In this piece Du Bois directly addresses the question of color bias, as well as what forms of education are best suited for blacks. In addition, he refers specifically to the idea of an educated or "Talented Tenth," which he elaborates on in more detail in an essay of the same name published the following year in the book *The Negro Problem* (see chapter 5 of this work, "The Talented Tenth," pages 75-92).

> Why, if the Soul can fling the Dust aside,
> And naked on the Air of Heaven ride,
> Were't not a Shame—were't not a Shame for him
> In this clay carcase crippled to abide?
> *OMAR KHAYYAM (FITZGERALD)*

From the shimmering swirl of waters where many, many thoughts ago the slave-ship first saw the square tower of Jamestown, have flowed down to our day three streams of thinking: one swollen from the larger world here and overseas, saying, the multiplying of human wants in culture-lands calls for the world-wide cooperation of men in satisfying them. Hence arises a new human unity, pulling the ends of earth nearer, and all men, black, yellow, and white. The larger humanity strives to feel in this contact of living Nations and sleeping hordes a thrill of new life in the world, crying, "If the contact of Life and Sleep be Death, shame on such Life." To be sure, behind this thought lurks the afterthought of force and dominion,—the making of brown men to delve when the temptation of beads and red calico cloys.

The second thought streaming from the death-ship and the curving river is the thought of the older South,—the sincere and passionate belief that somewhere between men and cattle, God created a tertium quid, and called it a Negro,—a clownish, simple creature, at times even lovable within its limitations, but straitly foreordained to walk within the Veil. To be sure, behind the thought lurks the afterthought,—some of them with favoring chance might become men, but in sheer self-defence we dare not let them, and we build about them walls so high, and hang between them and the light a veil so thick, that they shall not even think of breaking through.

And last of all there trickles down that third and darker thought,—the thought of the things themselves, the confused, half-conscious mutter of men who are black and whitened, crying "Liberty, Freedom, Opportunity—vouchsafe to us, O boastful World, the chance of living men!" To be sure, behind the thought lurks the afterthought,—suppose, after all, the World is right and we are less than men? Suppose this mad impulse within is all wrong, some mock mirage from the untrue?

So here we stand among thoughts of human unity, even through conquest and slavery; the inferiority of black men, even if forced by fraud; a shriek in the night for the freedom of men who themselves are not yet sure of their right to demand it. This is the tangle of thought and afterthought wherein we are called to solve the problem of training men for life.

Behind all its curiousness, so attractive alike to sage and dilettante, lie its dim dangers, throwing across us shadows at once grotesque and awful. Plain it is to us that what the world seeks through desert and wild we have within our threshold,—a stalwart laboring force, suited to the semi-tropics; if, deaf to the voice of the Zeitgeist, we refuse to use and develop these men, we risk poverty and loss. If, on the other hand, seized by the brutal afterthought, we debauch the race thus caught in our talons, selfishly sucking their blood and brains in the future as in the past, what shall save us from national decadence? Only that saner selfishness, which Education teaches, can find the rights of all in the whirl of work.

Again, we may decry the color-prejudice of the South, yet it remains a heavy fact. Such curious kinks of the human mind exist and must be reckoned with soberly. They cannot be laughed away, nor always successfully stormed at, nor easily abolished by act of legislature. And yet they must not be encouraged by being let alone. They must be recognized as facts, but unpleasant facts; things that stand in the way of civilization and religion and common decency. They can be met in but one way,—by the breadth and broadening of human reason, by catholicity of taste and culture. And so, too, the native ambition and aspiration of men, even though they be black, backward, and ungraceful, must not lightly be dealt with. To stimulate wildly weak and untrained minds is to play with mighty fires; to flout their striving idly is to welcome a harvest of brutish crime and shameless lethargy in our very laps. The guiding of thought and the deft coordination of deed is at once the path of honor and humanity.

And so, in this great question of reconciling three vast and partially contradictory streams of thought, the one panacea of Education leaps to the lips of all:—such human training as will best use the labor of all men without enslaving or brutalizing; such training as will give us poise to encourage the prejudices that bulwark society, and to stamp out those that in sheer barbarity deafen us to the wail of prisoned souls within the Veil, and the mounting fury of shackled men.

But when we have vaguely said that Education will set this tangle straight, what have we uttered but a truism? Training for life teaches living; but what training for the profitable living together of black men and white? A hundred and fifty years ago our task would have seemed easier. Then Dr. Johnson blandly assured us that education was needful solely for the embellishments of life, and was useless for ordinary vermin. Today we have climbed to heights where we would open at least the outer courts of knowledge to all, display its treasures to many, and select the few to whom its mystery of Truth is revealed, not wholly by birth or the accidents of the stock market, but at least in part according to deftness and aim, talent and character. This programme, however, we are sorely puzzled in carrying out through that part of the land where the blight of slavery fell hardest, and where we are dealing with two backward peoples. To make here in human education that ever necessary combination of the permanent and the contingent—of the ideal and the practical in workable equilibrium—has been there, as it ever must be in every age and place, a matter of infinite experiment and frequent mistakes.

In rough approximation we may point out four varying decades of work in Southern education since the Civil War. From the close of the war until 1876, was the period of uncertain groping and temporary relief. There were army schools, mission schools, and schools of the Freedmen's Bureau in chaotic disarrangement seeking system and co-operation. Then followed ten years of constructive definite effort toward the building of complete school systems in the South. Normal schools and colleges were founded for the freedmen, and teachers trained there to man the public schools. There was the inevitable tendency of war to underestimate the prejudices of the master and the ignorance of the slave, and all seemed clear sailing out of the wreckage of the storm. Meantime, starting in this decade yet especially developing from 1885 to 1895, began the industrial revolution of the South. The land saw glimpses of a new destiny and the stirring of new ideals. The educational system striving to complete itself saw new obstacles and a field of work ever broader and deeper. The Negro colleges, hurriedly founded, were inadequately equipped, illogically distributed, and of varying efficiency and grade; the normal and high schools were doing little more than common school work, and the common schools were training but a third of the children who ought to be in them, and training these too often poorly. At the same time the white South, by reason of its sudden conversion from the slavery ideal, by so much the more became set and strengthened in its racial prejudice, and crystallized it into harsh law and harsher custom; while the marvelous pushing forward of the poor white daily threatened to take even bread and butter from the mouths of the heavily handicapped sons of the freedmen. In the midst, then, of the larger problem of Negro education sprang up the more practical question of work, the inevitable economic quandary that faces a people in the transition from slavery to freedom, and especially those who make that change amid hate and prejudice, lawlessness and ruthless competition.

The industrial school springing to notice in this decade, but coming to full recognition in the decade beginning with 1895, was the proffered answer to this combined educational and economic crisis, and an answer of singular wisdom and timeliness. From the very first in nearly all the schools some attention had been given to training in handiwork, but now was this training first raised to a dignity that brought it in direct touch with the South's magnificent industrial development, and given an emphasis which reminded black folk that before the Temple of Knowledge swing the Gates of Toil.

Yet after all they are but gates, and when turning our eyes from the temporary and the contingent in the Negro problem to the broader question of the permanent uplifting and civilization of black men in America, we have a right to inquire, as this enthusiasm for material advancement mounts to its height, if after all the industrial school is the final and sufficient answer in the training of the Negro race; and to ask gently, but in all sincerity, the ever-recurring query of the ages, Is not life more than meat, and the body more than raiment? And men ask this today all the more eagerly because of sinister signs in recent educational movements. The tendency is here, born of slavery and quickened to renewed life by the crazy imperialism of the day, to regard human beings as among the material resources of a land to be trained with an eye single to future dividends. Race prejudices, which keep brown and black men in their "places," we are coming to regard as useful allies with such a theory, no matter how much they may dull the ambition and sicken the hearts of struggling human beings. And above all, we daily hear that an education that encourages aspiration, that sets the loftiest of ideals and seeks as an end culture and character rather than bread-winning, is the privilege of white men and the danger and delusion of black.

Especially has criticism been directed against the former educational efforts to aid the Negro. In the four periods I have mentioned, we find first, boundless, planless enthusiasm and sacrifice; then the preparation of teachers for a vast public school system; then the launching and expansion of that school system amid increasing difficulties; and finally the training of workmen for the new and growing industries. This development has been sharply ridiculed as a logical anomaly and flat reversal of nature. Soothly we have been told that first industrial and manual training should have taught the Negro to work, then simple schools should have taught him to read and write, and finally, after years, high and normal schools could have completed the system, as intelligence and wealth demanded.

That a system logically so complete was historically impossible, it needs but a little thought to prove. Progress in human affairs is more often a pull than a push, a surging forward of the exceptional man, and the lifting of his duller brethren slowly and painfully to his vantage-ground. Thus it was no accident that gave birth to universities centuries before the common schools, that made fair Harvard the first flower of our wilderness. So in the South: the mass of the freedmen at the end of the war lacked the intelligence so necessary to modern workingmen. They must first have the common school to teach them to read, write, and cipher; and they must have higher schools to teach teachers for the common schools. The white teachers who flocked South went to establish such a common school system. Few held the idea of founding colleges; most of them at first would have laughed at the idea. But they faced, as all men since them have faced, that central paradox of the South,—the social separation of the races. At that time it was the sudden volcanic rupture of nearly all relations between black and white, in work and government and family life. Since then a new adjustment of relations in economic and political affairs has grown up,—an adjustment subtle and difficult to grasp, yet singularly ingenious, which leaves still that frightful chasm at the color-line across which men pass at their peril. Thus, then and now, there stand in the South two separate worlds; and separate not simply in the higher realms of social intercourse, but also in church and school, on railway and streetcar, in hotels and theatres, in streets and city sections, in books and newspapers, in asylums and jails, in hospitals and graveyards. There is still enough of contact for large economic and group cooperation, but the separation is so thorough and deep that it absolutely precludes for the present between the races anything like that sympathetic and effective group-training and leadership of the one by the other, such as the American Negro and all backward peoples must have for effectual progress.

This the missionaries of '68 soon saw; and if effective industrial and trade schools were impracticable before the establishment of a common school system, just as certainly no adequate common schools could be founded until there were teachers to teach them. Southern whites would not teach them; Northern whites in sufficient numbers could not be had. If the Negro was to learn, he must teach himself, and the most effective help that could be given him was the establishment of schools to train Negro teachers. This conclusion was slowly but surely reached by every student of the situation until simultaneously, in widely separated regions, without consultation or systematic plan, there arose a series of institutions designed to furnish teachers for the untaught. Above the sneers of critics at the obvious defects of this procedure must ever stand its one crushing rejoinder: in a single generation they put thirty thousand black teachers in the South; they wiped out the illiteracy of the majority of the black people of the land, and they made Tuskegee possible.

Such higher training schools tended naturally to deepen broader development: at first they were common and grammar schools, then some became high schools. And finally, by 1900, some thirty-four had one year or more of studies of college grade. This development was reached with different degrees of speed in different institutions: Hampton is still a high school, while Fisk University started her college in 1871, and Spelman Seminary about 1896. In all cases the aim was identical,— to maintain the standards of the lower training by giving teachers and leaders the best practicable training; and above all, to furnish the black world with adequate standards of human culture and lofty ideals of life. It was not enough that the teachers of teachers should be trained in technical normal methods; they must also, so far as possible, be broad-minded, cultured men and women, to scatter civilization among a people whose ignorance was not simply of letters, but of life itself.

It can thus be seen that the work of education in the South began with higher institutions of training, which threw off as their foliage common schools, and later industrial schools, and at the same time strove to shoot their roots ever deeper toward college and university training. That this was an inevitable and necessary development, sooner or later, goes without saying; but there has been, and still is, a question in many minds if the natural growth was not forced, and if the higher training was not either overdone or done with cheap and unsound methods. Among white Southerners this feeling is widespread and positive. A prominent Southern journal voiced this in a recent editorial.

> The experiment that has been made to give the colored students classical training has not been satisfactory. Even though many were able to pursue the course, most of them did so in a parrot-like way, learning what was taught, but not seeming to appropriate the truth and import of their instruction, and graduating without sensible aim or

valuable occupation for their future. The whole scheme has proved a waste of time, efforts, and the money of the state.

While most fair-minded men would recognize this as extreme and overdrawn, still without doubt many are asking, Are there a sufficient number of Negroes ready for college training to warrant the undertaking? Are not too many students prematurely forced into this work? Does it not have the effect of dissatisfying the young Negro with his environment? And do these graduates succeed in real life? Such natural questions cannot be evaded, nor on the other hand must a Nation naturally skeptical as to Negro ability assume an unfavorable answer without careful inquiry and patient openness to conviction. We must not forget that most Americans answer all queries regarding the Negro a priori, and that the least that human courtesy can do is to listen to evidence.

The advocates of the higher education of the Negro would be the last to deny the incompleteness and glaring defects of the present system: too many institutions have attempted to do college work, the work in some cases has not been thoroughly done, and quantity rather than quality has sometimes been sought. But all this can be said of higher education throughout the land; it is the almost inevitable incident of educational growth, and leaves the deeper question of the legitimate demand for the higher training of Negroes untouched. And this latter question can be settled in but one way,—by a first-hand study of the facts. If we leave out of view all institutions which have not actually graduated students from a course higher than that of a New England high school, even though they be called colleges; if then we take the thirty-four remaining institutions, we may clear up many misapprehensions by asking searchingly, What kind of institutions are they? what do they teach? and what sort of men do they graduate?

And first we may say that this type of college, including Atlanta, Fisk, and Howard, Wilberforce and Claflin, Shaw, and the rest, is peculiar, almost unique. Through the shining trees that whisper before me as I write, I catch glimpses of a boulder of New England granite, covering a grave, which graduates of Atlanta University have placed there, with this inscription:

> "IN GRATEFUL MEMORY OF THEIR
> FORMER TEACHER AND FRIEND
> AND OF THE UNSELFISH LIFE HE
> LIVED, AND THE NOBLE WORK HE
> WROUGHT; THAT THEY, THEIR
> CHILDREN, AND THEIR CHILD-

REN'S CHILDREN MIGHT BE
BLESSED."

This was the gift of New England to the freed Negro: not alms, but a friend; not cash, but character. It was not and is not money these seething millions want, but love and sympathy, the pulse of hearts beating with red blood;—a gift which today only their own kindred and race can bring to the masses, but which once saintly souls brought to their favored children in the crusade of the sixties, that finest thing in American history, and one of the few things untainted by sordid greed and cheap vainglory. The teachers in these institutions came not to keep the Negroes in their place, but to raise them out of the defilement of the places where slavery had wallowed them. The colleges they founded were social settlements; homes where the best of the sons of the freedmen came in close and sympathetic touch with the best traditions of New England. They lived and ate together, studied and worked, hoped and harkened in the dawning light. In actual formal content their curriculum was doubtless old-fashioned, but in educational power it was supreme, for it was the contact of living souls.

From such schools about two thousand Negroes have gone forth with the bachelor's degree. The number in itself is enough to put at rest the argument that too large a proportion of Negroes are receiving higher training. If the ratio to population of all Negro students throughout the land, in both college and secondary training, be counted, Commissioner Harris assures us "it must be increased to five times its present average" to equal the average of the land.

Fifty years ago the ability of Negro students in any appreciable numbers to master a modern college course would have been difficult to prove. Today it is proved by the fact that four hundred Negroes, many of whom have been reported as brilliant students, have received the bachelor's degree from Harvard, Yale, Oberlin, and seventy other leading colleges. Here we have, then, nearly twenty-five hundred Negro graduates, of whom the crucial query must be made, How far did their training fit them for life? It is of course extremely difficult to collect satisfactory data on such a point,—difficult to reach the men, to get trustworthy testimony, and to gauge that testimony by any generally acceptable criterion of success. In 1900, the Conference at Atlanta University undertook to study these graduates, and published the results. First they sought to know what these graduates were doing, and succeeded in getting answers from nearly two-thirds of the living. The direct testimony was in almost all cases corroborated by the reports of the colleges where they graduated, so that in the main the reports were worthy of credence. Fifty-three per cent of these graduates were teachers,—presidents of institutions, heads of normal schools, principals of city school systems, and the like. Seventeen per cent were clergymen; another seventeen per cent were in the professions, chiefly as physicians. Over six per cent were merchants, farmers, and artisans, and four per cent were in the government civil-service. Granting even that a considerable proportion of the third unheard from are unsuccessful, this is a record of usefulness. Personally I know many hundreds of these graduates, and have corresponded with more than a thousand; through others I have followed carefully the life-work of scores; I have taught some of them and some of the pupils whom they have taught, lived in homes which they have builded, and looked at life through their eyes. Comparing them as a class with my fellow students in New England and in Europe, I cannot hesitate in saying that nowhere have I met men and women with a broader spirit of helpfulness, with deeper devotion to their life-work, or with more consecrated determination to succeed in the face of bitter difficulties than among Negro college-bred men. They have, to be sure, their proportion of ne'er-do-wells, their pedants and lettered fools, but they have a surprisingly small proportion of them; they have not that culture of manner which we instinctively associate with university men, forgetting that in reality it is the heritage from cultured homes, and that no people a generation removed from slavery can escape a certain unpleasant rawness and gaucherie, despite the best of training.

With all their larger vision and deeper sensibility, these men have usually been conservative, careful leaders. They have seldom been agitators, have withstood the temptation to head the mob, and have worked steadily and faithfully in a thousand communities in the South. As teachers, they have given the South a commendable system of city schools and large numbers of private normal schools and academies. Colored college-bred men have worked side by side with white college graduates at Hampton; almost from the beginning the backbone of Tuskegee's teaching force has been formed of graduates from Fisk and Atlanta. And today the institute is filled with college graduates, from the energetic wife of the principal down to the teacher of agriculture, including nearly half of the executive council and a majority of the heads of departments. In the professions, college men are slowly but surely leavening the Negro church, are healing and preventing the devastations of disease, and beginning to furnish legal protection for the liberty and property of the toiling masses. All this is needful work. Who would do it if Negroes did not? How could Negroes do it if they were not trained carefully for it? If white people need colleges to furnish teachers, ministers, lawyers, and doctors, do black people need nothing of the sort?

If it is true that there are an appreciable number of Negro youth in the land capable by character and talent to receive that higher training, the end of which is culture, and if the two and a half thousand who have had something of this training in the past have in the main proved themselves useful to their race and generation, the question then comes, What place in the future development of the South ought the Negro college and college-bred man to occupy? That the present social separation and acute race-sensitiveness must eventually yield to the influences of culture, as the South grows civilized, is clear. But such transformation calls for singular wisdom and patience. If, while the healing of this vast sore is progressing, the races are to live for many years side by side, united in economic effort, obeying a common government, sensitive to mutual thought and feeling, yet subtly and silently separate in many matters of deeper human intimacy,—if this unusual and dangerous development is to progress amid peace and order, mutual respect and growing intelligence, it will call for social surgery at once the delicatest and nicest in modern history. It will demand broad-minded, upright men, both white and black, and in its final accomplishment American civilization will triumph. So far as white men are concerned, this fact is today being recognized in the South, and a happy renaissance of university education seems imminent. But the very voices that cry hail to this good work are, strange to relate, largely silent or antagonistic to the higher education of the Negro.

Strange to relate! for this is certain, no secure civilization can be built in the South with the Negro as an ignorant, turbulent proletariat. Suppose we seek to remedy this by making them laborers and nothing more: they are not fools, they have tasted of the Tree of Life, and they will not cease to think, will not cease attempting to read the riddle of the world. By taking away their best equipped teachers and leaders, by slamming the door of opportunity in the faces of their bolder and brighter minds, will you make them satisfied with their lot? or will you not rather transfer their leading from the hands of men taught to think to the hands of untrained demagogues? We ought not to forget that despite the pressure of poverty, and despite the active discouragement and even ridicule of friends, the demand for higher training steadily increases among Negro youth: there were, in the years from 1875 to 1880, 22 Negro graduates from Northern colleges; from 1885 to 1890 there were 43, and from 1895 to 1900, nearly 100 graduates. From Southern Negro colleges there were, in the same three periods, 143, 413, and over 500 graduates. Here, then, is the plain thirst for training; by refusing to give this Talented Tenth the key to knowledge, can any sane man imagine that they will lightly lay aside their yearning and contentedly become hewers of wood and drawers of water?

No. The dangerously clear logic of the Negro's position will more and more loudly assert itself in that day when increasing wealth and more intricate social organization preclude the South from being, as it so largely is, simply an armed camp for intimidating black folk. Such waste of energy cannot he spared if the South is to catch up with civilization. And as the black third of the land grows in thrift and skill, unless skillfully guided in its larger philosophy, it must more and more brood over the red past and the creeping, crooked present, until it grasps a gospel of revolt and revenge and throws its new-found energies athwart the current of advance. Even today the masses of the Negroes see all too clearly the anomalies of their position and the moral crookedness of yours. You may marshal strong indictments against them, but their counter-cries, lacking though they be in formal logic, have burning truths within them which you may not wholly ignore, O Southern Gentlemen! If you deplore their presence here, they ask, Who brought us? When you cry, Deliver us from the vision of intermarriage, they answer that legal marriage is infinitely better than systematic concubinage and pro-stitution. And if in just fury you accuse their vagabonds of violating women, they also in fury quite as just may reply: The rape which your gentlemen have done against helpless black women in defiance of your own laws is written on the foreheads of two millions of mulattoes, and written in ineffaceable blood. And finally, when you fasten crime upon this race as its peculiar trait, they answer that slavery was the arch-crime, and lynching and lawlessness its twin abortions; that color and race are not crimes, and yet it is they which in this land receive most unceasing condemnation, North, East, South, and West.

I will not say such arguments are wholly justified,—I will not insist that there is no other side to the shield; but I do say that of the nine millions of Negroes in this nation, there is scarcely one out of the cradle to whom these arguments do not daily present themselves in the guise of terrible truth. I insist that the question of the future is how best to keep these millions from brooding over the wrongs of the past and the difficulties of the present, so that all their energies may be bent toward a cheerful striving and cooperation with their white neighbors toward a larger, juster, and fuller future. That one wise method of doing this lies in the closer knitting of the Negro to the great industrial possibilities of the South is a great truth. And this the common schools and the manual training and trade schools are working to accomplish. But these alone are not enough. The foundations of knowledge in this race, as in others, must be sunk deep in the college and university if we would build a solid, permanent structure. Internal problems of social advance must inevitably come,—problems of work and wages, of families and homes, of morals and the true valuing of the things of life; and all these and other inevitable problems of civilization the Negro must meet and solve largely for himself, by reason of his isolation; and can there be any possible solution other than by study and thought and an appeal to the rich experience of the past? Is there not, with such a group and in such a crisis, infinitely more danger to be apprehended from half-trained minds and shallow thinking than from over-education and over-refinement? Surely we have wit enough to found a Negro college so manned and equipped as to steer successfully between the dilettante and the fool. We shall hardly induce black men to believe that if their stomachs be full, it matters little about their brains. They already dimly perceive that the paths of peace winding between honest toil and dignified manhood call for the guidance of skilled thinkers, the loving, reverent comradeship between the black lowly and the black men emancipated by training and culture.

The function of the Negro college, then, is clear: it must maintain the standards of popular education, it must seek the social regeneration of the Negro, and it must help in the solution of problems of race contact and cooperation. And finally, beyond all this, it must develop men. Above our modern socialism, and out of the worship of the mass, must persist and evolve that higher individualism which the centres of culture protect; there must come a loftier respect for the sovereign human soul that seeks to know itself and the world about it; that seeks a freedom for expansion and self-development; that will love and hate and labor in its own way, untrammeled alike by old and new. Such souls afore-time have inspired and guided worlds, and if we be not wholly bewitched by our Rhinegold, they shall again. Herein the longing of black men must have respect: the rich and bitter depth of their experience, the unknown treasures of their inner life, the strange rendings of nature they have seen, may give the world new points of view and make their loving, living, and doing precious to all human hearts. And to themselves in these the days that try their souls, the chance to soar in the dim blue air above the smoke is to their finer spirits boon and guerdon for what they lose on earth by being black.

I sit with Shakespeare and he winces not. Across the color-line I move arm in arm with Balzac and Dumas, where smiling men and welcoming women glide in gilded halls. From out the caves of evening that swing between the strong-limbed earth and the tracery of the stars, I summon Aristotle and Aurelius and what soul I will, and they come all graciously with no scorn nor condescension. So, wed with Truth, I dwell above the Veil. Is this the life you grudge us, O knightly America? Is this the life you long to change into the dull red hideousness of Georgia? Are you so afraid lest peering from this high Pisgah, between Philistine and Amalekite, we sight the Promised Land?

CHAPTER FOUR

The Training of Negroes for Social Power

Du Bois begins this article, published in *Outlook* magazine in October 1903, with the argument, in the end, that American Negroes must be responsible in the end for their own social improvement. However, such efforts are meaningless if they are given responsibility without power. If blacks are to move beyond being a "subject child-race," then they must not be dealt with and trained as a subject case, but taught to think and lead for themselves.

In this essay Du Bois echoes the idea of cultivating a "Talented Tenth," or leadership class in the black population. This was an idea he was introducing simultaneously in a chapter he had contributed to the book *The Negro Problem* (see chapter 5 of this work, "The Talented Tenth," pages 75-92). He felt that those who would assume this leadership required a higher training. Not everyone, however, was suited to this training. As he explained:

> Not all men—indeed, not the majority of men, only the exceptional few among American negroes or among any other people—are adapted to this higher training, as, indeed, only the exceptional few are adapted to higher training in any line; but the to be measured by their numbers, but rather by the numbers of their pupils and followers who are destined to see the world through their eyes, hear it through their trained ears, and speak to it through the music of their words. (page 67 of this book)

The "spread of intelligence" was the first step in Du Bois's mind toward the improvement of the condition of blacks. The support of both free public education for blacks, as well as the development and support of Negro colleges, was key to this process.

Many of the ideas outlined in this essay are echoed in chapter 3, "Of the Training of Black Men," included in *The Souls of Black Folks*, which had been completed earlier in 1903. In the end, he asks his audience (one assumes almost exclusively made up of white readers) to view black colleges and universities as the foundation for training Negro leaders. It is these individuals—well-educated, critical and socially conscious blacks—whom Du Bois believes will provide the foundation for the regeneration of the

Negro people. He concludes the article with a challenge to the *Outlook*'s white readers: "Are you afraid to let them try?" In doing so, he calls for the empowerment of the Negro people through the education of its most talented individuals—its future leaders. In this process, education is key to black social empowerment.

The responsibility for their own social regeneration ought to be placed largely upon the shoulders of the negro people. But such responsibility must carry with it a grant of power; responsibility without power is a mockery and a farce. If, therefore, the American people are sincerely anxious that the negro shall put forth his best efforts to help himself, they must see to it that he is not deprived of the freedom and power to strive. The responsibility for dispelling their own ignorance implies that the power to overcome ignorance is to be placed in black men's hands; the lessening of poverty calls for the power of effective work; and the responsibility for lessening crime calls for control over social forces which produce crime.

Such social power means, assuredly, the growth of initiative among negroes, the spread of independent thought, the expanding consciousness of manhood; and these things today are looked upon by many with apprehension and distrust, and there is systematic and determined effort to avoid this inevitable corollary of the fixing of social responsibility. Men openly declare their design to train these millions as a subject caste, as men to be thought for, but not to think; to be led, but not to lead themselves.

Those who advocate these things forget that such a solution flings them squarely on the other horn of the dilemma: such a subject child-race could never be held accountable for its own misdeeds and shortcomings; its ignorance would be part of the Nation's design, its poverty would arise partly from the direct oppression of the strong and partly front thriftlessness which such oppression breeds; and, above all, its crime would be the legitimate child of that lack of self-respect which caste systems engender. Such a solution of the negro problem is not one which the saner sense of the Nation for a moment contemplates; it is utterly foreign to American institutions, and is unthinkable as a future for any self-respecting race of men. The sound afterthought of the American people must come to realize that the responsibility for dispelling ignorance and poverty and uprooting crime among negroes cannot be put upon their own shoulders unless they are given such independent leadership in intelligence, skill, and morality as will inevitably lead to an independent manhood which cannot and will not rest in bonds.

Let me illustrate my meaning particularly in the matter of educating negro youth.

The negro problem, it has often been said, is largely a problem of ignorance—not simply of illiteracy, but a deeper ignorance of the world and its ways, of the thought and experience of men; an ignorance of self and the possibilities of human souls. This can be gotten rid of only by training; and primarily such training must take the form of that sort of social leadership which we call education. To apply such leadership to themselves, and to profit by it, means that negroes would have among themselves men of careful training and broad culture, as teachers and teachers of teachers. There are always periods of educational evolution when it is deemed quite proper for pupils in the fourth reader to teach those in the third. But such a method, wasteful and ineffective at all times, is peculiarly dangerous when ignorance is widespread and when there are few homes and public institutions to supplement the work of the school. It is, therefore, of crying necessity among negroes that the heads of their educational system—the teachers in the normal schools, the heads of high schools, the principals of public systems, should be unusually well trained men; men trained not simply in common school branches, not simply in the technique of school management and normal methods, but trained beyond this, broadly and carefully, into the meaning of the age whose civilization it is their peculiar duty to interpret to the youth of a new race, to the minds of untrained people. Such educational leaders should be prepared by long and rigorous courses of study similar to those which the world over have been designed to strengthen the intellectual powers, fortify character, and facilitate the transmission from age to age of the stores of the world's knowledge.

Not all men—indeed, not the majority of men, only the exceptional few among American negroes or among any other people—are adapted to this higher training, as, indeed, only the exceptional few are adapted to higher training in any line; but the significance of such men is not to be measured by their numbers, but rather by the numbers of their pupils and followers who are destined to see the world through their eyes, hear it through their trained ears, and speak to it through the music of their words.

Such men, teachers of teachers and leaders of the untaught, Atlanta University and similar colleges seek to train. We seek to do our work thoroughly and carefully. We have no predilections or prejudices as to particular studies or methods, but we do cling to those time-honored sorts of discipline which the experience of the world has long since proven to be of especial value. We sift as carefully as possible the student material which offers itself, and we try by every conscientious method to give to students who have character and ability such years of discipline as shall make them stronger, keener, and better for their peculiar mission. The history of civilization seems to prove that no group or nation which seeks advancement and true development can despise or neglect the power of well-trained minds; and this power of intellectual leadership must be given to the talented tenth among American negroes before this race can seriously be asked to assume the responsibility of dispelling its own ignorance. Upon the foundation-stone of a few well equipped negro colleges of high and honest standards can be built a proper system of free common schools in the South for the masses of the negro people; any attempt to found a system of public schools on anything less than this—on narrow ideals, limited or merely technical training—is to call blind leaders for the blind.

The very first step toward the settlement of the negro problem is the spread of intelligence. The first step toward wider intelligence is a free public school system; and the first and most important step toward a public school system is the equipment and adequate support of a sufficient number of negro colleges. These are first steps, and they involve great movements: first, the best of the existent colleges must not be abandoned to slow atrophy and death, as the tendency is today; secondly, systematic attempt must be made to organize secondary education. Below the colleges and connected with them must come the normal and high schools, judiciously distributed and carefully manned. In no essential particular should this system of common and secondary schools differ from educational systems the world over. Their chief function is the quickening and training of human intelligence; they can do much in the teaching of morals and manners incidentally, but they cannot and ought not to replace the home as the chief moral teacher; they can teach valuable lessons as to the meaning of work in the world, but they cannot replace technical schools and apprenticeship in actual life, which are the real schools of work. Manual training can and ought to be used in these schools, but as a means and not as an end—to quicken intelligence and self-knowledge and not to teach carpentry; just as arithmetic is used to train minds and not skilled accountants.

Whence, now, is the money coming for this educational system? For the common schools the support should come from local communities, the State governments and the United States Government; for secondary education, support should come from local and State governments and private philanthropy; for the colleges, from private philanthropy and the United States Government. I make no apology for bringing the United States Government in thus conspicuously. The General Government must give aid to Southern education if illiteracy and ignorance are to cease threatening the very foundations of civilization within any reasonable time. Aid to common school education could be appropriated to the different States on the basis of illiteracy. The fund could be administered by State officials, and the results and needs reported upon by United States educational inspectors under the Bureau of Education. The States could easily distribute the funds so as to encourage local taxation and enterprise and not result in pauperizing the communities. As to higher training, it must be remembered that the cost of a single battle-ship like the Massachusetts would endow all the distinctively college work necessary for negroes during the next half-century; and it is without doubt true that the unpaid balance from bounties withheld from negroes in the Civil War would, with interest, easily supply this sum.

But spread of intelligence alone will not solve the negro problem. If this problem is largely a question of ignorance, it is also scarcely less a problem of poverty. If negroes are to assume the responsibility of raising the standards of living among themselves, the power of intelligent work and leadership toward proper industrial ideals must be placed in their hands. Economic efficiency depends on intelligence, skill, and thrift. The public school system is designed to furnish the necessary intelligence for the ordinary worker, the secondary school for the more gifted workers, and the college for the exceptional few. Technical knowledge and manual dexterity in learning branches of the world's work are taught by industrial and trade schools, and such schools are of prime importance in the training of colored children. Trade-teaching cannot be effectively combined with the work of the common schools because the primary curriculum is already too crowded, and thorough common school training should precede trade-teaching. It is, however, quite possible to combine some of the work of the secondary schools with purely technical training, the necessary limitations being matters of time and cost: the question whether the boy can afford to stay in school long enough to add parts of a high-school course to the trade course, and particularly the question whether the school can afford or ought to afford to give trade-training to high-school students who do not intend to become artisans. A system of trade-schools therefore, supported by State and private aid, should be added to the secondary school system.

An industrial school, however, does not merely teach technique. It is also a school—a center of moral influence and of mental discipline. As such it has peculiar problems in securing the proper teaching force. It demands broadly trained men: the teacher of carpentry must be more than a carpenter, and the teacher of the domestic arts more than a cook; for such teachers must instruct, not simply in manual dexterity, but in mental quickness and moral habits. In other words, they must be teachers as well as artisans. It thus happens that college-bred men and men from other higher schools have always been in demand in technical schools, and it has been the high privilege of Atlanta University to furnish during the thirty-six years of its existence a part of the teaching force of nearly every negro industrial school in the United States and today our graduates are teaching in more than ever such institutions. The same might be said of Fisk University and other higher schools. If the college graduates were today withdrawn from the teaching force of the chief negro industrial schools, nearly every one of them would have to close its doors. These facts are forgotten by such advocates of industrial training as oppose the higher schools. Strong; as the argument for industrial schools is—and its strength is undeniable—its cogency simply increases the urgency of the plea for higher training-schools and colleges to furnish broadly educated teachers.

But intelligence and skill alone will not solve the Southern problem of poverty. With these must go that combination of homely habits and virtues which we may loosely call thrift. Something of thrift may be taught in school, more must be taught at home; but both these agencies are helpless when organized economic society denies to workers the just rewards of thrift and efficiency. And this has been true of black laborers in the South from the tittle of slavery down through the scandal of the Freedmen's Bank to the peonage and croplien system of today. If the Southern negro is shiftless, it is primarily because over large areas a shiftless negro can get on in the world about as well as an industrious black man. This is not universally true in the South, but it is true to so large an extent as to discourage striving ill precisely that class of negroes who most need encouragement. What is the remedy? Intelligence—not simply the ability to read and write or to sew—but the intelligence of a society permeated by that larger vision of life and broader tolerance which are fostered by the college and university. Not that all men must be college-bred, but that some men, black and white, must be, to leaven the ideals of the lump. Can any serious student of the economic South doubt that this today is her crying need?

Ignorance and poverty are the vastest of the negro problems. But to these later years have added a third—the problem of negro crime. That a great problem of social morality must have become eventually the central problem of emancipation is as clear as day to any student of history. In its grosser form as a problem of serious crime it is already upon us. Of course it is false and silly to represent that white women in the South are in daily danger of black assaulters. On the contrary, white womanhood in the South is absolutely safe in the hands of ninety-five per cent of the black men—ten times safer than black womanhood is in the hands of white men. Nevertheless, there is a large and dangerous class of negro criminals, paupers, and outcasts. The existence and growth of such a class, far from causing surprise, should be recognized as the natural result of that social disease called the negro problem; nearly every untoward circumstance known to human experience has united to increase negro crime: the slavery of the past, the sudden emancipation, the narrowing of economic opportunity, the lawless environment of wide regions, the stifling of natural ambition, the curtailment of political privilege, the disregard of the sanctity of black men's homes, and, above all, a system of treatment for criminals calculated to breed crime far faster than all other available agencies could repress it. Such a combination of circumstances is as sure to increase the numbers of the vicious and outcast as the rain is to wet the earth. The phenomenon calls for no delicately drawn theories of race differences; it is a plain case of cause and effect.

But, plain as the causes may be, the results are just as deplorable, and repeatedly today the criticism is made that negroes do not recognize sufficiently their responsibility in this matter. Such critics forget how little power today negroes have over their own lower classes. Before the black murderer who strikes his victim today, the average black man stands far more helpless than the average white, and, too, suffers ten times more from the effects of the deed. The white man has political power, accumulated wealth, and knowledge of social forces; the black man is practically disfranchised, poor, and unable to discriminate between the criminal and the martyr. The negro needs the defense of the ballot, the conserving power of property, and, above all, the ability to cope intelligently with such vast questions of social regeneration and moral reform as confront him. If social reform among negroes be without organization or trained leadership from within, if the administration of law is always for the avenging of the white victim and seldom for the reformation of the black criminal, if ignorant black men misunderstand the functions of government because they have had no decent instruction, and intelligent black men are denied a voice in government because they are black—under such circumstances to hold negroes responsible for the suppression of crime among themselves is the cruelest of mockeries.

On the other hand, a sincere desire among the American peoples help the negroes undertake their own social regeneration means, first, that the negro be given the ballot on the same terms as other men, to protect him against injustice and to safeguard his interests in the administration of law; secondly, that through education and social organization he be trained to work, and save, and earn a decent living. But these are not all: wealth is not the only thing worth accumulating; experience and knowledge can be accumulated and handed down, and no people can be truly rich without them. Can the negro do without these? Can this training in work and thrift be truly effective without the guidance of trained intelligence and deep knowledge—without that same efficiency which has enabled modern peoples to grapple so successfully with the problems of the Submerged Tenth? There must surely be among negro leaders the philanthropic impulse, the uprightness of character and strength of purpose, but there must be more than these; philanthropy and purpose among blacks as well as among whites must be guided and curbed by knowledge and mental discipline—knowledge of the forces of civilization that make for survival, ability to organize and guide those forces, and realization of the true meaning of those broader ideals of human betterment which may in time bring heaven and earth a little nearer. This is social power—it is gotten in many ways by experience, by social contact, by what we loosely call the chances of life. But the systematic method of acquiring and imparting it is by the training of youth to thought, power, and knowledge in the school and college. And that group of people whose mental grasp is by heredity weakest, and whose knowledge of the past is for historic reasons the most imperfect, that group is the very one which needs above all, for the talented of its youth, this severe and careful course of training; especially if they are expected to take immediate part in modern competitive life, if they are to hasten the slower courses of human development, and if the responsibility for this is to be in their own hands.

Three things American slavery gave the negro—the habit of work, the English language, and the Christian religion; but one priceless thing it debauched, destroyed, and took from him, and that was the organized home. For the sake of intelligence and thrift, for the sake of work and morality, this home-life must be restored and regenerated with Newer ideals. How? The normal method would be by actual contact with a higher home-life among his neighbors, but this method the social separation of white and black precludes. A proposed method is by schools of domestic arts, but, valuable as these are, they are but subsidiary aids to the establishment of homes; for real homes are primarily centers of ideals and teaching and only incidentally centers of cooking. The restoration and raising of home ideals must, then, come from social life among negroes themselves; and does that social life need no leadership? It needs the best possible leadership of pure hearts and trained heads, the highest leadership of carefully trained men.

Such are the arguments for the negro college, and such is the work that Atlanta University and a few similar institutions seek to do. We believe that a rationally arranged college course of study for men and women able to pursue it is the best and only method of putting into the world negroes with ability to use the social forces of their race so as to stamp out crime, strengthen the home, eliminate degenerates, and inspire and encourage the higher tendencies of the race not only in thought and aspiration but in every-day toil. And we believe this, not simply because we have argued that such training ought to have these effects, or merely because we hope for such results in some dim future, but because already for years we have seen in the work of our graduates precisely such results as I have mentioned: successful teachers of teachers; intelligent and upright ministers, skilled physicians, principals of industrial schools, business men, and, above all, makers of model homes and leaders of social groups, out from which radiate subtle but tangible forces of uplift and inspiration. The proof of this lies scattered in every State of the South, and above all, in the half-unwilling testimony of men disposed to decry our work.

Between the Negro college and industrial school there are the strongest grounds for co-operation and unity. It is not a matter of mere emphasis, for we would be glad to see ten industrial schools to every college. It is not a fact that there are today too few negro colleges but rather that there are too many institutions attempting to do college work. But the danger lies in the fact that the best of the negro colleges are poorly equipped and are today losing support and countenance, and that, unless the Nation awakens to its duty, ten years will see the annihilation of higher negro training in the South. We need a few strong, well-equipped negro colleges, and we need them now, not tomorrow; unless we can have them and have them decently supported, negro education in the South, both common school and industrial, is doomed to failure and the forces of social regeneration will be fatally weakened, for the college today among negroes is, just as truly as it was yesterday among whites, the beginning and not the end of human training, the foundation and not the capstone of popular education.

Strange, is it not, my brothers, how often in America those great watchwords of human energy—"Be strong!" "Know thyself!" "Hitch your wagon to a star!"—how often these die away into dim whispers when we face these seething millions of black men? And yet do they not belong to them? Are they not their heritage as well as yours? Can they bear burdens without strength, know without learning, and aspire without ideals? Are you afraid to let them try? Fear rather, in this our common fatherland, lest we live to those great watchwords of Liberty and Opportunity which yonder in the eternal hills their fathers fought with your fathers to preserve.

CHAPTER FIVE

The Talented Tenth

"The Talented Tenth" is among the most important of Du Bois's early writings. It was published late in 1903 as the second chapter of *The Negro Problem*. Approximately forty years later in his autobiography *Dusk of Dawn*, Du Bois recalled:

> I believed in the higher education of the Talented tenth who through their knowledge of modern culture could guide the American Negro into a higher civilization. I knew that without this the Negro would have to accept white leadership, and that such leadership could not always be trusted to guide this group into self-realization and to its highest cultural possibilities. Mr. Washington on the other hand believed the Negro as an efficient worker could gain wealth and that eventually through his ownership of capital he would be able to achieve a recognized place in American culture and could then educate his children as he might wish and develop his possibilities. (Du Bois 1940, 605)

It is interesting to note that despite his sophistication as a social thinker, Du Bois never entirely escaped a personal model of elitism. While he objected to white domination of black people, he does not seem to have considered the possibility that a black elite or "Talented Tenth" could have had their own class and social biases that did not necessarily conform with the needs and interests of the black "masses."

In this context, Cornel West has criticized Du Bois for being disconnected to "suffering, yet striving ordinary blackfolk" (West 1999, 1967). Although as a student at Fisk, Du Bois spent several summers living and teaching in rural black Tennessee, and lived in black communities throughout his life, he was largely disconnected from "ordinary" blacks. West explained that Du Bois's "inability to immerse himself in black everyday life precluded his access to the distinctive black tragicomic sense and black encounter with the absurd. He certainly saw, analyzed and empathized with black sadness, sorrow and suffering…. His own personal and intellectual distance lifted him above them even as he addressed their plight in his progressive writings" (West 1999, 1967).

In the essay that follows, Du Bois's distance from the black masses is clear. He asks toward its end:

Can the masses of the Negro people be in any possible way more quickly raised than by the effort and example of this aristocracy of talent and character? Was there ever a nation on God's fair earth civilized from the bottom upward? Never; it is, ever was and ever will be from the top downward that culture filters. The Talented Tenth rises and pulls all that are worth the saving up to their vantage ground. This is the history of human progress. (page 80 of this book)

Du Bois's dream of the Talented Tenth did not have a chance of becoming reality until the Civil Rights movement of the 1960s. One would like to believe that something of his dream, even with its elitist limitations and liabilities, has been realized in the last forty years in the United States. Let the reader be the judge.

The Negro race, like all races, is going to be saved by its exceptional men. The problem of education, then, among Negroes must first of all deal with the Talented Tenth; it is the problem of developing the Best of this race that they may guide the Mass away from the contamination and death of the Worst, in their own and other races. Now the training of men is a difficult and intricate task. Its technique is a matter for educational experts, but its object is for the vision of seers. If we make money the object of man-training, we shall develop money-makers but not necessarily men; if we make technical skill the object of education, we may possess artisans but not, in nature, men. Men we shall have only as we make manhood the object of the work of the schools—intelligence, broad sympathy, knowledge of the world that was and is, and of the relation of men to it—this is the curriculum of that Higher Education which must underlie true life. On this foundation we may build bread winning, skill of hand and quickness of brain, with never a fear lest the child and man mistake the means of living for the object of life.

If this be true—and who can deny it—three tasks lay before me; first to show from the past that the Talented Tenth as they have risen among American Negroes have been worthy of leadership; secondly to show how these men may be educated and developed; and thirdly to show their relation to the Negro problem.

You misjudge us because you do not know us. From the very first it has been the educated and intelligent of the Negro people that have led and elevated the mass, and the sole obstacles that nullified and retarded their efforts were slavery and race prejudice; for what is slavery but the legalized survival of the unfit and the nullification of the work of natural internal leadership? Negro leadership therefore sought from the first to rid the race of this awful incubus that it might make way for natural selection and the survival of the fittest. In colonial days came Phillis Wheatley and Paul Cuffe striving against the bars of prejudice; and Benjamin Banneker, the almanac maker, voiced their longings when he said to Thomas Jefferson, "I freely and cheerfully acknowledge that I am of the African race and in colour which is natural to them, of the deepest dye; and it is under a sense of the most profound gratitude to the Supreme Ruler of the Universe, that I now confess to you that I am not under that state of tyrannical thraldom and inhuman captivity to which too many of my brethren are doomed, but that I have abundantly tasted of the fruition of those blessings which proceed from that free and unequalled liberty with which you are favored, and which I hope you will willingly allow, you have mercifully received from the immediate hand of that Being from whom proceedeth every good and perfect gift.

"Suffer me to recall to your mind that time, in which the arms of the British crown were exerted with every powerful effort, in order to reduce you to a state of servitude; look back, I entreat you, on the variety of dangers to which you were exposed; reflect on that period in which every human aid appeared unavailable, and in which even hope and fortitude wore the aspect of inability to the conflict, and you cannot but be led to a serious and grateful sense of your miraculous and providential preservation, you cannot but acknowledge, that the present freedom and tranquility which you enjoy, you have mercifully received, and that a peculiar blessing of heaven.

"This, sir, was a time when you clearly saw into the injustice of a state of Slavery, and in which you had just apprehensions of the horrors of its condition. It was then that your abhorrence thereof was so excited, that you publicly held forth this true and invaluable doctrine, which is worthy to be recorded and remembered in all succeeding ages: 'We hold these truths to be self evident, that all men are created equal; that they are endowed with certain inalienable rights, and that among these are life, liberty and the pursuit of happiness.'"

Then came Dr. James Derham, who could tell even the learned Dr. Rush something of medicine, and Lemuel Haynes, to whom Middlebury College gave an honorary A.M. in 1804. These and others we may call the Revolutionary group of distinguished Negroes—they were persons of marked ability, leaders of a Talented Tenth, standing conspicuously among the best of their time. They strove by word and deed to save the color line from becoming the line between the bond and free, but all they could do was nullified by Eli Whitney and the Curse of Gold. So they passed into forgetfulness.

But their spirit did not wholly die; here and there in the early part of the century came other exceptional men. Some were natural sons of unnatural fathers and were given often a liberal training and thus a race of educated mulattoes sprang up to plead for black men's rights. There was Ira Aldridge, whom all Europe loved to honor; there was that Voice crying in the Wilderness, David Walker, and saying:

> "I declare it does appear to me as though some nations think God is asleep, or that he made the Africans for nothing else but to dig their mines and work their farms, or they cannot believe history sacred or profane. I ask every man who has a heart, and is blessed with the privilege of believing —Is not God a God of justice to all his creatures? Do you say he is? Then if he gives peace and tranquility to tyrants and permits them to keep our fathers, our mothers, ourselves and our children in eternal ignorance and wretchedness to support them and their families, would he be to us a God of Justice? I ask, O, ye Christians, who hold us and our children in the most abject ignorance and degradation that ever a people were afflicted with since the world began—I say if God gives you peace and tranquility, and suffers you thus to go on afflicting us, and our children, who have never given you the least provocation—would He be to us a God of Justice? If you will allow that we are men, who feel for each other, does not the blood of our fathers and of us, their children, cry aloud to the Lord of Sabaoth against you for the cruelties and murders with which you have and do continue to afflict us?"

This was the wild voice that first aroused Southern legislators in 1829 to the terrors of abolitionism.

In 1831 there met that first Negro convention in Philadelphia, at which the world gaped curiously but which bravely attacked the problems of race and slavery, crying out against persecution and declaring that "Laws as cruel in themselves as they were unconstitutional and unjust, have in many places been enacted against our poor, unfriended and unoffending brethren (without a shadow of provocation on our part), at whose bare recital the very savage draws himself up for fear of contagion—looks noble and prides himself because he bears not the name of Christian." Side by side this free Negro movement, and the movement for abolition, strove until they merged in to one strong stream. Too little notice has been taken of the work which the Talented Tenth among Negroes took in the great abolition crusade. From the very day that a Philadelphia colored man became the first subscriber to Garrison's "Liberator," to the day when Negro soldiers made the Emancipation Proclamation possible, black leaders worked shoulder to shoulder with white men in a movement, the success of which would have been impossible without them. There was Purvis and Remond, Pennington and Highland Garnett, Sojourner Truth and Alexander Crummel, and above all, Frederick Douglass—what would the abolition movement have been without them? They stood as living examples of the possibilities of the Negro race, their own hard experiences and well wrought culture said silently more than all the drawn periods of orators—they were the men who made American slavery impossible. As Maria Weston Chapman once said, from the school of anti-slavery agitation, "a throng of authors, editors, lawyers, orators and accomplished gentlemen of color have taken their degree! It has equally implanted hopes and aspirations, noble thoughts, and sublime purposes, in the hearts of both races. It has prepared the white man for the freedom of the black man, and it has made the black man scorn the thought of enslavement, as does a white man, as far as its influence has extended. Strengthen that noble influence! Before its organization, the country only saw here and there in slavery some faithful Cudjoe or Dinah, whose strong natures blossomed even in bondage, like a fine plant beneath a heavy stone. Now, under the elevating and cherishing influence of the American Anti-Slavery Society, the colored race, like the white, furnishes Corinthian capitals for the noblest temples."

Where were these black abolitionists trained? Some, like Frederick Douglass, were self-trained, but yet trained liberally; others, like Alexander Crummell and McCune Smith, graduated from famous foreign universities. Most of them rose up through the colored schools of New York and Philadelphia and Boston, taught by college-bred men like Russworm, of Dartmouth, and college-bred white men like Neau and Benezet.

After emancipation came a new group of educated and gifted leaders: Langston, Bruce and Elliot, Greener, Williams and Payne. Through political organization, historical and polemic writing and moral regeneration, these men strove to uplift their people. It is the fashion of today to sneer at them and to say that with freedom Negro leadership should have begun at the plow and not in the Senate—a foolish and mischievous lie; two hundred and fifty years that black serf toiled at the plow and yet that toiling was in vain till the Senate passed the war amendments; and two hundred and fifty years more the half-free serf of today may toil at his plow, but unless he have political rights and righteously guarded civic status, he will still remain the poverty-stricken and ignorant plaything of rascals, that he now is. This all sane men know even if they dare not say it.

And so we come to the present—a day of cowardice and vacillation, of strident wide-voiced wrong and faint-hearted compromise; of double-faced dallying with Truth and Right. Who are today guiding the work of the Negro people? The "exceptions" of course. And yet so sure as this Talented Tenth is pointed out, the blind worshippers of the Average cry out in alarm: "These are exceptions, look here at death, disease and crime —these are the happy rule." Of course they are the rule, because a silly nation made them the rule: Because for three long centuries this people lynched Negroes who dared to be brave, raped black women who dared to be virtuous, crushed dark-hued youth who dared to be ambitious, and encouraged and made to flourish servility and lewdness and apathy. But not even this was able to crush all manhood and chastity and aspiration from black folk. A saving remnant continually survives and persists, continually aspires, continually shows itself in thrift and ability and character. Exceptional it is to be sure, but this is its chiefest promise; it shows the capability of Negro blood, the promise of black men. Do Americans ever stop to reflect that there are in this land a million men of Negro blood, well-educated, owners of homes, against the honor of whose womanhood no breath was ever raised, whose men occupy positions of trust and usefulness, and who, judged by any standard, have reached the full measure of the best type of modern European culture? Is it fair, is it decent, is it Christian to ignore these facts of the Negro problem, to belittle such aspiration, to nullify such leadership and seek to crush these people back into the mass out of which by toil and travail, they and their fathers have raised themselves?

Can the masses of the Negro people be in any possible way more quickly raised than by the effort and example of this aristocracy of talent and character? Was there ever a nation on God's fair earth civilized from the bottom upward? Never; it is, ever was and ever will be from the top downward that culture filters. The Talented Tenth rises and pulls all that are worth the saving up to their vantage ground. This is the history of human progress; and the two historic mistakes which have hindered that progress were the thinking first that no more could ever rise save the few already risen; or second, that it would better the uprisen to pull the risen down.

How then shall the leaders of a struggling people be trained and the hands of the risen few strengthened? There can be but one answer: The best and most capable of their youth must be schooled in the colleges and universities of the land. We will not quarrel as to just what the university of the Negro should teach or how it should teach it—I willingly admit that each soul and each race-soul needs its own peculiar curriculum. But this is true: A university is a human invention for the transmission of knowledge and culture from generation to generation, through the training of quick minds and pure hearts, and for this work no other human invention will suffice, not even trade and industrial schools.

All men cannot go to college but some men must; every isolated group or nation must have its yeast, must have for the talented few centers of training where men are not so mystified and befuddled by the hard and necessary toil of earning a living, as to have no aims higher than their bellies, and no God greater than Gold. This is true training, and thus in the beginning were the favored sons of the freedmen trained. Out of the colleges of the North came, after the blood of war, Ware, Cravath, Chase, Andrews, Bumstead and Spence to build the foundations of knowledge and civilization in the black South. Where ought they to have begun to build? At the bottom, of course, quibbles the mole with his eyes in the earth. Aye! truly at the bottom, at the very bottom; at the bottom of knowledge, down in the very depths of knowledge there where the roots of justice strike into the lowest soil of Truth. And so they did begin; they founded colleges, and up from the colleges shot normal schools, and out from the normal schools went teachers, and around the normal teachers clustered other teachers to teach the public schools; the college trained in Greek and Latin and mathematics, 2,000 men; and these men trained full 50,000 others in morals and manners, and they in turn taught thrift and the alphabet to nine millions of men, who today hold $300,000,000 of property. It was a miracle—the most wonderful peace-battle of the 19th century, and yet today men smile at it, and in fine superiority tell us that it was all a strange mistake; that a proper way to found a system of education is first to gather the children and buy them spelling books and hoes; afterward men may look about for teachers, if haply they may find them; or again they would teach men Work, but as for Life—why, what has Work to do with Life, they ask vacantly.

Was the work of these college founders successful; did it stand the test of time? Did the college graduates, with all their fine theories of life, really live? Are they useful men helping to civilize and elevate their less fortunate fellows? Let us see. Omitting all institutions which have not actually graduated students from a college course, there are today in the United States thirty-four institutions giving something above high school training to Negroes and designed especially for this race.

Three of these were established in border States before the War; thirteen were planted by the Freedmen's Bureau in the years 1864-1869; nine were established between 1870 and 1880 by various church bodies; five were established after 1881 by Negro churches, and four are state institutions supported by United States' agricultural funds. In most cases the college departments are small adjuncts to high and common schoolwork. As a matter of fact six institutions—Atlanta, Fisk, Howard, Shaw, Wilberforce and Leland, are the important Negro colleges so far as actual work and number of students are concerned. In all these institutions, seven hundred and fifty Negro college students are enrolled. In grade the best of these colleges are about a year behind the smaller New England colleges and a typical curriculum is that of Atlanta University. Here students from the grammar grades, after a three years' high school course, take a college course of 136 weeks. One-fourth of this time is given to Latin and Greek; one-fifth, to English and modern languages; one-sixth, to history and social science; one-seventh, to natural science; one-eighth to mathematics, and one-eighth to philosophy and pedagogy.

In addition to these students in the South, Negroes have attended Northern colleges for many years. As early as 1826 one was graduated from Bowdoin College, and from that time till today nearly every year has seen elsewhere, other such graduates. They have, of course, met much color prejudice. Fifty years ago very few colleges would admit them at all. Even today no Negro has ever been admitted to Princeton, and at some other leading institutions they are rather endured than encouraged. Oberlin was the great pioneer in the work of blotting out the color line in colleges, and has more Negro graduates by far than any other Northern college.

The total number of Negro college graduates up to 1899 (several of the graduates of that year not being reported) was as follows:

		Negro Colleges	White Colleges
Before	1876	137	75
	1875-80	143	22
	1880-85	250	31
	1885-90	413	43
	1890-95	465	66
	1895-99	475	88
Class Unknown		57	64
	Total	1,914	390

Of these graduates 2,079, were men and 252 were women; 50 per cent. of Northern-born college men come South to work among the masses of their people, at a sacrifice which few people realize; nearly 90 per cent. of the Southern-born graduates instead of seeking that personal freedom and broader intellectual atmosphere which their training has led them, in some degree, to conceive, stay and labor and wait in the midst of their black neighbors and relatives.

The most interesting question, and in many respects the crucial question, to be asked concerning college-bred Negroes, is: Do they earn a living? It has been intimated more than once that the higher training of Negroes has resulted in sending into the world of work, men who could find nothing to do suitable to their talents. Now and then there comes a rumor of a colored college man working at menial service, etc. Fortunately, returns as to occupations of college-bred Negroes, gathered by the Atlanta conference, are quite full—nearly sixty per cent of the total number of graduates.

This enables us to reach fairly certain conclusions as to the occupations of all college-bred Negroes. Of 1,312 persons reported, there were:

Teachers, 53.4%
Clergymen, 16.8%
Physicians, etc., 6.3%
Students, 5.6%
Lawyers, 4.7%
In Govt.Service, 4.0%
In Business, 3.6%
Farmers and Artisans, 2.7%
Editors, Secretaries and Clerks, 2.4%
Miscellaneous, .5%

Over half are teachers, a sixth are preachers, another sixth are students and professional men; over 6 per cent. are farmers, artisans and merchants, and 4 per cent. are in government service. In detail the occupations are as follows:

Occupations of College-Bred Men

701 Teachers:
> Presidents and Deans, 19
> Teacher of Music, 7
> Professors, Principals and Teachers, 675

221 Clergymen:
> Bishop, 1
> Chaplains U.S. Army, 2
> Missionaries, 9
> Presiding Elders, 12
> Preachers, 197

83 Physicians:
> Doctors of Medicine, 76
> Druggists, 4
> Dentists, 3

74 Students

62 Lawyers

53 in Civil Service:
> U.S. Minister Plenipotentiary, 1
> U.S. Consul, 1
> U.S. Deputy Collector, 1
> U.S. Gauger, 1
> U.S. Postmasters, 2
> U.S. Clerks, 44
> State Civil Service, 2
> City Civil Service, 1

47 Business Men:
> Merchants, etc., 30
> Managers, 13
> Real Estate Dealers, 4

26 Farmers

22 Clerks and Secretaries:
> Secretary of National Societies, 7
> Clerks, etc., 15

9 Artisans

9 Editors

5 Miscellaneous

These figures illustrate vividly the function of the college-bred Negro. He is, as he ought to be, the group leader, the man who sets the ideals of the community where he lives, directs its thoughts and heads its social movements. It need hardly be argued that the Negro people need social leadership more than most groups; that they have no traditions to fall back upon, no long established customs, no strong family ties, no well defined social classes. All these things must be slowly and painfully evolved. The preacher was, even before the war, the group leader of the Negroes, and the church their greatest social institution. Naturally this preacher was ignorant and often immoral, and the problem of replacing the older type by better educated men has been a difficult one. Both by direct work and by direct influence on other preachers, and on congregations, the college-bred preacher has an opportunity for reformatory work and moral inspiration, the value of which cannot be overestimated.

It has, however, been in the furnishing of teachers that the Negro college has found its peculiar function. Few persons realize how vast a work, how mighty a revolution has been thus accomplished. To furnish five millions and more of ignorant people with teachers of their own race and blood, in one generation, was not only a very difficult undertaking, but a very important one, in that it placed before the eyes of almost every Negro child an attainable ideal. It brought the masses of the blacks in contact with modern civilization, made black men the leaders of their communities and trainers of the new generation. In this work college-bred Negroes were first teachers, and then teachers of teachers. And here it is that the broad culture of college work has been of peculiar value. Knowledge of life and its wider meaning, has been the point of the Negro's deepest ignorance, and the sending out of teachers whose training has not been simply for bread winning, but also for human culture, has been of inestimable value in the training of these men.

In earlier years the two occupations of preacher and teacher were practically the only ones open to the black college graduate. Of later years a larger diversity of life among his people, has opened new avenues of employment. Nor have these college men been paupers and spendthrifts; 557 college-bred Negroes owned in 1899, $1,342,862.50 worth of real estate (assessed value), or $2,411 per family. The real value of the total accumulations of the whole group is perhaps about $10,000,000, or $5,000 a piece. Pitiful is it not beside the fortunes of oil kings and steel trusts, but after all is the fortune of the millionaire the only stamp of true and successful living? Alas! it is, with many and there's the rub.

The problem of training the Negro is today immensely complicated by the fact that the whole question of the efficiency and appropriateness of our present systems of education, for any kind of child, is a matter of active debate, in which final settlement seems still afar off. Consequently it often happens that persons arguing for or against certain systems of education for Negroes, have these controversies in mind and miss the real question at issue. The main question, so far as the Southern Negro is concerned, is: What under the present circumstance, must a system of education do in order to raise the Negro as quickly as possible in the scale of civilization? The answer to this question seems to me clear: It must strengthen the Negro's character, increase his knowledge and teach him to earn a living. Now it goes without saying that it is hard to do all these things simultaneously or suddenly and that at the same time it will not do to give all the attention to one and neglect the others; we could give black boys trades, but that alone will not civilize a race of ex-slaves; we might simply increase their knowledge of the world, but this would not necessarily make them wish to use this knowledge honestly; we might seek to strengthen character and purpose, but to what end if this people have nothing to eat or to wear? A system of education is not one thing, nor does it have a single definite object, nor is it a mere matter of schools. Education is that whole system of human training within and without the school house walls, which molds and develops men. If then we start out to train an ignorant and unskilled people with a heritage of bad habits, our system of training must set before itself two great aims— the one dealing with knowledge and character, the other part seeking to give the child the technical knowledge necessary for him to earn a living under the present circumstances. These objects are accomplished in part by the opening of the common schools on the one, and of the industrial schools on the other. But only in part, for there must also be trained those who are to teach these schools—men and women of knowledge and culture and technical skill who understand modern civilization, and have the training and aptitude to impart it to the children under them. There must be teachers, and teachers of teachers, and to attempt to establish any sort of a system of common and industrial school training, without *first* (and I say *first* advisedly) without *first* providing for the higher training of the very best teachers, is simply throwing your money to the winds. School houses do not teach themselves—piles of brick and mortar and machinery do not send out *men*. It is the trained, living human soul, cultivated and strengthened by long study and thought, that breathes the real breath of life into boys and girls and makes them human, whether they be black or white, Greek, Russian or American. Nothing, in these latter days, has so dampened the faith of thinking Negroes in recent educational movements, as the fact that such movements have been accompanied by ridicule and denouncement and decrying of those very institutions of higher training which made the Negro public school possible, and make Negro industrial schools thinkable. It was: Fisk, Atlanta, Howard and Straight, those colleges born of the faith and sacrifice of the abolitionists, that placed in the black schools of the South the 30,000 teachers and more, which some, who depreciate the work of these higher schools, are using to teach their own new experiments. If Hampton, Tuskegee and the hundred other industrial schools prove in the future to be as successful as they deserve to be, then their success in training black artisans for the South, will be due primarily to the white colleges of the North and the black colleges of the South, which trained the teachers who today conduct these institutions. There was a time when the American people believed pretty devoutly that a log of wood with a boy at one end and Mark Hopkins at the other, represented the highest ideal of human training. But in these eager days it would seem that we have changed all that and think it necessary to add a couple of saw-mills and a hammer to this outfit, and, at a pinch, to dispense with the services of Mark Hopkins. I would not deny, or for a moment seem to deny, the paramount necessity of teaching the Negro to work, and to work steadily and skillfully; or seem to depreciate in the slightest degree the important part industrial schools must play in the accomplishment of these ends, but I *do* say, and insist upon it, that it is industrialism drunk with its vision of success, to imagine that its own work can be accomplished without providing for the training of broadly cultured men and women to teach its own teachers, and to teach the teachers of the public schools.

But I have already said that human education is not simply a matter of schools; it is much more a matter of family and group life—the training of one's home, of one's daily companions, of one's social class. Now the black boy of the South moves in a black world—a world with its own leaders, its own thoughts, its own ideals. In this world he gets by far the larger part of his life training, and through the eyes of this dark world he peers into the veiled world beyond. Who guides and determines the education which he receives in his world? His teachers here are the group-leaders of the Negro people—the physicians and clergymen, the trained fathers and mothers, the influential and forceful men about him of all kinds; here it is, if at all, that the culture of the surrounding world trickles through and is handed on by the graduates of the higher schools. Can such culture training of group leaders be neglected? Can we afford to ignore it? Do you think that if the leaders of thought among Negroes are not trained and educated thinkers, that they will have no leaders? On the contrary a hundred half-trained demagogues will still hold the places they so largely occupy now, and hundreds of vociferous busy-bodies will multiply. You have no choice; either you must help furnish this race from within its own ranks with thoughtful men of trained leadership, or you must suffer the evil consequences of a headless misguided rabble.

I am an earnest advocate of manual training and trade teaching for black boys, and for white boys, too. I believe that next to the founding of Negro colleges the most valuable addition to Negro education since the war has been industrial training for black boys. Nevertheless, I insist that the object of all true education is not to make men carpenters, it is to make carpenters men; there are two means of making the carpenter a man, each equally important: the first is to give the group and community in which he works, liberally trained teachers and leaders to teach him and his family what life means; the second is to give him sufficient intelligence and technical skill to make him an efficient workman; the first object demands the Negro college and college-bred men—not a quantity of such colleges, but a few of excellent quality; not too many college-bred men, but enough to leaven the lump, to inspire the masses, to raise the Talented Tenth to leadership; the second object demands a good system of common schools, well-taught, conveniently located and properly equipped.

The Sixth Atlanta Conference truly said in 1901:

> "We call the attention of the Nation to the fact that less than one million of the three million Negro children of school age, are at present regularly attending school, and these attend a session which lasts only a few months.

> "We are today deliberately rearing millions of our citizens in ignorance, and at the same time limiting the rights of citizenship by educational qualifications. This is unjust. Half the black youth of the land have no opportunities open to them for learning to read, write and cipher. In the discussion as to the proper training of Negro children after they leave the public schools, we have forgotten that they are not yet decently provided with public schools.

> "Propositions are beginning to be made in the South to reduce the already meagre school facilities of Negroes. We congratulate the South on resisting, as much as it has, this pressure, and on the many millions it has spent on Negro education. But it is only fair to point out that Negro taxes and the Negroes' share of the income from indirect taxes and endowments have fully repaid this expenditure, so that the Negro public school system has not in all probability cost the white taxpayers a single cent since the war.

> "This is not fair. Negro schools should be a public burden, since they are a public benefit. The Negro has a right to demand good common school training at the hands of the States and the Nation since by their fault he is not in position to pay for this himself."

What is the chief need for the building up of the Negro public school in the South? The Negro race in the South needs teachers today above all else. This is the concurrent testimony of all who know the situation. For the supply of this great demand two things are needed—institutions of higher education and money for school houses and salaries. It is usually assumed that a hundred or more institutions for Negro training are today turning out so many teachers and college-bred men that the race is threatened with an over-supply. This is sheer nonsense. There are today less than 3,000 living Negro college graduates in the United States, and less than 1,000 Negroes in college. Moreover, in the 164 schools for Negroes, 95 per cent. of their students are doing elementary and secondary work, work which should be done in the public schools. Over half the remaining 2,157 students are taking high school studies. The mass of so-called "normal" schools for the Negro, are simply doing elementary common schoolwork, or, at most, high school work, with a little instruction in methods. The Negro colleges and the post-graduate courses at other institutions are the only agencies for the broader and more careful training of teachers. The work of these institutions is hampered for lack of funds. It is getting increasingly difficult to get funds for training teachers in the best modern methods, and yet all over the South, from State Superintendents, county officials, city boards and school principals comes the wail, "We need TEACHERS!" and teachers must be trained. As the fairest minded of all white Southerners, Atticus G. Haygood, once said: "The defects of colored teachers are so great as to create an urgent necessity for training better ones. Their excellencies and their successes are sufficient to justify the best hopes of success in the effort, and to vindicate the judgment of those who make large investments of money and service, to give to colored students opportunity for thoroughly preparing themselves for the work of teaching children of their people."

The truth of this has been strikingly shown in the marked improvement of white teachers in the South. Twenty years ago the rank and file of white public school teachers were not as good as the Negro teachers. But they, by scholarships and good salaries, have been encouraged to thorough normal and collegiate preparation, while the Negro teachers have been discouraged by starvation wages and the idea that any training will do for a black teacher. If carpenters are needed it is well and good to train men as carpenters. But to train men as carpenters, and then set them to teaching is wasteful and criminal; and to train men as teachers and then refuse them living wages, unless they become carpenters, is rank nonsense.

The United States Commissioner of Education says in his report for 1900: "For comparison between the white and colored enrollment in secondary and higher education, I have added together the enrollment in high schools and secondary schools, with the attendance on colleges and universities, not being sure of the actual grade of work done in the colleges and universities. The work done in the secondary schools is reported in such detail in this office, that there can be no doubt of its grade."

He then makes the following comparisons of persons in every million enrolled in secondary and higher education:

	Whole Country	*Negroes*
1880	4,362	1,289
1900	10,743	2,061

And he concludes: "While the number in colored high schools and colleges had increased somewhat faster than the population, it had not kept pace with the average of the whole country, for it had fallen from 30 per cent. to 24 per cent. of the average quota. Of all colored pupils, one (1) in one hundred was engaged in secondary and higher work, and that ratio has continued substantially for the past twenty years. If the ratio of colored population in secondary and higher education is to be equal to the average for the whole country, it must be increased to five times its present average." And if this be true of the secondary and higher education, it is safe to say that the Negro has not one-tenth his quota in college studies. How baseless, therefore, is the charge of too much training! We need Negro teachers for the Negro common schools, and we need first-class normal schools and colleges to train them. This is the work of higher Negro education and it must be done.

Further than this, after being provided with group leaders of civilization, and a foundation of intelligence in the public schools, the carpenter, in order to be a man, needs technical skill. This calls for trade schools. Now trade schools are not nearly such simple things as people once thought. The original idea was that the "Industrial" school was to furnish education, practically free, to those willing to work for it; it was to "do" things—i.e.: become a center of productive industry, it was to be partially, if not wholly, self-supporting, and it was to teach trades. Admirable as were some of the ideas underlying this scheme, the whole thing simply would not work in practice; it was found that if you were to use time and material to teach trades thoroughly, you could not at the same time keep the industries on a commercial basis and make them pay. Many schools started out to do this on a large scale and went into virtual bankruptcy. Moreover, it was found also that it was possible to teach a boy a trade mechanically, without giving him the full educative benefit of the process, and, vice versa, that there was a distinctive educative value in teaching a boy to use his hands and eyes in carrying out certain physical processes, even though he did not actually learn a trade. It has happened, therefore, in the last decade, that a noticeable change has come over the industrial schools. In the first place the idea of commercially remunerative industry in a school is being pushed rapidly to the background. There are still schools with shops and farms that bring an income, and schools that use student labor partially for the erection of their buildings and the furnishing of equipment. It is coming to be seen, however, in the education of the Negro, as clearly as it has been seen in the education of the youths the world over, that it is the *boy* and not the material product, that is the true object of education. Consequently the object of the industrial school came to be the thorough training of boys regardless of the cost of the training, so long as it was thoroughly well done.

Even at this point, however, the difficulties were not surmounted. In the first place modern industry has taken great strides since the war, and the teaching of trades is no longer a simple matter. Machinery and long processes of work have greatly changed the work of the carpenter, the ironworker and the shoemaker. A really efficient workman must be today an intelligent man who has had good technical training in addition to thorough common school, and perhaps even higher training. To meet this situation the industrial schools began a further development; they established distinct Trade Schools for the thorough training of better class artisans, and at the same time they sought to preserve for the purposes of general education, such of the simpler processes of elementary trade learning as were best suited therefor. In this differentiation of the Trade School and manual training, the best of the industrial schools simply followed the plain trend of the present educational epoch. A prominent educator tells us that, in Sweden, "In the beginning the economic conception was generally adopted, and everywhere manual training was looked upon as a means of preparing the children of the common people to earn their living. But gradually it came to be recognized that manual training has a more elevated purpose, and one, indeed, more useful in the deeper meaning of the term. It came to be considered as an educative process for the complete moral, physical and intellectual development of the child."

Thus, again, in the manning of trade schools and manual training schools we are thrown back upon the higher training as its source and chief support. There was a time when any aged and worn-out carpenter could teach in a trade school. But not so today. Indeed the demand for college-bred men by a school like Tuskegee, ought to make Mr. Booker T. Washington the firmest friend of higher training. Here he has as helpers the son of a Negro senator, trained in Greek and the humanities, and graduated at Harvard; the son of a Negro congressman and lawyer, trained in Latin and mathematics, and graduated at Oberlin; he has as his wife, a woman who read Virgil and Homer in the same class room with me; he has as college chaplain, a classical graduate of Atlanta University; as teacher of science, a graduate of Fisk; as teacher of history, a graduate of Smith,—indeed some thirty of his chief teachers are college graduates, and instead of studying French grammars in the midst of weeds, or buying pianos for dirty cabins, they are at Mr. Washington's right hand helping him in a noble work. And yet one of the effects of Mr. Washington's propaganda has been to throw doubt upon the expediency of such training for Negroes, as these persons have had.

Men of America, the problem is plain before you. Here is a race transplanted through the criminal foolishness of your fathers. Whether you like it or not the millions are here, and here they will remain. If you do not lift them up, they will pull you down. Education and work are the levers to uplift a people. Work alone will not do it unless inspired by the right ideals and guided by intelligence. Education must not simply teach work—it must teach Life. The Talented Tenth of the Negro race must be made leaders of thought and missionaries of culture among their people. No others can do this work and Negro colleges must train men for it. The Negro race, like all other races, is going to be saved by its exceptional men.

PART THREE

Du Bois on Elementary and Secondary Education

CHAPTER SIX

The Freedman's Bureau

In this article, first published in March 1901 in the *Atlantic Monthly*, Du Bois introduces the general public to what is his most famous quote: "The problem of the twentieth century is the problem of the color line." The quote was first used by him in public in London the previous year, and on the lead placard for the "Exhibit of the Georgia Negro," which he and his students from Atlanta University had displayed at the Paris 1900 International Exposition.

In this essay, Du Bois looks at the Freedman's Bureau as an attempt to deal with the "slave problem" and ultimately the "vast problems of race and social condition." It is an invaluable summary of the role of the Freedman's Bureau and a pioneering study in the history of black education in the United States. Much of the content of this essay was republished in 1903 in *The Souls of Black Folks.*

The problem of the twentieth century is the problem of the color line; the relation of the darker to the lighter races of men in Asia and Africa, in America and the islands of the sea. It was a phase of this problem that caused the Civil War; and however much they who marched south and north in 1861 may have fixed on the technical points of union and local autonomy as a shibboleth, all nevertheless knew, as we know, that the question of Negro slavery was the deeper cause of the conflict. Curious it was, too, how this deeper question ever forced itself to the surface, despite effort and disclaimer. No sooner had Northern armies touched Southern soil than this old question, newly guised, sprang from the earth,—What shall be done with slaves? Peremptory military commands, this way and that, could not answer the query; the Emancipation Proclamation seemed but to broaden and intensify the difficulties; and so at last there arose in the South a government of men called the Freedmen's Bureau, which lasted, legally, from 1865 to 1872, but in a sense from 1861 to 1876, and which sought to settle the Negro problems in the United States of America.

It is the aim of this essay to study the Freedmen's Bureau,—the occasion of its rise, the character of its work, and its final success and failure,—not only as a part of American history, but above all as one of the most singular and interesting of the attempts made by a great nation to grapple with vast problems of race and social condition.

No sooner had the armies, east and west, penetrated Virginia and Tennessee than fugitive slaves appeared within their lines. They came at night, when the flickering camp fires of the blue hosts shone like vast unsteady stars along the black horizon: old men, and thin, with gray and tufted hair; women with frightened eyes, dragging whimpering, hungry children; men and girls, stalwart and gaunt,—a horde of starving vagabonds, homeless, helpless, and pitiable in their dark distress. Two methods of treating these newcomers seemed equally logical to opposite sorts of minds. Said some, "We have nothing to do with slaves." "Hereafter," commanded Halleck, "no slaves should be allowed to come into your lines at all; if any come without your knowledge, when owners call for them, deliver them." But others said, "We take grain and fowl; why not slaves?" Whereupon Fremont, as early as August, 1861, declared the slaves of Missouri rebels free. Such radical action was quickly countermanded, but at the same time the opposite policy could not be enforced; some of the black refugees declared themselves freemen, others showed their masters had deserted them, and still others were captured with forts and plantations. Evidently, too, slaves were a source of strength to the Confederacy, and were being used as laborers and producers. "They constitute a military resource," wrote the Secretary of War, late in 1861; "and being such, that they should not be turned over to the enemy is too plain to discuss." So the tone of the army chiefs changed, Congress forbade the rendition of fugitives, and Butler's "contrabands" were welcomed as military laborers. This complicated rather than solved the problem; for now the scattering fugitives became a steady stream, which flowed faster as the armies marched.

Then the long-headed man, with care-chiseled face, who sat in the White House, saw the inevitable, and emancipated the slaves of rebels on New Year's, 1863. A month later Congress called earnestly for the Negro soldiers whom the act of July, 1862, had half grudgingly allowed to enlist. Thus the barriers were leveled, and the deed was done. The stream of fugitives swelled to a flood, and anxious officers kept inquiring: "What must be done with slaves arriving almost daily? Am I to find food and shelter for women and children?"

It was a Pierce of Boston who pointed out the way, and thus became in a sense the founder of the Freedmen's Bureau. Being specially detailed from the ranks to care for the freedmen at Fortress Monroe, he afterward founded the celebrated Port Royal experiment and started the Freedmen's Aid Societies. Thus, under the timid Treasury officials and bold army officers, Pierce's plan widened and developed. At first, the able-bodied men were enlisted as soldiers or hired as laborers, the women and children were herded into central camps under guard, and "superintendents of contrabands" multiplied here and there. Centres of massed freedmen arose at Fortress Monroe, Va., Washington, D.C., Beaufort and Port Royal, S.C., New Orleans, La., Vicksburg and Corinth, Miss., Columbus, Ky., Cairo, Ill., and elsewhere, and the army chaplains found here new and fruitful fields.

Then came the Freedmen's Aid Societies, born of the touching appeals for relief and help from these centres of distress. There was the American Missionary Association, sprung from the *Amistad*, and now full grown for work, the various church organizations, the National Freedmen's Relief Association, the American Freedmen's Union, the Western Freedmen's Aid Commission,—in all fifty or more active organizations, which sent clothes, money, school-books, and teachers southward. All they did was needed, for the destitution of the freedmen was often reported as "too appalling for belief," and the situation was growing daily worse rather than better.

And daily, too, it seemed more plain that this was no ordinary matter of temporary relief, but a national crisis; for here loomed a labor problem of vast dimensions. Masses of Negroes stood idle, or, if they worked spasmodically, were never sure of pay; and if perchance they received pay, squandered the new thing thoughtlessly. In these and in other ways were camp life and the new liberty demoralizing the freedmen. The broader economic organization thus clearly demanded sprang up here and there as accident and local conditions determined. Here again Pierce's Port Royal plan of leased plantations and guided workmen pointed out the rough way. In Washington, the military governor, at the urgent appeal of the superintendent, opened confiscated estates to the cultivation of the fugitives, and there in the shadow of the dome gathered black farm villages. General Dix gave over estates to the freedmen of Fortress Monroe, and so on through the South. The government and the benevolent societies furnished the means of cultivation, and the Negro turned again slowly to work. The systems of control, thus started, rapidly grew, here and there, into strange little governments, like that of General Banks in Louisiana, with its 90,000 black subjects, its 50,000 guided laborers, and its annual budget of $100,000 and more. It made out 4,000 pay rolls, registered all freedmen, inquired into grievances and redressed them, laid and collected taxes, and established a system of public schools. So too Colonel Eaton, the superintendent of Tennessee and Arkansas, ruled over 100,000, leased and cultivated 7,000 acres of cotton land, and furnished food for 10,000 paupers. In South Carolina was General Saxton, with his deep interest in black folk. He succeeded Pierce and the Treasury officials, and sold forfeited estates, leased abandoned plantations, encouraged schools, and received from Sherman, after the terribly picturesque march to the sea, thousands of the wretched camp followers.

Three characteristic things one might have seen in Sherman's raid through Georgia, which threw the new situation in deep and shadowy relief: the Conqueror, the Conquered, and the Negro. Some see all significance in the grim front of the destroyer, and some in the bitter sufferers of the lost cause. But to me neither soldier nor fugitive speaks with so deep a meaning as that dark and human cloud that clung like remorse on the rear of those swift columns, swelling at times to half their size, almost engulfing and choking them. In vain were they ordered back, in vain were bridges hewn from beneath their feet; on they trudged and writhed and surged, until they rolled into Savannah, a starved and naked horde of tens of thousands. There too came the characteristic military remedy: "The islands from Charleston south, the abandoned rice fields along the rivers for thirty miles back from the sea, and the country bordering the St. John's River, Florida, are reserved and set apart for the settlement of Negroes now made free by act of war." So read the celebrated field order.

All these experiments, orders, and systems were bound to attract and perplex the government and the nation. Directly after the Emancipation Proclamation, Representative Eliot had introduced a bill creating a Bureau of Emancipation, but it was never reported. The following June, a committee of inquiry, appointed by the Secretary of War, reported in favor of a temporary bureau for the "improvement, protection, and employment of refugee freedmen," on much the same lines as were afterward followed. Petitions came in to President Lincoln from distinguished citizens and organizations, strongly urging a comprehensive and unified plan of dealing with the freedmen, under a bureau which should be "charged with the study of plans and execution of measures for easily guiding, and in every way judiciously and humanely aiding, the passage of our emancipated and yet to be emancipated blacks from the old condition of forced labor to their new state of voluntary industry."

Some half-hearted steps were early taken by the government to put both freedmen and abandoned estates under the supervision of the Treasury officials. Laws of 1863 and 1864 directed them to take charge of and lease abandoned lands for periods not exceeding twelve months, and to "provide in such leases or otherwise for the employment and general welfare" of the freedmen. Most of the army officers looked upon this as a welcome relief from perplexing "Negro affairs;" but the Treasury hesitated and blundered, and although it leased large quantities of land and employed many Negroes, especially along the Mississippi, yet it left the virtual control of the laborers and their relations to their neighbors in the hands of the army.

In March, 1864, Congress at last turned its attention to the subject, and the House passed a bill, by a majority of two, establishing a Bureau for Freedmen in the War Department. Senator Sumner, who had charge of the bill in the Senate, argued that freedmen and abandoned lands ought to be under the same department, and reported a substitute for the House bill, attaching the Bureau to the Treasury Department. This bill passed, but too late for action in the House. The debate wandered over the whole policy of the administration and the general question of slavery, without touching very closely the specific merits of the measure in hand.

Meantime the election took place, and the administration, returning from the country with a vote of renewed confidence, addressed itself to the matter more seriously. A conference between the houses agreed upon a carefully drawn measure which contained the chief provisions of Charles Sumner's bill, but made the proposed organization a department independent of both the War and Treasury officials. The bill was conservative, giving the new department "general superintendence of all freedmen." It was to "establish regulations" for them, protect them, lease them lands, adjust their wages, and appear in civil and military courts as their "next friend." There were many limitations attached to the powers thus granted, and the organization was made permanent. Nevertheless, the Senate defeated the bill, and a new conference committee was appointed. This committee reported a new bill, February 28, which was whirled through just as the session closed, and which became the act of 1865 establishing in the War Department a "Bureau of Refugees, Freedmen, and Abandoned Lands."

This last compromise was a hasty bit of legislation, vague and uncertain in outline. A Bureau was created, "to continue during the present War of Rebellion, and for one year thereafter," to which was given "the supervision and management of all abandoned lands, and the control of all subjects relating to refugees and freedmen," under "such rules and regulations as may be presented by the head of the Bureau and approved by the President." A commissioner, appointed by the President and Senate, was to control the Bureau, with an office force not exceeding ten clerks. The President might also appoint commissioners in the seceded states, and to all these offices military officials might be detailed at regular pay. The Secretary of War could issue rations, clothing, and fuel to the destitute, and all abandoned property was placed in the hands of the Bureau for eventual lease and sale to ex-slaves in forty-acre parcels.

Thus did the United States government definitely assume charge of the emancipated Negro as the ward of the nation. It was a tremendous undertaking. Here, at a stroke of the pen, was erected a government of millions of men,—and not ordinary men, either, but black men emasculated by a peculiarly complete system of slavery, centuries old; and now, suddenly, violently, they come into a new birthright, at a time of war and passion, in the midst of the stricken, embittered population of their former masters. Any man might well have hesitated to assume charge of such a work, with vast responsibilities, indefinite powers, and limited resources. Probably no one but a soldier would have answered such a call promptly; and indeed no one but a soldier could be called, for Congress had appropriated no money for salaries and expenses.

Less than a month after the weary emancipator passed to his rest, his successor assigned Major General Oliver O. Howard to duty as commissioner of the new Bureau. He was a Maine man, then only thirty-five years of age. He had marched with Sherman to the sea, had fought well at Gettysburg, and had but a year before been assigned to the command of the Department of Tennessee. An honest and sincere men, with rather too much faith in human nature, little aptitude for systematic business and intricate detail, he was nevertheless conservative, hard-working, and, above all, acquainted at first-hand with much of the work before him. And of that work it has been truly said, "No approximately correct history of civilization can ever be written which does not throw out in bold relief, as one of the great landmarks of political and social progress, the organization and administration of the Freedmen's Bureau."

On May 12, 1865, Howard was appointed, and he assumed the duties of his office promptly on the 15th, and began examining the field of work. A curious mess he looked upon: little despotisms, communistic experiments, slavery, peonage, business speculations, organized charity, unorganized almsgiving,—all reeling on under the guise of helping the freedman, and all enshrined in the smoke and blood of war and the cursing and silence of angry men. On May 19 the new government—for a government it really was—issued its constitution; commissioners were to be appointed in each of the seceded states, who were to take charge of "all subjects relating to refugees and freedmen," and all relief and rations were to be given by their consent alone. The Bureau invited continued cooperation with benevolent societies, and declared, "It will be the object of all commissioners to introduce practicable systems of compensated labor," and to establish schools. Forthwith nine assistant commissioners were appointed. They were to hasten to their fields of work; seek gradually to close relief establishments, and make the destitute self-supporting; act as courts of law where there were no courts, or where Negroes were not recognized in them as free; establish the institution of marriage among ex-slaves, and keep records; see that freedmen were free to choose their employers, and help in making fair contracts for them; and finally, the circular said, "Simple good faith, for which we hope on all hands for those concerned in the passing away of slavery, will especially relieve the assistant commissioners in the discharge of their duties toward the freedmen, as well as promote the general welfare."

No sooner was the work thus started, and the general system and local organization in some measure begun, than two grave difficulties appeared which changed largely the theory and outcome of Bureau work. First, there were the abandoned lands of the South. It had long been the more or less definitely expressed theory of the North that all the chief problems of emancipation might be settled by establishing the slaves on the forfeited lands of their masters,—a sort of poetic justice, said some. But this poetry done into solemn prose meant either wholesale confiscation of private property in the South, or vast appropriations. Now Congress had not appropriated a cent, and no sooner did the proclamations of general amnesty appear than the 800,000 acres of abandoned lands in the hands of the Freedmen's Bureau melted quickly away. The second difficulty lay in perfecting the local organization of the Bureau throughout the wide field of work. Making a new machine and sending out officials of duly ascertained fitness for a great work of social reform is no child's task; but this task was even harder, for a new central organization had to be fitted on a heterogeneous and confused but already existing system of relief and control of ex-slaves; and the agents available for this work must be sought for in an army still busy with war operations,—men in the very nature of the case ill fitted for delicate social work,—or among the questionable camp followers of an invading host. Thus, after a year's work, vigorously as it was pushed, the problem looked even more difficult to grasp and solve than at the beginning. Nevertheless, three things that year's work did, well worth the doing: it relieved a vast amount of physical suffering; it transported 7,000 fugitives from congested centres back to the farm; and, best of all, it inaugurated the crusade of the New England schoolma'am.

The annals of this Ninth Crusade are yet to be written, the tale of a mission that seemed to our age far more quixotic than the quest of St. Louis seemed to his. Behind the mists of ruin and rapine waved the calico dresses of women who dared, and after the hoarse mouthings of the field guns rang the rhythm of the alphabet. Rich and poor they were, serious and curious. Bereaved now of a father, now of a brother, now of more than these, they came seeking a life work in planting New England schoolhouses among the white and black of the South. They did their work well. In that first year they taught 100,000 souls, and more.

Evidently, Congress must soon legislate again on the hastily organized Bureau, which had so quickly grown into wide significance and vast possibilities. An institution such as that was well-nigh as difficult to end as to begin. Early in 1866 Congress took up the matter, when Senator Trumbull, of Illinois, introduced a bill to extend the Bureau and enlarge its powers. This measure received, at the hands of Congress, far more thorough discussion and attention than its predecessor. The war cloud had thinned enough to allow a clearer conception of the work of emancipation. The champions of the bill argued that the strengthening of the Freedmen's Bureau was still a military necessity; that it was needed for the proper carrying out of the Thirteenth Amendment, and was a work of sheer justice to the ex-slave, at a trifling cost to the government. The opponents of the measure declared that the war was over, and the necessity for war measures past; that the Bureau, by reason of its extraordinary powers, was clearly unconstitutional in time of peace, and was destined to irritate the South and pauperize the freedmen, at a final cost of possibly hundreds of millions. Two of these arguments were unanswered, and indeed unanswerable: the one that the extraordinary powers of the Bureau threatened the civil rights of all citizens; and the other that the government must have power to do what manifestly must be done, and that present abandonment of the freedmen meant their practical enslavement. The bill which finally passed enlarged and made permanent the Freedmen's Bureau. It was promptly vetoed by President Johnson, as "unconstitutional," "unnecessary," and "extrajudicial," and failed of passage over the veto. Meantime, however, the breach between Congress and the President began to broaden, and a modified form of the lost bill was finally passed over the President's second veto, July 16.

The act of 1866 gave the Freedmen's Bureau its final form,—the form by which it will be known to posterity and judged of men. It extended the existence of the Bureau to July, 1868; it authorized additional assistant commissioners, the retention of army officers mustered out of regular service, the sale of certain forfeited lands to freedmen on nominal terms, the sale of Confederate public property for Negro schools, and a wider field of judicial interpretation and cognizance. The government of the un-reconstructed South was thus put very largely in the hands of the Freedmen's Bureau, especially as in many cases the departmental military commander was now made also assistant commissioner. It was thus that the Freedmen's Bureau became a full-fledged government of men. It made laws, executed them and interpreted them; it laid and collected taxes, defined and punished crime, maintained and used military force, and dictated such measures as it thought necessary and proper for the accomplishment of its varied ends. Naturally, all these powers were not exercised continuously nor to their fullest extent; and yet, as General Howard has said, "scarcely any subject that has to be legislated upon in civil society failed, at one time or another, to demand the action of this singular Bureau."

To understand and criticise intelligently so vast a work, one must not forget an instant the drift of things in the later sixties: Lee had surrendered, Lincoln was dead, and Johnson and Congress were at loggerheads; the Thirteenth Amendment was adopted, the Fourteenth pending, and the Fifteenth declared in force in 1870. Guerrilla raiding, the ever present flickering after-flame of war, was spending its force against the Negroes, and all the Southern land was awakening as from some wild dream to poverty and social revolution. In a time of perfect calm, amid willing neighbors and streaming wealth, the social uplifting of 4,000,000 slaves to an assured and self-sustaining place in the body politic and economic would have been an herculean task; but when to the inherent difficulties of so delicate and nice a social operation were added the spite and hate of conflict, the Hell of War; when suspicion and cruelty were rife, and gaunt Hunger wept beside Bereavement,—in such a case, the work of any instrument of social regeneration was in large part foredoomed to failure. The very name of the Bureau stood for a thing in the South which for two centuries and better men had refused even to argue,—that life amid free Negroes was simply unthinkable, the maddest of experiments. The agents which the Bureau could command varied all the way from unselfish philanthropists to narrow-minded busybodies and thieves; and even though it be true that the average was far better than the worst, it was the one fly that helped to spoil the ointment. Then, amid all this crouched the freed slave, bewildered between friend and foe. He had emerged from slavery: not the worst slavery in the world, not a slavery that made all life unbearable,—rather, a slavery that had here and there much of kindliness, fidelity, and happiness,—but withal slavery, which, so far as human aspiration and desert were concerned, classed the black man and the ox together. And the Negro knew full well that, whatever their deeper convictions may have been, Southern men had fought with desperate energy to perpetuate this slavery, under which the black masses, with half-articulate thought, had writhed and shivered. They welcomed freedom with a cry. They fled to the friends that had freed them. They shrank from the master who still strove for their chains. So the cleft between the white and black South grew. Idle to say it never should have been; it was as inevitable as its results were pitiable. Curiously incongruous elements were left arrayed against each other: the North, the government, the carpetbagger, and the slave, here; and there, all the South that was white, whether gentleman or vagabond, honest man or rascal, lawless murderer or martyr to duty.

Thus it is doubly difficult to write of this period calmly, so intense was the feeling, so mighty the human passions, that swayed and blinded men. Amid it all two figures ever stand to typify that day to coming men: the one a gray-haired gentleman, whose fathers had quit themselves like men, whose sons lay in nameless graves, who bowed to the evil of slavery because its abolition boded untold ill to all; who stood at last, in the evening of life, a blighted, ruined form, with hate in his eyes. And the other, a form hovering dark and mother-like, her awful face black with the mists of centuries, had aforetime bent in love over her white master's cradle, rocked his sons and daughters to sleep, and closed in death the sunken eyes of his wife to the world; ay, too, had laid herself low to his lust and borne a tawny man child to the world, only to see her dark boy's limbs scattered to the winds by midnight marauders riding after Damned Niggers. These were the saddest sights of that woeful day; and no man clasped the hands of these two passing figures of the present-past; but hating they went to their long home, and hating their children's children live today.

Here, then, was the field of work for the Freedmen's Bureau; and since, with some hesitation, it was continued by the act of 1868 till 1869, let us look upon four years of its work as a whole. There were, in 1868, 900 Bureau officials scattered from Washington to Texas, ruling, directly and indirectly, many millions of men. And the deeds of these rulers fall mainly under seven heads,—the relief of physical suffering, the overseeing of the beginnings of free labor, the buying and selling of land, the establishment of schools, the paying of bounties, the administration of justice, and the financiering of all these activities. Up to June, 1869, over half a million patients had been treated by Bureau physicians and surgeons, and sixty hospitals and asylums had been in operation. In fifty months of work 21,000,000 free rations were distributed at a cost of over $4,000,000,—beginning at the rate of 30,000 rations a day in 1865, and discontinuing in 1869. Next came the difficult question of labor. First, 30,000 black men were transported from the refuges and relief stations back to the farms, back to the critical trial of a new way of working. Plain, simple instructions went out from Washington,—the freedom of laborers to choose employers, no fixed rates of wages, no peonage or forced labor. So far so good; but where local agents differed *toto coelo* in capacity and character, where the personnel was continually changing, the outcome was varied. The largest element of success lay in the fact that the majority of the freedmen were willing, often eager, to work. So contracts were written,—50,000 in a single state,—laborers advised, wages guaranteed, and employers supplied. In truth, the organization became a vast labor bureau; not perfect, indeed,—notably defective here and there,—but on the whole, considering the situation, successful beyond the dreams of thoughtful men. The two great obstacles which confronted the officers at every turn were the tyrant and the idler: the slaveholder, who believed slavery was right, and was determined to perpetuate it under another name; and the freedman, who regarded freedom as perpetual rest. These were the Devil and the Deep Sea.

In the work of establishing the Negroes as peasant proprietors the Bureau was severely handicapped, as I have shown. Nevertheless, something was done. Abandoned lands were leased so long as they remained in the hands of the Bureau, and a total revenue of $400,000 derived from black tenants. Some other lands to which the nation had gained title were sold, and public lands were opened for the settlement of the few blacks who had tools and capital. The vision of landowning, however, the righteous and reasonable ambition for forty acres and a mule which filled the freedmen's dreams, was doomed in most cases to disappointment. And those men of marvelous hind-sight, who today are seeking to preach the Negro back to the soil, know well, or ought to know, that it was here, in 1865, that the finest opportunity of binding the black peasant to the soil was lost. Yet, with help and striving, the Negro gained some land, and by 1874, in the one state of Georgia, owned near 350,000 acres.

The greatest success of the Freedmen's Bureau lay in the planting of the free school among Negroes, and the idea of free elementary education among all classes in the South. It not only called the schoolmistress through the benevolent agencies, and built them schoolhouses, but it helped discover and support such apostles of human development as Edmund Ware, Erastus Cravath, and Samuel Armstrong. State superintendents of education were appointed, and by 1870 150,000 children were in school. The opposition to Negro education was bitter in the South, for the South believed an educated Negro to be a dangerous Negro. And the South was not wholly wrong; for education among all kinds of men always has had, and always will have, an element of danger and revolution, of dissatisfaction and discontent. Nevertheless, men strive to know. It was some inkling of this paradox, even in the unquiet days of the Bureau, that allayed an opposition to human training, which still today lies smouldering, but not flaming. Fisk, Atlanta, Howard, and Hampton were founded in these days, and nearly $6,000,000 was expended in five years for educational work, $750,000 of which came from the freedmen themselves. Such contributions, together with the buying of land and various other enterprises, showed that the ex-slave was handling some free capital already. The chief initial source of this was labor in the army, and his pay and bounty as a soldier. Payments to Negro soldiers were at first complicated by the ignorance of the recipients, and the fact that the quotas of colored regiments from Northern states were largely filled by recruits from the South, unknown to their fellow soldiers. Consequently, payments were accompanied by such frauds that Congress, by joint resolution in 1867, put the whole matter in the hands of the Freedmen's Bureau. In two years $6,000,000 was thus distributed to 5000 claimants, and in the end the sum exceeded $8,000,000. Even in this system, fraud was frequent; but still the work put needed capital in the hands of practical paupers, and some, at least, was well spent.

The most perplexing and least successful part of the Bureau's work lay in the exercise of its judicial functions. In a distracted land where slavery had hardly fallen, to keep the strong from wanton abuse of the weak, and the weak from gloating insolently over the half-shorn strength of the strong, was a thankless, hopeless task. The former masters of the land were peremptorily ordered about, seized and imprisoned, and punished over and again, with scant courtesy from army officers. The former slaves were intimidated, beaten, raped, and butchered by angry and revengeful men. Bureau courts tended to become centres simply for punishing whites, while the regular civil courts tended to become solely institutions for perpetuating the slavery of blacks. Almost every law and method ingenuity could devise was employed by the legislatures to reduce the Negroes to serfdom,—to make them the slaves of the state, if not of individual owners; while the Bureau officials too often were found striving to put the "bottom rail on top," and give the freedmen a power and independence which they could not yet use. It is all well enough for us of another generation to wax wise with advice to those who bore the burden in the heat of the day. It is full easy now to see that the man who lost home, fortune, and family at a stroke, and saw his land ruled by "mules and niggers," was really benefited by the passing of slavery. It is not difficult now to say to the young freedman, cheated and cuffed about, who has seen his father's head beaten to a jelly and his own mother namelessly assaulted, that the meek shall inherit the earth. Above all, nothing is more convenient than to heap on the Freedmen's Bureau all the evils of that evil day, and damn it utterly for every mistake and blunder that was made.

All this is easy, but it is neither sensible nor just. Some one had blundered, but that was long before Oliver Howard was born; there was criminal aggression and heedless neglect, but without some system of control there would have been far more than there was. Had that control been from within, the Negro would have been reenslaved, to all intents and purposes. Coming as the control did from without, perfect men and methods would have bettered all things; and even with imperfect agents and questionable methods, the work accomplished was not undeserving of much commendation. The regular Bureau court consisted of one representative of the employer, one of the Negro, and one of the Bureau. If the Bureau could have maintained a perfectly judicial attitude, this arrangement would have been ideal, and must in time have gained confidence; but the nature of its other activities and the character of its personnel prejudiced the Bureau in favor of the black litigants, and led without doubt to much injustice and annoyance. On the other hand, to leave the Negro in the hands of Southern courts was impossible.

What the Freedmen's Bureau cost the nation is difficult to determine accurately. Its methods of bookkeeping were not good, and the whole system of its work and records partook of the hurry and turmoil of the time. General Howard himself disbursed some $15,000,000 during his incumbency; but this includes the bounties paid colored soldiers, which perhaps should not be counted as an expense of the Bureau. In bounties, prize money, and all other expenses, the Bureau disbursed over $20,000,000 before all of its departments were finally closed. To this ought to be added the large expenses of the various departments of Negro affairs before 1865; but these are hardly extricable from war expenditures, nor can we estimate with any accuracy the contributions of benevolent societies during all these years.

Such was the work of the Freedmen's Bureau. To sum it up in brief, we may say: it set going a system of free labor; it established the black peasant proprietor; it secured the recognition of black freemen before courts of law; it founded the free public school in the South. On the other hand, it failed to establish good will between ex-masters and freedmen; to guard its work wholly from paternalistic methods that discouraged self-reliance; to make Negroes landholders in any considerable numbers. Its successes were the result of hard work, supplemented by the aid of philanthropists and the eager striving of black men. Its failures were the result of bad local agents, inherent difficulties of the work, and national neglect. The Freedmen's Bureau expired by limitation in 1869, save its educational and bounty departments. The educational work came to an end in 1872, and General Howard's connection with the Bureau ceased at that time. The work of paying bounties was transferred to the adjutant general's office, where it was continued three or four years longer.

Such an institution, from its wide powers, great responsibilities, large control of moneys, and generally conspicuous position, was naturally open to repeated and bitter attacks. It sustained a searching congressional investigation at the instance of Fernando Wood in 1870. It was, with blunt discourtesy, transferred from Howard's control, in his absence, to the supervision of Secretary of War Belknap in 1872, on the Secretary's recommendation. Finally, in consequence of grave intimations of wrongdoing made by the Secretary and his subordinates, General Howard was court-martialed in 1874. In each of these trials, and in other attacks, the commissioner of the Freedmen's Bureau was exonerated from any willful misdoing, and his work heartily commended. Nevertheless, many unpleasant things were brought to light: the methods of transacting the business of the Bureau were faulty; several cases of defalcation among officials in the field were proven, and further frauds hinted at; there were some business transactions which savored of dangerous speculation, if not dishonesty; and, above all, the smirch of the Freedmen's Bank, which, while legally distinct from, was morally and practically a part of the Bureau, will ever blacken the record of this great institution. Not even ten additional years of slavery could have done as much to throttle the thrift of the freedmen as the mismanagement and bankruptcy of the savings bank chartered by the nation for their especial aid. Yet it is but fair to say that the perfect honesty of purpose and unselfish devotion of General Howard have passed untarnished through the fire of criticism. Not so with all his subordinates, although in the case of the great majority of these there were shown bravery and devotion to duty, even though sometimes linked to narrowness and incompetency.

The most bitter attacks on the Freedmen's Bureau were aimed not so much at its conduct or policy under the law as at the necessity for any such organization at all. Such attacks came naturally from the border states and the South, and they were summed up by Senator Davis, of Kentucky, when he moved to entitle the act of 1866 a bill "to promote strife and conflict between the white and black races . . . by a grant of unconstitutional power." The argument was of tremendous strength, but its very strength was its weakness. For, argued the plain common sense of the nation, if it is unconstitutional, unpracticable, and futile for the nation to stand guardian over its helpless wards, then there is left but one alternative: to make those wards their own guardians by arming them with the ballot. The alternative offered the nation then was not between full and restricted Negro suffrage; else every sensible man, black and white, would easily have chosen the latter. It was rather a choice between suffrage and slavery, after endless blood and gold had flowed to sweep human bondage away. Not a single Southern legislature stood ready to admit a Negro, under any conditions, to the polls; not a single Southern legislature believed free Negro labor was possible without a system of restrictions that took all its freedom away; there was scarcely a white man in the South who did not honestly regard emancipation as a crime, and its practical nullification as a duty. In such a situation, the granting of the ballot to the black man was a necessity, the very least a guilty nation could grant a wronged race. Had the opposition to government guardianship of Negroes been less bitter, and the attachment to the slave system less strong, the social seer can well imagine a far better policy: a permanent Freedmen's Bureau, with a national system of Negro schools; a carefully supervised employment and labor office; a system of impartial protection before the regular courts; and such institutions for social betterment as savings banks, land and building associations, and social settlements. All this vast expenditure of money and brains might have formed a great school of prospective citizenship, and solved in a way we have not yet solved the most perplexing and persistent of the Negro problems.

That such an institution was unthinkable in 1870 was due in part to certain acts of the Freedmen's Bureau itself. It came to regard its work as merely temporary, and Negro suffrage as a final answer to all present perplexities. The political ambition of many of its agents and proteges led it far afield into questionable activities, until the South, nursing its own deep prejudices, came easily to ignore all the good deeds of the Bureau, and hate its very name with perfect hatred. So the Freedmen's Bureau died, and its child was the Fifteenth Amendment.

The passing of a great human institution before its work is done, like the untimely passing of a single soul, but leaves a legacy of striving for other men. The legacy of the Freedmen's Bureau is the heavy heritage of this generation. Today, when new and vaster problems are destined to strain every fibre of the national mind and soul, would it not be well to count this legacy honestly and carefully? For this much all men know: despite compromise, struggle, war, and struggle, the Negro is not free. In the backwoods of the Gulf states, for miles and miles, he may not leave the plantation of his birth; in well-nigh the whole rural South the black farmers are peons, bound by law and custom to an economic slavery, from which the only escape is death or the penitentiary. In the most cultured sections and cities of the South the Negroes are a segregated servile caste, with restricted rights and privileges. Before the courts, both in law and custom, they stand on a different and peculiar basis. Taxation without representation is the rule of their political life. And the result of all this is, and in nature must have been, lawlessness and crime. That is the large legacy of the Freedman's Bureau, the work it did not do because it could not.

I have seen a land right merry with the sun; where children sing, and rolling hills lie like passioned women, wanton with harvest. And there in the King's Highway sat and sits a figure, veiled and bowed, by which the traveler's footsteps hasten as they go. On the tainted air broods fear. Three centuries' thought has been the raising and unveiling of that bowed human heart, and now, behold, my fellows, a century new for the duty and the deed. The problem of the twentieth century is the problem of the color line.

CHAPTER SEVEN

Heredity and the Public Schools

Heredity and the Public Schools is based on a lecture Du Bois delivered in 1904 under the sponsorship of the Principals' Association of the Colored Schools in Washington, D.C. It was subsequently published as a pamphlet. In this piece, Du Bois asks the question: "Is the average Negro child capable of essentially the same training and development as the average white child?"

Du Bois makes it clear that his position is:

> the Negro races are from every physical standpoint full and normally developed men; their stature and muscular development, their keenness of sense and their physical measurement show absolutely no variation from the European type sufficient to base any theory of essentially human difference upon. (pages 119-120 of this book)

For Du Bois, environment was the critical factor in determining the difference between the performances of black and white students in school. In comparing a black student to a white student, Du Bois notes how the difference in their environment has shaped their ability to learn.

> Here are two boys being trained for life; six hours a day they are in school; three hours they are in the street; fifteen hours they are at home. The schools they are in are similar—the teachers are of the same sort; but one walks and plays in alleys, with sordid companions, amid poverty and perhaps crime; the other lives on clean streets, with pavements, quiet and well-dressed, and well-behaved people; the home of one is dark, cheerless and empty; the home of the other is large, cheerful, filled with books and pictures, music and instruction; the parents of the one are ignorant, driven by the shadow of poverty, harassed by doubt and dream, worn with querulousness, fretting and scolding; the other has hands to lead him, hearts to soothe him, heads to guide him and correct him. Would you expect these two boys after ten years of this training to be equal in endowment and accomplishment? Would the difference be due to the shadowy unknown physical heredity of these children or to the perfectly tangible and well-known spiritual training—the social heritage of these two sons of men? (page 120-121 of this book)

Du Bois is of the conviction that black children are in no way inferior to their white counterparts. Instead, the differences between them are a result of their different environments. By itself, education (even when it is the same as for the white child) cannot bring about equality. In the case of black children, Du Bois notes that: "Even where they have equal chances of education the social heritage into which they are trained is poorer, lower, and more depressing." (page 122 of this book)

The social improvement of blacks, according to Du Bois, could not simply be addressed by the increased efficiency of the public schools, but instead, had to include "social reform," which would open the "gates of opportunity" for black children. In this context, Du Bois prophetically understood that education, learning and social growth and development are inextricably connected to the more general environment in which the individual lives. In this regard, he echoes progressive social reformers like Jacob Riis, Jane Addams, and John Dewey, who all believed that environment played a crucial role in the shaping of the individual.

There is perhaps no single subject upon which so much has in recent years been said, and from which so many widely varying conclusions have been drawn as upon the subject of heredity. And I want to speak to you about it because I continually find among our thinking classes much of misapprehension as to the real implications of certain arguments which have been used in regard to our race and which have without doubt tended to discourage many of our best workers with the prospects of successfully uplifting a nation of ten million men. And I particularly want to speak to you because you are teachers. I know you have been told this—have had the trite saying dinned into your ears, that the teacher above all men has the moulding of the next generation and according to his will can raise or lower the standards of efficiency and goodness. Consciously or unconsciously you have answered this question by throwing off a large part of your responsibility on that magic word, heredity. Nor is the fault yours, for the same shifting of burdens is seen all about you—for the evil of the world in politics, religion, social reform and race contact we have seen the world almost scuttling to place on the shoulders of this new god of the Philistines, the responsibility for all evil and shortcoming and mistake. Indeed, heredity with us becomes a sort of dignified rag-bag into which we carelessly or impatiently put the ideals and dreams of what we fear was an over-credulous past.

It would indeed be queer if we as parts of this nation escaped this contagion. We have not escaped it. Some of us have already thrown up our hands in half despair, saying the burden before us is the burden of shoulders broader than ours—of an intelligence all knowing of powers infinite in range and unwearied in doing. Others of us have made a brave appearance and spoken confidently and yet within has lurked the fear and the doubt.

It is a shadow of that old picture—the swaying gray-haired man, lifting his arms to God in dark despair: "It is enough, O Lord, I am not better than my fathers."

To no class of us is this tendency to despair of the very constitution of things more prevalent than among us as teachers. Nor is the reason far to seek—we see the material raw and in the moulding and we are in a profession where above all others the doctrine of heredity as enunciated to day—now carelessly, now vaguely, now curiously—has been deemed especially and peculiarly applicable.

For this reason and because of similar signs in the air I want today to go with you frankly to the kernel of a problem which we usually hover about and whisper over, but seldom frankly and openly and exhaustively discuss. And this question is: Is the average Negro child capable of essentially the same training and development as the average white child?

Now to answer this question it is necessary to examine certain fundamental ideas. And you will pardon me if I say right here that the development of this subject must of necessity be dry and not entertaining and that unless you work with me we will not accomplish all that I want to do in laying before you certain clear ideas.

One of the first questions that comes to every inquiring mind is: how did things happen to be as they are? Here is earth and air and sea and sky—above all here are men curious in thought and ability, intricate in body and muscle—how did they happen? And above all how did they happen just so?

Now the first answer that thinking men gave to these question was: these men were made, and they were made in the form they are for certain obvious purposes: here is a hand, it is clearly made for grasping—separate fingers for twining themselves, joints for bending, tendrils and cords and blocks and tackles for tightening the grasp; hardened extremities to save the wear and tear and hard tough covering within for rough usage. Was there ever a more obvious case of a thing created for a certain definite purpose? Or look this being over. Where in the human body can you find accident: here high in front are eyes—no mistake—they were not placed in the heels, or the small of the back, but aloft in a tower to survey the world; notice the balancing of this mass of 150 lbs. of matter—see the muscles; and its guiding, its delicate telegraphy; where does it center? away up out of the dust in a carefully covered casket of marvellous workmanship. I remember once that Professor James, the greatest of American psychologists, said to a class in which I was: the argument for purposive creation, of means foreordained to certain ends was, a century ago, practically unanswerable. And yet today you hear scarce a word of it, and the reason is that since the day of Charles Darwin the world has spoken a new language.

But let us not be too easily misled. Purposive creation is not negatived but certain accompanying misconceptions have been swept away; and the chief of these misconceptions is that of the sudden "Fiat" creation and that of the way in which purpose is manifested. Man is a dramatic animal: given a great conception like that of the creation of a world and he dressed it out in glamour and regalia. The vision of a mighty arm leaped to his eyes the roaring of primeval chaos and the Voice sweeping across the waters, crying let there be light. One element alone of creation he could not hold in his imagination, and that was Time—of a creation in a minute, in the twinkling of an eye, he could think and dream and paint, but not of a creative force working silently, continuously a hundred, a thousand a million years. And here was the first correction that came to the older ideas. There was a day when men were hanged for daring to suggest that it took longer than six days to build a mountain, guide a river, and set the stars above the seas. But today we realize the element of time in creation and read into the early chapters of Genesis a new meaning. It seems to some that the poetry and truth of the picture has been spoiled and the bases of religious faith shaken; to others it seems that we have received a conception at once vaster and truer and more sublime.

Then again the conception of the working of purpose was changed by Charles Darwin's epoch-making work. He said the hands are surely made to grasp; strangely made, beautifully adjusted, but how came it so? Not again by sudden fiat, but quick creation. First it was a hoof, then it became a paw, then a two or three fingered limb and finally a human hand. No sooner however, had this conception of growth come than the question followed why did it grow this way; why did it progress from the less useful to the more useful; the less facile to the delicately adaptable? The answer to this query was an epoch-making leap of the human mind: and that answer was: the animals with hands were able to survive under given conditions of life better than animals with paws; consequently the animals with hands multiplied and increased, and the increase of the animals with paws was checked and so on through nature hunted by its enemies the animals which by reason of their color and form could hide survived while those whose color was unfavorable perished, the strong of muscle survived, the weak perished, the beautiful were chosen for mating, the ugly died unmated and so on thro' the world by a strange natural selection those attributes and habits and limbs and organs were by the physical surroundings of animals and their circumstances of life chosen out and kept alive, while death carried the rest away. And this is what we mean by the survival of the fittest.

But there is, as many of you must know, one curious hitch in this otherwise brilliant demonstration. How did it happen that any animal so varied from the type as to present a new feature which proved valuable for helping him live—in a world of hoofed animals how did it happen that a split-hoofed animal appeared and then a five fingered man? The answer tentatively given to this was that this happened thro' inexplicable and yet evident variation from type. From the parents without apparent cause there is suddenly born offspring that does not wholly resemble either—it varies; perhaps slightly, perhaps considerably from the parent type. If the variation is useless it has no effect on animal life; if it is useful it gives the possessor a new means of getting on in the world—an advantage over its rivals; if lastly the new variation from type is a hindrance it will handicap and eventually kill its possessor or his descendants. As to the hidden forces determining this variation, science too returns no definite; but when once the variation occurs there is an application of the great law of inertia which tends to make the new thing permanent in the race and this tendency to permanence in acquired character is what is known as heredity.

The recognition of the wonderful part which heredity and variation play in animal life literally changed the world's language in the earlier half of the 19th century and especially did the phrase: "*the survival of the fittest.*" Undoubtedly this phrase led to a hardening of human hearts.

Certain animals, certain races survive, and the reason of this survival was because they were fit to survive. The exact explanation of this fitness, however, varied from time to time. Some people meant by, fitness the fact that this particular race or this particular group were the best representatives of humanity or of the animal world. Scientists, however, meant simply that this particular race or group were the strongest people or the more cunning, or in some way best adapted to overcome their enemies in the animal world or in the physical world. And moreover it became increasingly clearer that much of the ability of survival a group or an animal possessed depended upon his reason; that those races of men for instance, with the strongest reasoning powers must of necessity over-reach those with weaker minds; so that out of a tendency to regard survival in the world as merely mechanical and as inevitable a fatalistic thing that must occur, there grew up by degrees the larger conception that survival depended upon human ability; and it was upon this thought that, several decades ago, were based the whole argument for the public school. It was said here is a nation; if that nation expects to survive it must think; if it is going to think it must think clearly; it must have large funds of knowledge, and have at its fingers' ends the facts of this multitudinous world; consequently the children of this people must be trained, not simply some of the children but all of the children; and as they are trained through the effects of the great law of heredity, the acquired ability is going to be transmitted to their children; and thus the race and the nation is going to be bettered.

I do not doubt but that most people take it that this is the argument for the public schools today; in a sense it is; and yet there has come a subtle change in the application and in the way in which the world's keener minds conceive it; and that change in conception depends upon a change in the conception of what heredity really means and how it really works in animal life. The older and cruder doctrine of heredity said: "The child is born; it grows to youth and manhood; it learns certain things; acquires certain habits, the things which it learns and acquires, it transmits to its children, and they in turn transmit what was transmitted to them in addition to what they themselves have acquired." And so there goes on in the line of individual descent an accumulation of acquired characteristics; and it is such acquired characteristics, in addition to the original endowment which makes the civilized man. Now this conception of heredity has been very seriously questioned; and I think it fair to say today that it is practically overthrown, and the man who did the overthrowing, Weismann of Germany, has shown us a newer and more subtle conception.

Weismann's conception is that no acquired characteristics of the individual after birth are ever transmitted to his descendants; that each individual is, as it were, the ripened fruit fallen from the parent tree, and once so separated from the parent he begins an independent development of his own which can not be influenced physically by the original tree, nor can any of the acquired characteristics be handed down generation after generation; that the child resembles parent from the fact that they both spring from the same great seed and not because the characteristics acquired by the father were given to the son. Now it may seem to you that this after all makes but little difference, and yet upon this distinction is based nearly all the modern doctrine of higher and lower races, of superior and inferior nations: for it is said how impossible it is to make an Anglo-Saxon out of a Zulu, since no matter how educated the individual Zulu may become his acquired education can never be transmitted to his children; Zulu in stock and birth he must continue Zulu to the world's end; he can never be raised or lowered; he is fated to be what by inexplicable creation he was made. If any of you have noted, in the last decade or so, a weakening of interest in the public school, a lessening of faith in what human training may accomplish, and a general tendency to sit back and watch the lower classes and the lower races waver arid wander on, unhelped and with little sympathy from above, you may be sure that the source of this new attitude is the conception of heredity which I have already mentioned. But in the last decade this evidently incomplete picture of what human life really is has received a strange and notable reinforcement and adjustment to larger truth. Let it be granted that men do not receive from their fathers, through sheer physical heredity, that new and wonderful endowment which the world has given to growing sons of the twentieth century, and yet it nevertheless remains true that he does receive the endowment, or in other words physical heredity by no means the only heredity in the world nor is it in all probability the more important heredity. The human child receives its body and the physical bases of life from its parents, but it receives its thoughts, the larger part of its habits, its tricks of doing, its religion; its whole conception of what it is and what the whole world about it is from the society in which it is placed; and this heredity which is not physical at all has been aptly called social heredity. It is easy to illustrate this; take for instance a boy; he is born and reared in the slums of New York; conceive now a boy of exactly similar endowment, born on a farm in Ohio; that you are going to have two entirely different men under such circumstances is as clear as noonday. But why? It is not all necessary that they should have had, a different beginning in the world, that they should have sprung from a different kind of human seed; we may indeed conceive them to be own brothers; and yet in the one place the social influences of the slums of New York are going to form a street Arab, quick, keen, depraved, perhaps criminal, while the surroundings of the other boy are going to give to the world a slower, more honest, and more open nature; nor is it the mere physical surroundings that are going to make this difference; it is the spiritual surroundings, the thought, the talk, the economic organization, the different ways in which these two different worlds conceive themselves as parts of some larger world; and so vast and important are these social surroundings to any human being, either today or yesterday, that it is undoubtedly true that nine tenths of what a man is, depends on social rather than on physical heredity.

Now while people for centuries have known this and partially grasped the idea and expressed it in varying ways, yet it is not until the present decade perhaps that the idea has received that scientific formulation that enables us to comprehend it broadly, and when people do comprehend it, it is going to revolutionize modern thought and modern conceptions of education.

Now I want to go back again over the way which we have come, that is account of the varying conceptions of creation and the development of the conceptions of heredity, and bring to your minds how these varying conceptions have influenced our ideas of the inter-relations in the world of men. In the first place, when purposive creation in its more child-like form, was dominant it tried to explain one thing that has ever faced men, and that is the difference in the human condition; the difference between high and low, good and bad, prosperous and unfortunate; and first if explained them simply and crudely, that men were divided into the elect and the damned; that the elect were happy and the damned unhappy, and when it became evident that this did not explain all the intricacies of human inequality there was added to this the larger idea of a second story to the world where the happiness of the elect would be more assured and the punishment of the damned more certain. When, however even before the days of Charles Darwin, men had begun to notice how dependent we are upon physical environment and how the circumstances of life changed life there was a tendency toward a more fatalistic conception of life, and more emphasis placed upon climate and circumstances as determining whether men should be happy or unhappy, whether races should survive or perish.

Then when the tendency was to put the stress on human capabilities and acquirements as the bases of race accomplishment men were disposed to measure brain capacitys and look for the exceptional individual. If a single Negro could read Greek it showed that some Negroes were among the gifted and that the lines of superiority were not entirely racial. But when we come down further to the idea that individual accomplishment was spasmodic that only those great lines of descent of certain families natures furnish the seed of surviving peoples, then again our way of thinking was changed. The world thought less of the exceptional man and began to look at the average man as typical of the race. Finally; with the knowledge that thought and words, and right and deed influence men even more than their original physical endowment there has arisen the whole movement of social reform to inspire and arouse men, and to furnish by social heredity that which they otherwise lack.

I know all this seems dry and far-fetched and much of it is trite and yet we can not get too sure a grasp of it. Humanity was created with a purpose, but, that purpose slowly fulfilled itself and was made effective by the way in which, surrounding circumstances life helped or, hindered individuals with certain characteristics. Favorable and unfavorable characteristics were handed down by heredity, but those individuals with the unfavorable traits died, the others survived; the acquirement of favorable characteristics may come in two ways: by physical descent, by social influence. Those acquired by physical descent are fixed by laws beyond our knowledge and control, but the vastly larger and more important number are acquired by the individual after he is grown by the thoughts, soul, and deeds which influence and mold his life.

And this resume brings me to the center of my theme. The public school of today is the largest and most efficient single organ for transmitting the social heritage of men. This was not the original conception of the school. It was for years conceived simply as a place where men were to be given religious precepts for guidance in a world of clearly manifest purpose. Then it was conceived of as a place of apprenticeship for boys and girls to learn the technique of fighting a physical world of heat and cold, of rocks and hills, of air and water. Then we thought that schools were to develop exceptional men—those endowed by nature with genius, and finally we came to a day when we know that the public school is a force for giving to men that knowledge and power which will enable them to live under modern conditions of life.

How does all this apply to the American Negro? In many ways. In the earlier days of the world's history there was nowhere a hint that in the creation of the world the Lord graded ability or desert according to color. This was natural because civilization began in the torrid zone among the darker races; when however it moved to the lighter races of the temperate zone, here and there the idea arose of a certain misfortune in the darker races because of the climate of the lands and their physical conformation. The Darwinian theory added to this the idea that the white races were about to inherit the earth because of a certain innate superiority and the Weismannic theory clinched this by denying that even the appearance of exceptional Negroes could disprove the general rule.

What now are the facts in the case and the fair deductions? First, as to sheer physical heredity: are the black races degenerate or undeveloped specimens of humanity? The answer to this is clear and unequivocal and has never for a moment been disputed by any scientific evidence; the Negro races are from every physical standpoint full and normally developed men; their stature and muscular development, their keenness of sense and their physical measurement show absolutely no variation from the European type sufficient to base any theory of essentially human difference upon. There were some brain measurements taken once which have been often quoted to the Negro's disadvantage, but the experiment was ridiculous as a crucial test from the small number of cases, and the prejudgment of the issue. It is interesting to know that one of the latest methods of measuring physical race differences came to the interesting results of placing English men and African Bantus in the semi-tall long headed type. The Negroes have their degenerate types in the dwarfs and Hottentots—so have the Europeans; they have their mixed types of all degrees and kinds of mixture—so have the Europeans. But it is an unproved and to all appearance an unprovable thesis that the physical development of men shows any color line below which is a black pelt and above the white.

Nevertheless it is true that if here in the city of Washington we gather haphazard a hundred white children and a hundred black children of the same age; the white would be further advanced, somewhat brighter in intellect and quicker in adaptability. This is not simply true in Washington, in Atlanta, in Chicago, but practically throughout the United States. People who discover this fact usually greet it either with a gasp of astonishment or a word of apology, and many a thoughtless person has without argument or inquiry taken this as self-evident proof of race inferiority. Now they say: here is the same curriculum, teachers tested by the same requirements, children starting at the same age and manifesting in the earlier years the same native ability, and yet as the course progresses fewer Negro children pass, and the quality of work as the student progresses often falls more or less below the average white child.

What does this prove? Let us look at the facts narrowly, Here are two boys being trained for life; six hours a day they are in school; three hours they are in the street; fifteen hours they are at home. The schools they are in are similar—the teachers are of the same sort; but one walks and plays in alleys, with sordid companions, amid poverty and perhaps crime; the other lives on clean streets, with pavements, quiet and well-dressed, and well-behaved people; the home of one is dark, cheerless and empty; the home of the other is large, cheerful, filled with books and pictures, music and instruction; the parents of the one are ignorant, driven by the shadow of poverty, harassed by doubt and dream, worn with querulousness, fretting and scolding; the other has hands to lead him, hearts to soothe him, heads to guide him and correct him. Would you expect these two boys after ten years of this training to be equal in endowment and accomplishment? Would the difference be due to the shadowy unknown physical heredity of these children or to the perfectly tangible and well-known spiritual training—the social heritage of these two sons of men? You may well say that there is not much difference between all white and black boys in Washington. It is perfectly true that hundreds of black children in the city have far better homes than hundreds of whites;

but it is also true, and the history of the past tells us why it is true, that there are thousands of white, children whose homes are better than the corresponding thousands of black so that the average in this city and throughout the United States is such that black children must of necessity receive a training in street and church and home so poor that it cannot be wholly offset by the better training of the school, and the total training of any child depends vastly more upon his home life, his contact with people, his knowledge of the world's daily thoughts, than it does upon the teachings of the schools, nor is this strange; the teacher has twenty, thirty, or fifty pupils for the fourth of a day; the home has one, three or five for three-fourths of the day. Ought not then the home training to be even times as influential as the school training? And can any technical change in school curriculum or teaching force make up for deficiencies that lie far beyond the school-room walls?

Now this, of course, is no new thought, and yet it is seldom clearly expressed. We are so fond of explaining differences of men by the enigmatical word "heredity" that we forget how far those differences depend upon homely, every day life, and we are so eager to seize any excuse for shirking our great responsibility toward the weak and lowly and unfortunate that we hasten on the slightest pretext to attribute to the act of God or to unknown forces of nature obviously and perfectly intelligible results of the deeds of men. I repeat, then, that the schools can and ought to do but little part in the training of the children. The larger part of the training of human beings must come from the social surroundings in which they live, and when they are found deficient, when the results of their training are not what we wish, we must seek not simply to improve the schools but just as strenuously to improve the social surroundings, the social opportunities, and the social heritage of the unfortunate and untrained. There is today without doubt a tendency among the American people to be particularly blind as to this fact. Whenever, by chance, Negroes are seen not to be doing quite as well as their neighbors who are having better chances to do well, then instead of taking every precaution to help the Negroes to do better, the distinct tendency is to cut off some of the privileges they already have. If for instance, the Negro public schools have for obvious reasons a smaller percentage of success than the white public schools, the proposal is made to lower the standards of those schools; that is class education, the beginning of a caste system is proposed instead of sticking by the standards and stimulating the other organs of social education so the public schools may have better material to work upon. This tendency must be resisted to the last ditch. There is a system of caste in the United States, but it must extend no further than it has already gone. The proposals to train black boys and girls to be something less than men and women, something less than free-born American citizens is a tendency born of the devil and to be resisted by every possible measure. In native endowment, the black children of this land are not a whit behind the white children. In every privilege of education they have far less opportunity, save in the North, and in some cities like Washington. Even where they have equal chances of education the social heritage into which they are trained is poorer, lower, and more depressing. If then we are to increase the efficiency of public schools in such places we must increase the work of social reform, open the gates of opportunity, and inspire instead of discourage these millions of growing youth. And after all, my fellows, inspiration is what the Negro needs, the uplifting presence of morning on the hills of God, the whistle of birds in the treetops of the dawn, the flare of the flaming sword in the hands of that dread angel who keeps the way of life.

CHAPTER EIGHT

Negro Education

In this review, published in *The Crisis* in 1918, Du Bois reviews a report on Negro education prepared by the Phelps Stokes Fund. It is important in its call to oppose the report's call to restrict higher education for blacks to industrial and manual training. It also opposes Southern black colleges and universities "cooperating" with conservative Southern whites, an issue that would come to the fore in Du Bois's criticisms of Fisk University in the mid-1920s. His criticism is summarized at the conclusion of the review where he argues that the "weakness and sinister danger" of the report lies in its call "for a union of philanthropic effort with no attempt to make sure of the proper and just lines along which this united effort should work." (page 131 of this book)

The casual reader has greeted this study of Negro education with pleasure. It is the first attempt to cover the field of secondary and higher education among colored Americans with anything like completeness. It is published with the sanction and prestige of the United States government and has many excellent points as, for instance, full statistics on such matters as the public expenditure for Negro school systems, the amount of philanthropy given private schools, Negro property, etc.; there is excellent and continued insistence upon the poor support which the colored public schools are receiving today. The need of continued philanthropic aid to private schools is emphasized and there are several good maps. Despite, then, some evidently careless proofreading (pages 59, 129, 157), the ordinary reader unacquainted with the tremendous ramifications of the Negro problem will hail this report with unstinted praise.

Thinking Negroes, however, and other persons who know the problem of educating the American Negro will regard the Jones report, despite its many praiseworthy features, as a dangerous and in many respects unfortunate publication.

The Thesis of the Report

This report again and again insists by direct statements, by inference, and by continued repetition on three principles of a thesis which we may state as follows: *First*, that the present tendency toward academic and higher education among Negroes should be restricted and replaced by a larger insistence on manual training, industrial education, and agricultural training; *secondly,* the private schools in the South must "cooperate" with the Southern whites; and, *third,* that there should be more thoroughgoing unity of purpose among education boards and foundations working among Negroes.

The Negro College

The whole trend of Mr. Jones' study and of his general recommendations is to make the higher training of Negroes practically difficult, if not impossible, despite the fact that his statistics show (in 1914-15) only 1,643 colored students studying college subjects in all the private Negro schools out of 12,726 pupils. He shows that there are (in proportion to population) ten times as many whites in the public high schools as there are colored pupils and only sixty-four public high schools for Negroes in the whole South! He shows that even at present there are few Negro colleges and that they have no easy chance for survival. What he is criticizing, then, is not the fact that Negroes are tumbling into college in enormous numbers, but their wish to go to college and their endeavor to support and maintain even poor college departments.

What, in fact, is back of this wish? Is it merely a silly desire to study "Greek," as Mr. Jones several times intimates, or is it not rather a desire on the part of American Negroes to develop a class of thoroughly educated men according to modern standards? If such a class is to be developed these Negro colleges must be planned as far as possible according to the standards of white colleges, otherwise colored students would be shut out of the best colleges of the country.

The curriculum offered at the colored southern colleges, however, brings the author's caustic criticism. Why, for instance, should "Greek and Latin" be maintained to the exclusion of economics, sociology, and "a strong course in biology"?

The reason for the maintenance of these older courses of study in the colored colleges is not, at all, as the author assumes, that Negroes have a childish love for "classics." It is very easily and simply explicable. Take, for instance, Fisk University. Fisk University maintained Greek longer than most northern colleges, for the reason that it had in Adam K. Spence not simply a finished Greek scholar, pupil of the great D'Ooge, but a man of singularly strong personality and fine soul. It did not make much difference whether the students were studying Greek or biology—the great thing was that they were studying under Spence. So, in a large number of cases the curriculum of the southern Negro college has been determined by the personnel of the available men. These men were beyond price and working for their devotion to the cause. The college was unable to call men representing the newer sciences young sociologists and biologists. They were unable to equip laboratories, but they did with infinite pains and often heartbreaking endeavor keep within touch of the standard set by the higher northern schools and the proof that they did well came from the men they turned out and not simply from the courses they studied.

This, Mr. Jones either forgets or does not know and is thus led into exceedingly unfortunate statements as when, for instance, he says that the underlying principle of the industrial school "is the adaptation of educational activities whether industrial or literary to the needs of the pupils and the community," which is, of course, the object of any educational institution and it is grossly unfair to speak of it as being the object of only a part of the great Negro schools of the South. Any school that does not have this for its object is not a school but a fraud.

The Public Schools

Not only does this report continually decry the Negro college and its curriculum but, on the other hand, it seeks to put in its place schools and courses of study which make it absolutely impossible for Negro students to be thoroughly trained according to modern standards. To illustrate: Mr. Jones shows (page 90) that in Butte, Mont., manual training has been put into the elementary schools at the rate of *half a day a week* during the first six years and two *half days a week* in the seventh and eighth grades. When, however, it comes to the smaller elementary industrial schools of the South Mr. Jones recommends *one-half day* classroom work and *one-half* practice in the field and shops *every day*.

What, now, is the real difference between these two schemes of education? The difference is that in the Butte schools for white pupils, a chance is held open for the pupil to go through high school and college and to advance at the rate which the modern curriculum demands; that in the colored schools, on the other hand, a program is being made out that will land the boy at the time he becomes self-conscious and aware of his own possibilities in an educational *impasse*. He cannot go on in the public schools even if he should move to a place where there are good public schools because he is too old. Even if he has done the elementary work in twice the time that a student is supposed to, it has been work of a kind that will not admit him to a northern high school. No matter, then, how gifted the boy may be, he is absolutely stopped from a higher education. This is not only unfair to the boy but it is grossly unfair to the Negro race.

The argument, then, against the kind of school that is being foisted upon Negroes in the name of industrial education is not any dislike on the part of the Negroes for having their children trained in vocations, or in having manual training used as a means of education; it is rather in having a series of schools established which deliberately shut the door of opportunity in the face of bright Negro students.

Industrial Training

With the drive that has been made to industrialize elementary schools before the children have learned to read and write and to turn the high schools to vocational teaching without giving any of the pupils a chance to train for college, it is, of course, beside the mark to criticize the colored colleges because the children that come to them are poorly trained.

Much of the criticism of colored teachers is also unfair. Even well-trained teachers are having curious pressure put upon them. . . .

With its insistent criticizing of Negro colleges this report touches with curious hesitation and diffidence upon the shortcomings of industrial schools. Their failure to distinguish between general education and technical trade training has resulted in sending out numbers of so-called teachers from educational schools who cannot read and write the English language and who are yet put in public and other schools as teachers. They may show children how to make tin pans and cobble shoes, but they are not the right persons to train youth, mentally or morally. In the second place, most of the trades taught by these trade schools are, because of hostile public opinion and poverty, decadent trades: carpentry, which is rapidly falling below the level of skilled trades; the patching of shoes; blacksmithing, in the sense of repair work, etc. The important trades of the world that are today assembled in factories and call for skilled technique and costly machinery are not taught in the vast majority of Negro industrial schools. Moreover, the higher industrial training calls for more education than the industrial schools give. . . .

That the course of study in the southern schools as well as in the schools of the nation has got to be changed and adapted is absolutely true, but the object of a school system is to carry the child as far as possible in its knowledge of the accumulated wisdom of the world and then when economic or physical reasons demand that this education must stop, vocational training to prepare for life work should follow. That some of this vocational training may be made educational in object is true; that normal training may use manual training and even to some extent vocational training is true, but it is not true that the industrializing of any curriculum necessarily makes it better or that you can at one and the same time educate the race in modern civilization and train it simply to be servants and laborers. Anyone who suggests by sneering at books and "literary courses" that the great heritage of human thought ought to be displaced simply for the reason of teaching the technique of modern industry is pitifully wrong and, if the comparison must be made, more wrong than the man who would sacrifice modern technique to the heritage of ancient thought.

Cooperation

The second part of Mr. Jones' thesis lies in an insistence that the private schools of the Negro should "cooperate" with the South. He stresses the adaptation of education to the needs of the "community" (page 18), evidently meaning the *white* community. He quotes on page 25 the resolution of the white Southern Educational Association which deplores that the Negro schools are isolated from the "community," meaning again the *white* community. He instances Willcox County, Ala., where there are almost no public schools and recommends that the private schools established there be put under "community" authorities (page 149). Now what is this "community" with which the colored people are to cooperate?

In the first place, Mr. Jones admits (pages 4 and 5), that it is only the progressive few in the white South that care anything at all about Negro schools. He might go even further and acknowledge that if a plebescite were taken tomorrow in the South the popular vote of white people would shut every single Negro school by a large majority. The hostile majority is kept from such radical action by the more progressive minority and by fear of northern interference, but the condition in which they have today left the colored schools is shown by this report to be truly lamentable.

Mr. Jones quotes from southern white men who speak of Negro school houses as "miserable beyond all description," of teachers as "absolutely untrained" and paid "the princely fortune of $80.92 for the whole term." He goes on with fact after fact to show the absolute inadequacy in the provision for colored children in the public schools of the South. On the other hand, he shows the increase in Negro property, the larger and larger amounts which Negroes are contributing to the school funds; and with all this he practically asks that the domination of the Negro private schools, which are now bearing the burden of nearly all the secondary and higher education of the Negro and much of the elementary education—that the domination of these schools be put into the hands of the same people who are doing so little for the public schools!

There is not in the whole report a single word about taxation without representation. There is not a single protest against a public school system in which the public which it serves has absolutely no voice, vote, or influence. There is no defense of those colored people of vision who see the public schools being used as training schools for cheap labor and menial servants instead of for education and who are protesting against this by submitting to double taxation in the support of private schools; who cannot see that these schools should be turned over to people who by their actions prove themselves to be enemies of the Negro race and its advancement.

Until the southern Negro has a vote and representation on school boards public control of his education will mean his spiritual and economic death and that despite the good intentions of the small white minority in the South who believe in justice for the Negro. It is, therefore, contradictory for this report to insist, on the one hand, on the continuation of northern philanthropy for these schools and, on the other, to commend various southern schools in proportion as they have gained the approval of the white community.

Compare, for instance, Fisk University and Atlanta University. Both Cravath of Fisk and Ware of Atlanta were men radical in their belief in Negro possibility and in their determination to establish well equipped Negro colleges. Cravath, however, lived in a more enlightened community which was earlier converted to his ideals. He did not yield his opinion any more than Ware, but Ware lived in a community that to this day will not furnish even a high school for its colored pupils. To say that Fisk should receive on this account more support than Atlanta is rank injustice; if anything Atlanta deserves the greater credit.

Cooperation with the white South means in many cases the surrender of the very foundations of self-respect. Mr. Jones inserts in his report one picture of a colored principal and his assistant waiting on table while the white trustees of his school sat. The colored people of the South do not care a rap whether white folks eat with them or not, but if white officials are coming into their schools as persons in control or advisors, then to ask that in those schools and in their homes the colored people shall voluntarily treat themselves as inferiors is to ask more than any self
-respecting man is going to do.

The white community, undoubtedly, wants to keep the Negro in the country as a peasant under working conditions least removed from slavery. The colored man wishes to escape from those conditions. Mr. Jones seeks to persuade him to stay there by asserting that the advance of the Negro in the rural South has been greatest (pages 97 and 123), and he refers to the "delusion" of city life even among white people. This may be all good enough propaganda but, in fact, it is untrue. Civilization has always depended upon the cities. The advance of the cities has been greatest for all people, white and colored, and for any colored man to take his family to the country districts of South Georgia in order to grow and develop and secure education and uplift would be idiotic.

Mr. Jones touches the State schools very lightly. Here are cases where the whites have control and stories of graft and misappropriation of funds and poor organization are well known to everybody with the slightest knowledge of southern conditions. Teachers there and in the public schools are often selected not from the best available, but from the wbrst or most complacent. In small towns and country districts white trustees may maintain their mistresses as teachers and the protest of the colored people has fallen upon deaf ears. Until, then, colored people have a voice in the community, surrender to the domination of the white South is unthinkable.

Northern Philanthropy

This brings us to the third part of Mr. Jones' thesis, namely, that the boards working for southern education should unite as far as possible with one policy. This is an unfortunate and dangerous proposal for the simple reason that the great dominating philanthropic agency, the General Education Board, long ago surrendered to the white South by practically saying that the educational needs of the white South must be attended to before any attention should be paid to the education of Negroes; that the Negro must be trained according to the will of the white South and not as the Negro desires to be trained. It is this board that is spending more money today in helping Negroes learn how to can vegetables than in helping them to go through college. It is this board that by a system of interlocking directorates bids fair to dominate philanthropy toward the Negro in the United States. Indeed, the moving thought back of the present report is the idea of a single authority who is to say which Negro school is right or is wrong, which system is right and which is wrong, etc.

No one doubts the efficiency of concentration and unity in certain lines of work but always, even in work that can be unified, the question

                    Negro Education

is *whose* influence is going to dominate; it may well be that diversity and even a certain chaos would be better than unity under a wrong idea. This is even more true in educational than in economic matters. Of course, the economic foundation of all recent educational philanthropy, particularly toward the Negro, is evident. Mr. Jones rather naively speaks of the fact that at certain times of the year "it is exceedingly difficult to prevail upon children to attend school" in the colored South which is, of course, another way of saying that bread and butter in the cotton fields is of more importance than trained intelligence.

Undoubtedly, there has already been a strong public opinion manufactured in the country which looks upon the training of Negroes in the South as cheap, contented labor to be used in emergency and for keeping white union labor from extravagant demands as a feasible and workable program. It is, in fact, one of the most dangerous programs ever thought out and is responsible for much of the lynching, unrest, and unhappiness in the South. Its genesis came easily with the idea of working for the Negro rather than working *with* him, a thing which Mr. Jones condemns, but hardly lives up to his condemnation.

In this very report the Negro was practically unrepresented. Instead of choosing a strong, experienced colored man to represent the Negro race (like W. T. B. Williams, or President Young of Tallahassee, or President Hope of Morehouse) an inexperienced young man was taken, of excellent character but absolutely without weight or influence. Of course, back of all this is the great difficulty of ordinary social intercourse. The reason that boards of trustees like those that control the Phelps Stokes Fund find it so much easier to work for the Negro than *with* him; the reason that forgetting the investigations by Negroes at Atlanta University they turned to white institutions to encourage investigation and neglected established and worthy work is because if they are going to cooperate with the dominant white South and even with certain classes of Northerners they cannot meet Negroes as men. The propaganda that is so largely carried on and the influence that is so often formed through social intercourse must always, at present, be offered with the Negro unrepresented and unheard.

There follows easily the habit of having no patience with the man who does not agree with the decisions of such boards. The Negro who comes with his hat in his hand and flatters and cajoles the philanthropist—that Negro gets money. If these foundations raise, as they do in this report, the cry of fraud they have themselves to thank. They more than any other agency have encouraged that kind of person. On the other hand, the Negro who shows the slightest independence of thought or character is apt to be read out of all possible influence not only by the white South but by the philanthropic North.

If philanthropic agencies could unite for certain obvious great movements how splendid it would be! Take, for instance, the duplication of higher educational schools which Mr. Jones repeatedly denounces and which, undoubtedly, is a source of weakness. The General Education Board could settle the matter with the greatest ease. Let it offer in Atlanta an endowment of $500,000 for a single Negro college, provided that there be but one college there for Negroes. The boards of the different schools immediately would have something to act upon. As it is, nothing that they can do individually would really better the situation. A new college formed by a federation of colored colleges in Atlanta, Marshall, Texas, and elsewhere, would be easily possible if an endowment was in sight.

Summary

Here, then, is the weakness and sinister danger of Mr. Jones' report. It calls for a union of philanthropic effort with no attempt to make sure of the proper and just lines along which this united effort should work. It calls for cooperation with the white South without insisting on the Negro being represented by voice and vote in such "cooperation," and it calls for a recasting of the educational program for Negroes without insisting on leaving the door of opportunity open for the development of a thoroughly trained class of leaders at the bottom, in the very beginnings of education, as well as at the top.

CHAPTER NINE

Does the Negro Need Separate Schools?

This article, published in July 1935 in the *Journal of Negro Education*, is among Du Bois's most important statements about education. In this work he raises the question of whether or not separate schools are needed for blacks at the elementary and secondary level, as well as for colleges and universities.

Du Bois answers this question in a manner that is specifically linked to the cultural conditions and meaning of American life at that time. According to him, separate black schools and colleges are needed as long "as they are necessary for the proper education of the Negro race" (page 135 of this book). Under the existing conditions of racism in the United States, Du Bois maintained that "the Negro not only needs the vast majority of these schools, but it is a grave question if, in the near future, he will not need more such schools, both to take care of his natural increase, and to defend him against the growing animosity of the whites" (page 135 of this book). Contrary to popular opinion, Du Bois did not believe that the "Color Line" was softening and the races were drawing together.

Even in those cases in Northern colleges where blacks were admitted, Du Bois concluded that the racism that often dominated these institutions made it impossible for the blacks attending them to be adequately educated. He came to the conclusion that "there is no room for argument whether the Negro needs separate schools or not. The plain fact faces us, that either he will have separate schools or he will not be educated" (page 136 of this book).

Du Bois called for the black community to respect the teachers in its black schools and to see that they are paid decent salaries. He also argued that the best and brightest black students must not aspire to be educated in white schools—whether at the elementary, secondary or university level—simply because they were white institutions. As he explained:

As long as the Negro student wishes to graduate from Columbia, not because Columbia is an institution of learning, but because it is attended by white students; as long as a Negro student is ashamed to attend Fisk or Howard because these institutions are largely run by black folk, just so long the main problem of Negro education will not be segregation but self-knowledge and self-respect. (page 138 of this book)

In reference to the Negro public school system, Du Bois argued that the efforts of the NAACP and other organizations to desegregate the schools was incomplete if they did not have the courage to also address the fact that black schools received anywhere from one-tenth to half as much of the funding received by white schools for the education of their children. According to Du Bois, they failed to pursue the issue of equal funding for separate schools, since it would concede the idea of separate schooling being an acceptable condition.

Du Bois called for blacks to empower themselves. Without doing so, they would remain helpless in the white world. Du Bois asked:

> Does the Negro need separate schools? God knows he does. But what he needs more than separate schools is a firm and unshakable belief that twelve million American Negroes have the inborn capacity to accomplish just as much BLS any nation of twelve million anywhere in the world ever accomplished, and that this is not because they are Negroes but because they are human. (page 140 of this book)

Besides overcoming the hostile environment of mixed schools, Du Bois believed that there was an additional advantage to the development of Negro institutions: they would have the potential to more directly address problems and issues facing black culture. By calling for the inclusion of black historical and cultural figures in the education of African-Americans at all levels, Du Bois foreshadowed the development of African-American Studies programs and traditions such as Black History Week at the elementary and secondary level, as well as the Black Power movement.

There are in the United States some four million Negroes of school age, of whom two million are in school, and of these, four-fifths are taught by forty-eight thousand Negro teachers in separate schools. Less than a half million are in mixed schools in the North, where they are taught almost exclusively by white teachers. Beside this, there are seventy-nine Negro universities and colleges with one thousand colored teachers, beside a number of private secondary schools.

The question which I am discussing is: Are these separate schools and institutions needed? And the answer, to my mind, is perfectly clear. They are needed just so far as they are necessary for the proper education of the Negro race. The proper education of any people includes sympathetic touch between teacher and pupil; knowledge on the part of the teacher, not simply of the individual taught, but of his surroundings and background, and the history of his class and group; such contact between pupils, and between teacher and pupil, on the basis of perfect social equality, as will increase this sympathy and knowledge; facilities for education in equipment and housing, and the promotion of such extra-curricular activities as will tend to induct the child into life.

If this is true, and if we recognize the present attitude of white America toward black America, then the Negro not only needs the vast majority of these schools, but it is a grave question if, in the near future, he will not need more such schools, both to take care of his natural increase, and to defend him against the growing animosity of the whites. It is of course fashionable and popular to deny this; to try to deceive ourselves into thinking that race prejudice in the United States across the Color Line is gradually softening and that slowly but surely we are coming to the time when racial animosities and class lines will be so obliterated that separate schools will be anachronisms.

Certainly, I shall welcome such a time. Just as long as Negroes are taught in Negro schools and whites in white schools; the poor in the slums, and the rich in private schools; just as long as it is impracticable to welcome Negro students to Harvard, Yale and Princeton; just as long as colleges like Williams, Amherst and Wellesley tend to become the property of certain wealthy families, where Jews are not solicited; just so long we shall lack in America that sort of public education which will create the intelligent basis of a real democracy.

Much as I would like this, and hard as I have striven and shall strive to help realize it, I am no fool; and I know that race prejudice in the United States today is such that most Negroes cannot receive proper education in white institutions. If the public schools of Atlanta, Nashville, New Orleans and Jacksonville were thrown open to all races tomorrow, the education that colored children would get in them would be worse than pitiable. It would not be education. And in the sauce way, there are many public school systems in the North where Negroes are admitted and tolerated, but they are not educated; they are crucified. There are certain Northern universities where Negro students, no matter what their ability, desert, or accomplishment, cannot get fair recognition, either in classroom or on the campus, in dining halls and student activities, or in common human courtesy. It is well-known that in certain faculties of the University of Chicago, no Negro has yet received the doctorate and seldom can achieve the mastership in arts; at Harvard, Yale and Columbia, Negroes are admitted but not welcomed; while in other institutions, like Princeton, they cannot even enroll.

Under such circumstances, there is no room for argument as to whether the Negro needs separate schools or not. The plain fact faces us, that either he will have separate schools or he will not be educated. There may be, and there is, considerable difference of opinion as to how far this separation in schools is today necessary. There can be argument as to what our attitude toward further separation should be. Suppose, for instance, that in Montclair, New Jersey, a city of wealth and culture, the Board of Education is determined to establish separate schools for Negroes; suppose that, despite the law, separate Negro schools are already established in Philadelphia, and pressure is being steadily brought to extend this separation at least to the junior high school; what must be our attitude toward this?

Manifestly, no general and inflexible rule can be laid down. If public opinion is such in Montclair that Negro children cannot receive decent and sympathetic education in the white schools, and no Negro teachers can be employed, there is for us no choice. We have got to accept Negro schools. Any agitation and action aimed at compelling a rich and powerful majority of the citizens to do what they will not do, is useless. On the other hand, we have a right and a duty to assure ourselves of the truth concerning this attitude; by careful conferences, by public meetings and by petitions, we should convince ourselves whether this demand for separate schools is merely the agitation of a prejudiced minority, or the considered and final judgment of the town.

There are undoubtedly cases where a minority of leaders force their opinions upon a majority, and induce a community to establish separate schools, when as a matter of fact, there is no general demand for it; there has been no friction in the schools; and Negro children have been decently treated. In that case, a firm and intelligent appeal to public opinion would eventually settle the matter. But the futile attempt to compel even by law a group to do what it is determined not to do, is a silly waste of money, time, and temper.

On the other hand, there are also cases where there has been no separation in schools and no movement toward it. And yet the treatment of Negro children in the schools, the kind of teaching and the kind of advice they get, is such that they ought to demand either a thorough-going revolution in the official attitude toward Negro students, or absolute separation in educational facilities. To endure bad schools and wrong education because the schools are "mixed" is a costly if not fatal mistake. I have long been convinced, for instance, that the Negroes in the public schools of Harlem are not getting an education that is in any sense comparable in efficiency, discipline, and human development with that which Negroes are getting in the separate public schools of Washington, D.C. And yet on its school situation, black Harlem is dumb and complacent, if not actually laudatory.

Recognizing the fact that for the vast majority of colored students in elementary, secondary, and collegiate education, there must be today separate educational institutions because of an attitude on the part of the white people which is not going materially to change in our time, our customary attitude toward these separate schools must be absolutely and definitely changed. As it is today, American Negroes almost universally disparage their own schools. They look down upon them; they often treat the Negro teachers in them with contempt; they refuse to work for their adequate support; and they refuse to join public movements to increase their efficiency.

The reason for this is quite clear, and may be divided into two parts: (1) the fear that any movement which implies segregation even as a temporary, much less as a relatively permanent institution, in the United States, is a fatal surrender of principle, which in the end will rebound and bring more evils on the Negro than he suffers today. (2) The other reason is at bottom an utter lack of faith on the part of Negroes that their race can do anything really well. If Negroes could conceive that Negroes could establish schools quite as good as or even superior to white schools; if Negro colleges were of equal grade in accomplishment and in scientific work with white colleges; then separation would be a passing incident and not a permanent evil; but as long as American Negroes believe that their race is constitutionally and permanently inferior to white people, they necessarily disbelieve in every possible Negro Institution.

The first argument is more or less metaphysical and cannot be decided *a priori* for every case. There are times when one must stand up for principle at the cost of discomfort, harm, and death. But in the case of the education of the young, you must consider not simply yourself but the children and the relation of children to life. It is difficult to think of anything more important for the development of a people than proper training for their children; and yet I have repeatedly seen wise and loving colored parents take infinite pains to force their little children into schools where the white children, white teachers, and white parents despised and resented the dark child, made mock of it, neglected or bullied it, and literally rendered its life a living hell. Such parents want their child to "fight" this thing out, but, dear God, at what a cost! Sometimes, to be sure, the child triumphs and teaches the school community a lesson; but even in such cases, the cost may be high, and the child's whole life turned into an effort to win cheap applause at the expense of healthy individuality. In other cases, the result of the experiment may be complete ruin of character, gift, and ability and ingrained hatred of schools and men. For the kind of battle thus indicated, most children are under no circumstances suited. It is the refinement of cruelty to require it of them. Therefore, in evaluating the advantage and disadvantage of accepting race hatred as a brutal but real fact, or of using a little child as a battering ram upon which its nastiness can be thrust, we must give greater value and greater emphasis to the rights of the child's own soul. We shall get a finer, better balance of spirit; an infinitely more capable and rounded personality by putting children in schools where they are wanted, and where they are happy and inspired, than in thrusting them into hells where they are ridiculed and bated.

Beyond this, lies the deeper, broader fact. If the American Negro really believed in himself; if he believed that Negro teachers can educate children according to the best standards of modern training; if he believed that Negro colleges transmit and add to science, as well as or better than other colleges, then he would bend his energies, not to escaping inescapable association with his own group, but to seeing that his group had every opportunity for its best and highest development. He would insist that his teachers be decently paid; that his schools were properly housed and equipped; that his colleges be supplied with scholarship and research funds; and he would be far more interested in the efficiency of these institutions of learning, than in forcing himself into other institutions where he is not wanted.

As long as the Negro student wishes to graduate from Columbia, not because Columbia is an institution of learning, but because it is attended by white students; as long as a Negro student is ashamed to attend Fisk or Howard because these institutions are largely run by black folk, just so long the main problem of Negro education will not be segregation but self-knowledge and self-respect.

There are not many teachers in Negro schools who would not esteem it an unparalleled honor and boast of it to their dying day, if instead of teaching black folk, they could get a chance to teach poor-whites, Irishmen, Italians or Chinese in a "white" institution. This is not unnatural. This is to them a sort of acid test of their worth. It is but the logical result of the "white" propaganda which has swept civilization for the last thousand years, and which is now bolstered and defended by brave words, high wages, and monopoly of opportunities. But this state of mind is suicidal and must be fought, and fought doggedly and bitterly: first, by giving Negro teachers decent wages, decent schoolhouses and equipment, and reasonable chances for advancement; and then by kicking out and leaving to the mercy of the white world those who do not and cannot believe in their own.

Lack of faith in Negro enterprise leads to singular results: Negroes will fight frenziedly to prevent segregated schools; but if segregation is forced upon them by dominant white public opinion, they will suddenly lose interest and scarcely raise a finger to see that the resultant Negro schools get a fair share of the public funds so as to have adequate equipment and housing; to see that real teachers are appointed, and that they are paid as much as white teachers doing the same work. Today, when the Negro public school system gets from half to one-tenth of the amount of money spent on white schools, and is often consequently poorly run and poorly taught, colored people tacitly if not openly join with white people in assuming that Negroes cannot run Negro enterprises, and cannot educate themselves, and that the very establishment of a Negro school means starting an inferior school.

The NAACP and other Negro organizations have spent thousands of dollars to prevent the establishment of segregated Negro schools, but scarcely a single cent to see that the division of funds between white and Negro schools, North and South, is carried out with some faint approximation of justice. There can be no doubt that if the Supreme Court were overwhelmed with cases where the blatant and impudent discrimination against Negro education is openly acknowledged, it would be compelled to hand down decisions which would make this discrimination impossible. We Negroes do not dare to press this point and force these decisions because, forsooth, it would acknowledge the fact of separate schools, a fact that does not need to be acknowledged, and will not need to be for two centuries.

Howard, Fisk, and Atlanta are naturally unable to do the type and grade of graduate work which is done at Columbia, Chicago, and Harvard; but why attribute this to a defect in the Negro race, and not to the fact that the large white colleges have from one hundred to one thousand times the funds for equipment and research that Negro colleges can command? To this, it may logically he answered, all the more reason that Negroes should try to get into better-equipped schools, and who pray denies this? But the opportunity for such entrance is becoming more and more difficult, and the training offered less and less suited to the American Negro of today. Conceive a Negro teaching in a Southern school the economics which lie learned at the Harvard Business School! Conceive a Negro teacher of history retailing to his black students the sort of history that is taught at the University of Chicago! Imagine the history of Reconstruction being handed by a colored professor from the lips of Columbia professors to the ears of the black belt! The results of this kind of thing are often fantastic, and call for Negro history and sociology, and even physical science taught by men who understand their audience, and are not afraid of the truth.

There was a time when the ability of Negro brains to do first-class work had to be proven by facts and figures, and I was a part of the movement that sought to set the accomplishments of Negro ability before the world. But the world before which I was setting this proof was a disbelieving white world. I did not need the proof for myself. I did not dream that my fellow Negroes needed it; but in the last few years, I have become curiously convinced that until American Negroes believe in their own power and ability, they are going to be helpless before the white world, and the white world, realizing this inner paralysis and lack of self-confidence, is going to persist in its insane determination to rule the universe for its own selfish advantage.

Does the Negro need separate schools? God knows he does. But what he needs more than separate schools is a firm and unshakable belief that twelve million American Negroes have the inborn capacity to accomplish just as much BLS any nation of twelve million anywhere in the world ever accomplished, and that this is not because they are Negroes but because they are human.

So far, I have noted chiefly negative arguments for separate Negro institutions of learning based on the fact that in the majority of cases Negroes are not welcomed in public schools and universities nor treated as fellow human beings. But beyond this, there are certain positive reasons due to the fact that American Negroes have, because of their history, group experiences and memories, a distinct entity, whose spirit and reactions demand a certain type of education for its development.

In the past, this fact has been noted and misused for selfish purposes. On the ground that Negroes needed a type of education "suited" to them, we have an attempt to train them as menials and dependents; or in the case of West Indians, an attempt to perpetuate their use as low-paid laborers by limiting their knowledge; or in the case of African natives, efforts to deprive them of modern languages and modern science in order to seal their subordination to outworn mores, reactionary native rulers, industrialization.

What I have in mind is nothing like this. It is rather an honest development of the premises from which this plea for special education starts. It is illustrated by these facts: Negroes must know the history of the Negro race in America, and this they will seldom get in white institutions. Their children ought to study textbooks like Brawley's "Short History," the first edition of Woodson's "Negro in Our History," and Cromwell, Turner and Dykes' "Readings from Negro Authors." Negroes who celebrate the birthdays of Washington and Lincoln, and the worthy, but colorless and relatively unimportant "founders" of various Negro colleges, ought not to forget the 5th of March, that first national holiday of this country, which commemorates the martyrdom of Crispus Attucks. They ought to celebrate Negro Health Week and Negro History Week. They ought to study intelligently and from their own point of view, the slave trade, slavery, emancipation, Reconstruction, and present economic development.

Beyond this, Negro colleges ought to be studying anthropology, psychology, and the social sciences, from the point of view of the colored races. Today, the anthropology that is being taught, and the expeditions financed for archeological and ethnographical explorations, are for the most part straining every nerve to erase the history of black folk from the record. One has only to remember that the majority of anthropologists have peopled the continent of Africa itself with almost no Negroes, while men like Sayce and Reisner have even declared that the Ethiopians have no Negro blood! All this has been done by the legerdemain and metaphysics of nomenclature, and in the face of the great and important history of black blood in the world.

Recently, something has been done by colored scholars to correct the extraordinary propaganda of post-war psychology which sent men like Brigham and McDougall rushing into scientific proof of Negro congenital inferiority. But much more is necessary and demanded of Negro scholarship. In history and the social sciences the Negro school and college has an unusual opportunity and role. It does not consist simply in trying to parallel the history of white folk with similar boasting about black and brown folk, but rather an honest evaluation of human effort and accomplishment, without color blindness, and without transforming history into a record of dynasties and prodigies.

Here, we have in America, a working class which in our day has achieved physical freedom, and mental clarity. An economic battle has just begun. It can be studied and guided; it can teach consumers' cooperation, democracy, and socialism, and be made not simply a record and pattern for the Negro race, but a guide for the rise of the working classes throughout the world, just at the critical time when these classes are about to assume their just political domination which is destined to become the redemption of mankind.

Much has been said of the special esthetic ability of the Negro race. Naturally, it has been exaggerated. Naturally, it is not a racial characteristic in the sense of hereditary, inborn, and heritable difference; but there is no doubt but what the tremendous psychic history of the American and West Indian groups has made it possible for the present generation to accumulate a wealth of material which, with encouragement and training, could find expression in the drama, in color and form, and in music. And no where could this training better be pursued than in separate Negro schools under competent and intelligent teachers? What little has already been done in this line is scarcely a beginning of what is possible, provided the object is not simple entertainment or bizarre efforts at money raising.

In biology, the pioneering work of Carolyn Bond Day could be extended indefinitely in Negro laboratories; and in the purely physical and chemical sciences, the need of Negroes familiar with the intricate technical basis of modern civilization would not only help them to find their place in the industrial scene for their own organization, but also enable them to help Abyssinia, India, China, and the colored world, to maintain their racial integrity, and their economic independence. It could easily be the mission and duty of American Negroes to master this scientific basis of modern invention, and give it to all mankind.

Thus, instead of our schools being simply separate schools, forced on us by grim necessity, they can become centers of a new and beautiful effort at human education, which may easily lead and guide the world in many important and valuable aspects. It is for this reason that when our schools are separate, the control of the teaching force, the expenditure of money, the choice of textbooks, the discipline and other administrative matters of this sort ought, also, to come into our hands, and be incessantly demanded and guarded.

I remember once, in Texas, reading in a high-school textbook for colored students, the one anecdote given concerning Abraham Lincoln: he was pictured as chasing Negro thieves all night through the woods from his Mississippi flatboat! Children could read that history in vain to learn any word of what had been accomplished in American history by Benjamin Banneker, Jan Matseliger, Elijah McCoy, Frederick Douglass, or James Dunn. In fact, one of the peculiar tragedies of the smaller Southern colleges is that they hire as teachers of history, economics and sociology, colored men trained in Northern institutions where not a word of any information concerning these disciplines, so far as Negroes are concerned, has ever been imparted to them. I speak from experience, because I came to Atlanta University to teach history in 1897, without the slightest idea from my Harvard tuition, that Negroes ever had any history!

I know that this article will forthwith be interpreted by certain illiterate "nitwits" as a plea for segregated Negro schools and colleges. It is not. It is simply calling a spade a spade. It is saying in plain English: that a separate Negro school, where children are treated like human beings, trained by teachers of their own race, who know what it means to be black in the year of salvation 1935, is infinitely better than making our boys and girls doormats to be spit and trampled upon and lied to by ignorant social climbers, whose sole claim to superiority is the ability to kick "niggers" when they are down. I say, too, that certain studies and discipline necessary to Negroes can seldom be found in white schools.

It means this, and nothing more.

To sum up this: theoretically, the Negro needs neither segregated schools nor mixed schools. What he needs is Education. What he trust remember is that there is no magic, either in mixed schools or in segregated schools. A mixed school with poor and unsympathetic teachers, with hostile public opinion, and no teaching of truth concerning black folk, is bad. A segregated school with ignorant placeholders, inadequate equipment, poor salaries, and wretched housing, is equally bad. Other things being equal, the mixed school is the broader, more natural basis for the education of all youth. It gives wider contacts; it inspires greater self-confidence; and suppresses the inferiority complex. But other things seldom are equal, and in that case, Sympathy, Knowledge, and the Truth, outweigh all that the mixed school can offer.

CHAPTER TEN

How Negroes Have Taken Advantage
of Educational Opportunities
Offered by Friends

It is easy to forget that besides his writing on social issues and race, as well as his work as the editor of the NAACP's *The Crisis*, Du Bois was also an historian. His doctoral dissertation, *The Suppression of the African Slave, 1638-1870*, published in 1896 as the first volume of the Harvard Historical Studies, is a seminal work in African-American history. His 1909 biography of John Brown also stands as an important book in the field.

Several of Du Bois's historical essays deal with black education and schooling. His 1901 article on the Freedman's Bureau, which was published in the *Atlantic Monthly* and later used in *The Souls of Black Folks*, is a pioneering work in not only black history, but also in the history of American education.

The essential elements of Du Bois's Freedman's article are available in numerous editions of *The Souls of Black Folks*. A less well know historical essay, published in 1938 in the *Journal of Negro Education*, "How Negroes Have Taken Advantage of Educational Opportunities Offered by Friends," provides another example of his work as an educational historian. In this work, Du Bois not only outlines the efforts of the Friends, or Quakers, to advance the cause of blacks, but also discusses the response by the African-American community to their program of social improvement.

I have not sufficient accurate information to confine my paper strictly to the limits set down. It would be interesting work to study in careful detail exactly what Quakers have done toward the education of Negroes. But in this paper, while I am seeking to note their main efforts, I have also taken into account the efforts of others; and with the knowledge that I have it would be rather difficult to distinguish wholly the Quaker contributions to Negro education from the efforts of many others.

Early Educational Endeavors

Nevertheless, the Quakers were early in the field of those who broadly and insistently advocated the education of emancipated slaves and of Negroes eventually to be emancipated. To be sure there were others that were thinking along the same lines and some of these might claim actual priority. The Catholics, especially Jesuits in Louisiana, began some teaching of Negroes in the 17th century, on no large scale and with no clear philosophy as to the future. The Society for the Propagation of the Gospel in Foreign Parts authorized by the Established Church of England in 1701 did considerable teaching. They had a school of 20 Negroes in South Carolina as early as 1695 and another in New York in 1704 which with some viscisitudes lasted until Negroes were admitted into the public schools of that state. Dr. Bray and the Bray Associates continued this teaching in Maryland and eventually furnished part of the funds for the Negro school started by Quakers. The French Black Code of 1685 provided for the education of Negroes but was systematically disregarded in that as in other respect. George Whitefield, the Methodist who advocated slavery in Georgia, nevertheless wanted them educated after they came and in 1740 purchased a tract of land in Pennsylvania in order to found a Negro school. In all these cases, however, there developed no sustained philosophy and no movement which put any of these forces consistently and continuously in back of Negro education.

On the other hand, George Fox as early as 1672 was thinking not only of emancipation for Negroes but of their education. A few years later he was speaking boldly and his ideas were supported by George Keith and perhaps partially by William Penn himself. From this time on there was an increasing number of Quakers who insisted on education for Negroes and at no time did the continuity of this line of endeavor lapse or suffer serious interruption. Early in the 18th century this thought took the inevitable distraction of colonization and African missionaries; but it was soon brought back to practicalities by the inner struggle with the problem by Quakers in the Border States, Virginia and the Carolinas, as well as in the North. North Carolina tried to stop Quakers from teaching Negroes as early as 1731; and in Virginia in 1782 there was a remarkable proposal by Robert Pleasants, a Quaker, to establish a free school for the instruction of Negroes. But such development could not go far in the South if slavery was to become a permanent economic institution.

In the North, on the other hand, the spread of the emancipation movement during and after the Revolutionary War was supplemented by certain Quakers with renewed demand for Negro education. While

Hepburn, Coleman and Sandiford were attacking slavery, Benjamin Lay was working for Negro education as the step toward emancipation. Into this struggle came Anthony Benezet. He was a persecuted French protestant who migrated first to England and then to Philadelphia. For some time he taught a fashionable school for young ladies. Then he joined the Quakers and afterwards became interested in Negroes and began attacking the slave trade and especially advocated Negro education. With the help of the Philadelphia Yearly Meeting he opened a Negro school in 1770 and found a friend in Benjamin Franklin who with the Abolitionists came to the support of the school in 1774. On Benezet's death in 1784 he left his small wealth to educate Negroes and Indians. His bequest was supplemented with funds from England and with a gift of 300 pounds from Thomas Sidney, a Negro of Philadelphia. A school house was finally built in 1787. We may not forget here that the freedom which shrieked when Kosciusko died, doubtless remembered the fortune which he left in 1798 in the hands of Thomas Jefferson to endow Negro education.

The Negro Response

From such beginnings the effort to educate Negroes grew and this paper is interested not so much in what Quakers and others did for Negroes as in the response which their efforts inspired among the Negroes themselves. There was a series of events which aroused the American Negro during and after the Revolutionary War at a time when he numbered 750,000 living among something over three million whites. First there was his participation in the Revolutionary War, where it seems probable that as many Negroes in proportion to their population fought in the army as whites. Secondly, there was the culmination of the Abolition Movement which emancipated slaves completely in New England and gradually in New York, Pennsylvania, and New Jersey. There was also a large movement of fugitive slaves from the South into the new free territory; and finally, there came in the dawn of the 19th century that vast industrial revolution of the modern world caused by black labor and free land, which sent increasing quantities of tobacco, sugar, and cotton into Europe and started the domination of the modern machine and capitalistic industry.

All these movements stirred American Negroes and with the bits of education that they had gained here and there from Catholics, Episcopalians, Methodists, Quakers, and others they began definite efforts for their own uplift. Perhaps the first significant and far reaching step was the revolt of Richard Allen and Absalom Jones. Richard Allen, a slave in the Chew family; and Absalom Jones, a Delaware Negro, had both been educated in Benezet's school. They were men of intelligence and real leadership. They had bought their freedom and that of their families by hiring their time and paying their former masters for their own bodies. They risked their lives in the Philadelphia epidemic of 1792, helping to bury the dead and even spending their own money; they were publicly commended by the mayor in 1794.

But they did not like the treatment which they were receiving at Saint George's Methodist Church, Fourth and Vine; and when they were forced to retire to the gallery, they left. They formed the Free African Society and for a while, I surmise, rather hoped that they were going to be invited to join the Quakers. But the Quakers hesitated. After all this was taking a rather presumptious social attitude; and besides, behind these leaders were a mass of uneducated, poverty-stricken, working folk who scarcely seemed fitted to Quaker fellowship. For the Quaker way of solving the more difficult of our social problems was the simple one of leaving ignorance and sin outside the fold, and dealing with these things at long range. But, after all, the ignorant and degraded exist and must go somewhere. Jones took a part of the flock into the Episcopal Church where, on terms but slightly better than the Methodists offered, he became a priest, segregated, insulted, and half recognized and yet his flock survives today in the 50,000 Negroes who hold membership in the Episcopal Church and are represented by a well-trained priesthood and on the bishop's bench. Allen, however, did the more startling and logical thing. He organized an independent Negro church, the African Methodist, which today has 550,000 members, 7,000 churches and property worth $32,000,000. The church has staggered desperately through a 150 years of development, fighting single-handed and without the aid of the Rich, the Good and the Pure—poverty, ignorance, disease, and superstition; and surviving under remarkable and often distinguished leadership and with some astonishing if not perfect accomplishments in religion, education, and social work.

Everywhere Negroes helped in their own education, cooperated with those who were working for them and even beyond this, established in many cases and financed their own schools early in the 19th century. Three free Negroes founded the first Negro school in the District of Columbia in 1807 and supported it for a number of years. It was closed for a while and then revived in 1818 and is the foundation upon which the present magnificent Negro school system of Washington is built. The Negroes of Cincinnati opened their own schools; the Negroes of New York rallied to the support of the old Neau school; the Negroes of Boston taxed themselves for a school.

Not only was this movement hastened in the North but even in the slave-ridden South. The Haitian Revolution drove both whites and blacks out of the West Indies. Some of them came to Baltimore, and colored Catholic women educated in France and in the Islands began Negro schools. Nelson Wells, a Baltimore Negro, left $10,000 for Negro education in 1835. In Charleston, South Carolina, a school was opened as early as 1744 for the free Negroes taught by a black West Indian; in New Orleans and Savannah schools opened and such schools in various other Southern cities were kept running more or less openly during the early 19th century.

In the meantime, however, other forces were beginning to work. Between 1790 and 1800 the Negro population of Philadelphia, for instance, more than doubled, increasing 176 per cent. This was the result of gradual emancipation; but it increased the poverty and distress in the city. Despite this increase of social problems, however; despite the Haitian Revolution, Abolitionist sentiment stiffened. Anti-slavery supporters refused to let the word "white" be inserted in the Constitution of 1790 which thus allowed free Negro property holders to vote. The U.S. export slave trade was forbidden in 1794 and Absalom Jones in 1800 petitioned the Legislature for immediate abolition of slavery and petitioned Congress against the fugitive slave law. There was uproar in the House of Representatives, and the Negroes were roundly censured for their contumely.

Between 1800 and 1810 the city Negro population of Philadelphia continued to increase. The Negro school had 400 pupils and there were six churches and many benevolent societies. Men like James Forten arose to leadership; he too was educated by Benezet, and was a "gentleman by nature, easy in manner, and able in intercourse." He helped raise colored troops when in 1814 the British burned Washington. By 1815 Negroes held $250,000 of city property.

As late as 1794 some Quakers still held slaves. Nevertheless, the mass of Quaker opinion was definitely set against slavery and a strong part of it toward education. This showed itself most effectively in the training of unusual and gifted colored men: Paul Cuffee of Massachusetts who fought for the entrance of Negroes into public schools and took some of the first immigrants to Liberia on his own ship; Benjamin Banneker who convinced Thomas Jefferson, at least partially, of the possibilities of the Negro mind and who helped lay out the city of Washington; and always men like Frederick Douglass and women like Sojourner Truth found some of their best friends among the Quakers.

The Beginning of Reaction

With 1820 new difficulties loomed in Philadelphia, in New York, in the West, and in the South. In the South came a series of attempted slave revolts, not actually very effective but terribly arresting in their possibilities. There was Gabriel in Virginia in 1800; Denmark Vesey in Charleston in 1822; and finally, the murderous and intrepid Nat Turner in Virginia in 1831. David Walker of Massachusetts published his burning appeal in 1829: "Can our condition be any worse," he shrieked. "Can it be more mean or abject. I appeal to heaven for my motive in writing. My object is, if possible, to awaken in the breasts of my afflicted, degraded and slumbering brethren a sympathy of inquiry and investigation respecting our misery and wretchedness, in this republican land of liberty!!" South Carolina tried to make Massachusetts extradite him. But Massachusetts refused in 1829 as she did in 1837.

Reactionary laws were passed in the South and in the North; new forces were at work. There was the re-bound after the War of 1812. There was the beginning of foreign immigration. There was the nationwide spread of the abolition controversy attacking slavery even in the South. The tide set against the Negro stronger and the whole period from 1820 to 1840 became a time of retrogression for the mass of Negroes and of discontenance and repression on the part of the whites; especially was there a fierce battle for economic survival between the Negroes and the new foreign immigrants. They fought for bread and butter; for the same jobs; and riots broke out in Boston, New York, Philadelphia, and Cincinnati. Perhaps it will be enough to notice the extraordinary series of riots in Philadelphia.

In June, 1829, a Scotch woman, Fannie Wright Darusmont, gave a series of addresses in Philadelphia, advocating emancipation and social equality between the races. There was great excitement; and late in the fall, a riot. The legislature proposed to make free Negroes carry passes. The Quakers hastened to advise against sending fugitive slaves into the city "as the effects of such a measure would probably be disastrous to the peace and comfort of the whole colored population in Pennsylvania." Edward Bettle was afraid that the personal liberty laws would be repealed and slave kidnappers given a free hand. There was a demonstration against Abolitionists in 1833 and the next year serious riots occurred. On an August night, 1834, hundreds of boys and men armed with clubs marched down 7th Street to the Pennsylvania Hospital. On South Street near 8th, 400 or 500 people engaged in a free street fight. Buildings were torn down and inmates beaten. The policemen and constables quieted the tumult but the very next night the mob wrecked a

Negro church and tore down 20 Negro dwellings. The houses of the whites had lights in the windows to guide the rioters. Steven James, "an honest, industrious colored man was killed."

In 1835 rioting began again and Negro houses on 8th Street were set on fire. In 1838 the mob again marched. They burned Pennsylvania Hall, the Shelter for Colored Orphans, and damaged Bethel Church. In a last riot of this series in 1842 the district between 5th and 8th Streets was looted and burned; a Negro hall and church burned; and the rioting lasted two days until it was stopped by the militia with artillery!

Meantime the courts in 1836 decided that free Negroes could not vote despite the Constitution of 1790 and the Reform Convention over the earnest protests of Negroes and their friends inserted the work "white" in the constitution of 1837 thus disfranchizing the Negroes of Pennsylvania for 35 years.

The case of the "Amistad" and "Creole," slavers captured by their slaves and brought to American and English waters in 1839 and 1841, aroused bitter controversy and gave birth to the American Missionary Society, which founded the Negro College after the war.

In the Cincinnati riots of 1829, 1,200 Negroes were driven out of the city and further riots took place in 1836 and 1841. In New York from 1834 to 1836 there were 25 or more efforts to break up abolition meetings and New York made a discriminatory property qualification against Negro voters in 1821. At the same time despite or because of these happenings, an extraordinary succession of Negro leaders arose: men in many and vital respects equal and sometimes superior to their white fellows and yet almost unknown outside their race because of color—Dr. James McCune Smith, graduated in Medicine at the University of Glasgow; William C. Nell and William Wells Brown, writers; Charles Reason, a great teacher; Samuel Ward the orator; and black preachers like Crummel of Cambridge University, England; and Pennington of Heidelberg.

The fine thing about the situation was that with such leaders the Negroes did not despair and did not give up their efforts. They proved in 1832 by actual tax receipts that they owned $350,000 worth of taxable property in Philadelphia alone. They had then in 1837, 1,700 children in schools, taught mainly by colored teachers; 16 churches and 100 benevolent societies. The record in the West and in the East is equally good. But it was clear to the Negroes that some positive action must repel this nation-wide assault upon their liberty and privileges.

The First National Convention of Negroes

They called together in Philadelphia in 1831 and again in 1833 the first National Convention of Negroes in the United State. Five to eight states were represented, and William Lloyd Garrison and leading Quakers visited and spoke at the convention. The convention took up two problems: first, what was to be done for the Negroes of Ohio who were being driven by mobs out of Cincinnati and other places; their schools ruined and their occupations taken away. The state laws were against them; and the convention of 1831 arranged for assisted migration to Canada. In this way the Canadian settlements of Negroes above the Great Lakes began. It became a center for education and agitation and it was here that John Brown repaired for volunteers when he was planning his raid on Harper's Ferry. These settlements became a refuge for fugitive slaves and for emissaries who like Harriet Tubman and Josiah Henson ranged through the South encouraging slaves to run away. Thus Negroes planned and instigated the escape of fugitives while white Quakers and others concealed and protected the Negroes on their way North. This was the celebrated Underground Railroad.

The second problem of the conventions of 1831 and 1833 was the problem of education. They had schools scattered here and there chiefly in cities but only enough to begin the training of the increasing numbers of black, who demanded it. They were especially weak in trade schools and means of training young Negroes to earn a living. The convention sought to establish such a school. They sought to gain admission to certain private schools in the North which resulted in the well known incident of Prudence Crandall. They increased the number of their self-supported schools in various cities and encouraged each other in the fight for emancipation and education.

Richard Humphreys, a West Indian ex-slave owner, living in Philadelphia at the time, bequeathed at his death in 1832, $10,000 to found an institution "having for its object the benevolent design of instructing the descendants of the African race in school learning in the various branches of the mechanical arts and trades and in agriculture. In order to prepare, to fit, and qualify them to act as teachers." The institution was founded in 1837 and at first taught farming and shoemaking to boys on a country tract of land. In 1842, it was incorporated and Jonathan Zane another Quaker added $18,000 to the endowment. An evening school was added and then a day school in 1852. Finally a building was erected on Lombard Street known as the Institute of Colored Youth with Charles L. Reason of New York, in charge. Other Quakers furnished further funds and in 1866 the Institute was located on Bainbridge above 9th, where it stayed until it was moved here to Cheyney.

Between 1840 and 1870 this problem of earning a living faced the Negroes more insistently. White migration drove them steadily out of the trades but in New York and especially in Philadelphia they built up a new and successful career in private catering. The caterers of Philadelphia became celebrated throughout the nation from Robert Bogle through Augustin, the Prossers, Jones, Dorsey, and Minton. The social condition of Negroes improved. Nearly 2,000 Negroes were in the Philadelphia schools in 1847 and the Negroes had $400,000 in real estate and 19 churches. This improvement kept on until the Civil War and Emancipation.

The Post-War Scene

Leaving now the more local history of Negro education and its benefactor, we pass into that great crusade which undertook the education of 4,000,000 emancipated slaves and another 1,000,000 black free men after the Civil War. It was an astonishing movement which has not been wholly evaluated and appreciated even up to our day. In this movement the Quaker lagged behind. Among the sects the Congregationalists took distinctly the lead followed by the Methodists and at a greater distance the Baptists and Presbyterians. The Quakers helped in general contributions to the work but perhaps on the whole from tradition were rather skeptical about a vast edifice of education erected so suddenly and with such unlimited ambition. They did not generally believe in Negro suffrage, and neither for that matter did William Lloyd Garrison. The Quaker conception of democracy was straitly limited. They were not sure that Negroes needed colleges. And Negro colleges were planted in the South which aimed to be universities. High schools and normal schools were widespread and a system of elementary schools was set up in the South for the first time in its history by the black voters under the Reconstruction Governments.

The education movement among Negroes rose to a flood. Some 90,000 were in school in 1866 and 150,000 in 1870. Twenty years later were 1,250,000; 1,600,000 in 1910; and in 1930, 2,500,000. Yet this represented no complete triumph in education because the task of educating a whole population far outstriped the Negro funds of philanthropists and the meagre provisions of the government. Only 60 per cent of the Negro children attend school today and hardly one-third of these have really adequate modern equipment and attention. Short terms, poor teaching, double sessions, inadequate finance, and lack of housing still leave the problem of Negro education woefully unsolved.

The whole structure was at first poorly conceived and vulnerable but without a shadow of doubt it was the salvation of the Negro not only in America but in the world. No half-way measures at that time were possible. Unless the Negro and his friends had made every effort to establish in America a distinct educated Negro leadership the reaction after the war and the economic imperialism of Europe over the darker races would have held American Negroes in a much more certain caste and bondage than they are in today. For with all the Negro's disadvantages in America he has this tremendous advantage over Negro groups in West, South, and East Africa and in the West Indies and even over colored groups in India—not to mention the difficulties of China and the South Seas. He has so large and well-constituted a group of educated leadership that it has been able to convince the modern world that permanent color caste is unthinkable and that the continued holding of the darker races in subjection to the whites is no longer a feasible nor a desirable program. For this consummation, the Negro has the right to thank the unselfish efforts of his own fathers in the 18th and 19th centuries; he has the duty of being especially grateful to the mass of abolitionists and their co-workers during and after the Civil War who established Negro education. But above all he has to thank that little group of Quaker thinkers who in the 18th and 19th centuries began to differentiate between two problems: the problem of freedom and the problem of education—and began to see that the emancipation of the Negro was not enough; that education even before they were free and certainly afterwards was the primary and important thing for the race and for the world. If their descendants hesitated before the logical implications of this thesis, all the greater honor to the fathers who did not hesitate. Indeed one part of the program for Negro education the Quakers never dropped, and that was the keeping of the door of opportunity open for the individual Negro who showed unusual talent. Not that all Quakers did this always then or now but it was continually the saving grace of a man like Alfred Cope who supported the first Negro doctor of philosophy at Yale. And then down far below this came a renewed, even if limited, activity in orphanages for the under-privileged which sought at the very beginning of life to see that the stream of ability and health was not hopelessly blocked.

The response of the Negroes to all this help from the day of George Fox to Cheyney has been continuous and unquestioned; and with everything that we may point to of failure and carping criticism, there has nevertheless been a solid accomplishment and an extraordinary social advance among these people which is one of the world wonders of our day.

CHAPTER ELEVEN

Two Hundred Years
Of Segregated Schools

In this speech, delivered in February 1955, just a year after the Supreme Court decision of *Brown vs. Topeka*, Du Bois provides an overview of the history of segregation and schooling in the United States. In doing so, he not only analyzes the significance of the court's decision, but also the possibilities increasingly opening themselves to blacks in the United States.

The African slave in America had tried physical force against oppression from the time of Columbus to the day of Nat Turner. In every island and every slave state, as Herbert Aptheker has shown us, there were hundreds of slave revolts which prove, as Haitian historians say, that the French Revolution did not spread from France to the West Indies but from the West Indies to France. Negro revolt under the Maroons culminated in Haiti where Britain, France and Spain were worsted and the United States was frightened into stopping the slave trade. The United States then got the territory west of the Mississippi as a gift.

Nevertheless, against force wielded by slaves, greater force brought to bear by organization and arms in white America kept the shackles riveted on many of the Negroes. These Negroes therefore became determined to achieve freedom by brain if not by muscle.

In the early eighteenth century two free Negroes of Massachusetts built schools and opened them to all who would attend. Then Negroes had schools furnished for them in New York, Philadelphia and Cincinnati. Teachers first were white and funds came from missionary organizations like the British Society for the Propagation of the Gospel and from individual philanthropists like Thomas Bray and Anthony Benezet. Sometimes Negroes took over the teaching, like Katy Ferguson who established the Sunday Schools in New York for white and colored; and John Chavis of North Carolina, who taught some of the most distinguished whites.

In the early nineteenth century free Negroes conducted schools in New York, Charleston, Savannah, New Orleans and elsewhere. As free public schools became common in the North, a few Negroes entered here and there, but the barriers closed against them and they began to fight. Alexander Crummel and two companions secured admission to a New

Hampshire semiprivate school but enraged whites dragged the schoolhouse into a swamp. Prudence Crandall received a colored girl into her seminary in New Haven and was crucified in spirit and property. By 1855, led by William C. Nell, the segregated school system of Massachusetts was abolished.

Then there grew up later in the century distinct Negro public school systems, supported by the state, usually with colored principals but not as well equipped as the white schools. These systems spread in northern cities like New York, Philadelphia and Cincinnati. Private higher schools also were established for Negroes, especially by churches. Lincoln in Pennsylvania, run by white Presbyterians, and Wilberforce in Ohio, run by colored Methodists, gave secondary school instruction and some college work about 1854. In 1850 there were 4,000 colored children in school in the South and 22,000 in the North.

After emancipation there arose a complete Negro public school system in Washington and in several other cities; while in the South Negro voters demanded a public school system of the reluctant whites. The Civil War and emancipation also brought Negro schools under the Freedmen's Bureau and northern missions. This system, which covered much of the South, became the southern system of free public education under the Reconstruction governments.

As I have written elsewhere, "The first great mass movement for public education at the expense of the state in he South came from Negroes. Many white leaders before the war had advocated general education for white children but few had been listened to. Schools for indigents and pauper white children were supported here and there and more or less spasmodically. Some states had elaborate plans but they were not carried out. Public education for all at public expense was, in the South, a Negro idea."

The question of separating races in these schools was not at first regarded as important. Negroes wanted education on any terms. In theory of course they knew that the mixed school was the democratic ideal and they were sure that the cost of a double system would eventually force a mixed system. They accepted temporarily separate schools, therefore, without much objection.

The action of the states varied. With Reconstruction, public schools were opened in Charleston, South Carolina, without distinction of color. Twenty-five of the forty-two teachers were colored. The South Carolina Act of 1870 for a system of free schools was the most complete legislation that the state had ever enacted. Textbooks were provided at cost or free to the poor but the schools were separated by race.

In Louisiana, by the Constitution of *1863* all children were admitted to schools regardless of color. That prevailed until *1877,* although often by administrative action colored children were kept out of white schools. Finally segregated schools prevailed. In Mississippi, separate schools by race were demanded in *1875.* In Florida, the colored superintendent, Jonathan E. Gibbs, established schools which at first were mixed but afterward they became by law separated by color.

The state system of schools for North Carolina in 1869 called for separation by race. In Virginia the constitution did not provide for separate schools but laws passed in *1869* separated the schools by color. In the District of Columbia, Negroes from *1807* ran self-supported schools. In *1864* public schools were provided with separate and poorer schools for Negroes. By *1867* the Negro schools began to receive a proportionate share of the funds and there came two separate systems, white and colored, each with its own superintendent. About *1890* the system became unified, with a colored assistant superintendent in charge of the schools for Negroes.

Gradually the South, backed by the dictates of the Supreme Court, settled down to a system of public education with separation of whites and Negroes. There were separate buildings and facilities. Teachers in colored schools were usually colored, although in Charleston and Richmond southern white teachers were long retained, to the disgust of Negroes and retardation of Negro children. The superintendence of the colored systems was entirely in the hands of the whites, save in a few cases of powerless local colored trustees. The white school authorities could allocate the school funds as they pleased and often did not have to report even to the federal government on federal funds.

There came into use a custom, encouraged by the Southern Education Board and its successor, the General Education Board, where discrimination against Negroes was excused, with the dogma of "first educate the whites and later the Negroes." This changed soon to deliberately poorer and cheaper Negro schools. Then the South moved North and planted "Jim Crow" in schools in localities in twenty northern states. This situation finally became so great a national disgrace that Negroes and many whites began systematically to complain.

It long seemed useless to bring the matter to the courts. When the Supreme Court declared in *1896* that separate but equal schools meant separate but not equal; and when later to the astonishment even of the white South decreed that the city of Augusta, Georgia, could provide an elaborate high school and night schools for whites and none for Negroes, the Negroes were in despair for years. They were reduced to begging local white school authorities for some pretense of decent treatment and only in case of federal appropriations to demand directly from Congress equal shares.

As Negro voting increased, Congress got an improved sense of hearing. First, Negroes secured some increase of justice in the distribution and administration of federal funds. The shares of the Negro Land Grant colleges began slowly to increase and the crisis came in the matter of the home or in the church where, under current Christian custom, segregation by race and class will remain until the last possible moment.

Despite all this we Negroes will stand fast and pull through. Some of our literature will for a season descend into the "white folks' n---- " type, with fulsome praise of what "good white folk" have done for us. Our leadership in social studies may well succumb to money which millionaires will drop into the laps of young white southern "scholars" and subservient blacks to undertake the study of Negroes, which Negro scholars began.

Yet we will survive. The labor unions are open now for us as never before and beginning to receive us not with condescension but in brotherhood. Europe is listening to us and not so exclusively to the "professional" whites to tell them about kind slave drivers and "black mammies." Asia has risen to her feet and taken her stand against white supremacy: and finally Africa too, despite American dollars, artillery and atom bombs imported to back Malan. It's just one more long battle, but we are ready to fight it.

PART FOUR

Du Bois, Washington and the Hampton Model

CHAPTER TWELVE

Of Mr. Booker T. Washington and Others

This is perhaps the most important single piece of writing by Du Bois. It represents Du Bois's main attack on the "Tuskegee Machine" and the "Hampton Model." The controversy between Du Bois and Washington was historic and has been analyzed in detail by others, as well as in the introduction to this volume. In *Dusk of Dawn*, Du Bois explained that the controversy that developed between him and Washington became far more controversial than he "had ever dreamed." Many years later he summarized the conflict:

> I believed in the higher education of the Talented Tenth who through their knowledge of modern culture could guide the American Negro into higher civilization. I knew that without this the Negro would have to accept white leadership, and that such leadership could not always be trusted to guide this group into self-realization and to its highest cultural possibilities. (604)

This was Du Bois at his very best. As much as any other black leader, he understood that what was at stake in the controversy over Tuskegee and the Hampton Model was more than a disagreement with Washington and his model of education. Instead, it was an act of conscious opposition to a system of economic and social discrimination that dominated the United States.

Easily the most striking thing in the history of the American Negro since 1876 is the ascendancy of Mr. Booker T. Washington. It began at the time when war memories and ideals were rapidly passing; a day of astonishing commercial development was dawning; a sense of doubt and hesitation overtook the freedmen's sons—then it was that his leading began. Mr. Washington came, with a simple definite programme, at the psychological moment when the nation was a little ashamed of having bestowed so much sentiment on Negroes, and was concentrating its energies on Dollars. His programme of industrial education, conciliation of the South, and submission and silence as to civil and political rights, was not wholly original; the Free Negroes from 1830 up to war-time had striven to build industrial schools, and the

American Missionary Association had from the first taught various trades; and Price and others had sought a way of honorable alliance with the best of the Southerners. But Mr. Washington first indissolubly linked these things; he put enthusiasm, unlimited energy, and perfect faith into this programme, and changed it from a by-path into a veritable Way of Life. And the tale of the methods by which he did this is a fascinating study of human life.

It startled the nation to hear a Negro advocating such a programme after many decades of bitter complaint; it startled and won the applause of the South, it interested and won the admiration of the North; and after a confused murmur of protest, it silenced if it did not convert the Negroes themselves.

To gain the sympathy and cooperation of the various elements comprising x, the white South was Mr. Washington's first task; and this, at the time Tuskegee was founded, seemed, for a black man, well-nigh impossible. And yet ten years later it was done in the word spoken at Atlanta: "In all things purely social we can be as separate as the five fingers, and yet one as the hand in all things essential to mutual progress." This "Atlanta Compromise" is by all odds the most notable thing in Mr. Washington's career. The South interpreted it in different ways: the radicals received it as a complete surrender of the demand for civil and political equality; the conservatives, as a generously conceived working basis for mutual understanding. So both approved it, and today its author is certainly the most distinguished Southerner since Jefferson Davis, and the one with the largest personal following.

Next to this achievement comes Mr. Washington's work in gaining place and consideration in the North. Others less shrewd and tactful had formerly essayed to sit on these two stools and had fallen between them; but as Mr. Washington knew the heart of the South from birth and training, so by singular insight he intuitively grasped the spirit of the age which was dominating the North. . . .

And yet this very singleness of vision and thorough oneness with his age are a mark of the successful man. It is as though Nature must needs make men narrow in order to give them force. So Mr. Washington's cult has gained unquestioning followers, his work has wonderfully prospered, his friends are legion, and his enemies are confounded. Today he stands as the one recognized spokesman of his ten million fellows, and one of the most notable figures in a nation of seventy millions. One hesitates, therefore, to criticise a life which, beginning with so little, has done so much. And yet the time is come when one may speak in all sincerity and utter courtesy of the mistakes and shortcomings of Mr. Washington's career, as well as of his triumphs, without being thought captious or envious, and without forgetting that it is easier to do ill than well in the world.

The criticism that has hitherto met Mr. Washington has not always been of this broad character. In the South especially has he had to walk warily to avoid the harshest judgments—and naturally so, for he is dealing with the one subject of deepest sensitiveness to that section. Twice—once when at the Chicago celebration of the Spanish-American War he alluded to the color prejudice that is "eating away the vitals of the South," and once when he dined with President Roosevelt—has the resulting Southern criticism been violent enough to threaten seriously his popularity. In the North the feeling has several times forced itself into words, that Mr. Washington's counsels of submission overlooked certain elements of true manhood, and that his educational programme was unnecessarily narrow. Usually, however, such criticism has not found open expression, although, too, the spiritual sons of the Abolitionists have not been prepared to acknowledge that the schools founded before Tuskegee, by men of broad ideals and self-sacrificing spirit, were wholly failures or worthy of ridicule. While, then, criticism has not failed to follow Mr. Washington, yet the prevailing public opinion of the land has been but too willing to deliver the solution of a wearisome problem into his hands, and say, "If that is all you and your race ask, take it."

Among his own people, however, Mr. Washington has encountered the strongest and most lasting opposition, amounting at times to bitterness, and even today continuing strong and insistent even though largely silenced in outward expression by the public opinion of the nation. . . .

But the hushing of the criticism of honest opponents is a dangerous thing. It leads some of the best of the critics to unfortunate silence and paralysis of effort, and others to burst into speech so passionately and intemperately as to lose listeners. . . .

Now in the past the American Negro has had instructive experience in the choosing of group leaders, founding thus a peculiar dynasty which in the light of present conditions is worth while studying. When sticks and stones and beasts form the sole environment of a people, their attitude is largely one of determined opposition to and conquest of natural forces. But when to earth and brute is added an environment of men and ideas, then the attitude of the imprisoned group may take three main forms—a feeling of revolt and revenge; an attempt to adjust all thought and action to the will of the greater group; or, finally, a determined effort at self-realization and self-development despite environing opinion. The influence of all of these attitudes at various times can be traced in the history of the American Negro, and in the evolution of his successive leaders.

Before 1750, while the fire of African freedom still burned in the veins of the slaves, there was in all leadership or attempted leadership but the one motive of revolt and revenge—typified in the terrible Maroons, the Danish blacks, and Cato of Stono, and veiling all the Americas in fear of insurrection. The liberalizing tendencies of the latter half of the eighteenth century brought, along with kindlier relations between black and white, thoughts of ultimate adjustment and assimilation. Such aspiration was especially voiced in the earnest songs of Phyllis, in the martyrdom of Attucks, the fighting of Salem and Poor, the intellectual accomplishments of Banneker and Derham, and the political demands of the Cuffes.

Stern financial and social stress after the war cooled much of the previous humanitarian ardor. The disappointment and impatience of the Negroes at the persistence of slavery and serfdom voiced itself in two movements. The slaves in the South, aroused undoubtedly by vague rumors of the Haytian [sic] revolt, made three fierce attempts at insurrection—in 1800 under Gabriel in Virginia, in 1822 under Vesey in Carolina, and in 1831 again in Virginia under the terrible Nat Turner. In the Free States, on the other hand, a new and curious attempt at self-development was made. In Philadelphia and New York color-prescription led to a withdrawal of Negro communicants from white churches and the formation of a peculiar socio-religious institution among the Negroes known as the African Church—an organization still living and controlling in its various branches over a million of men.

Walker's wild appeal against the trend of the times showed how the world was changing after the coming of the cotton-gin. By 1830 slavery seemed hopelessly fastened on the South, and the slaves thoroughly cowed into submission. The free Negroes of the North, inspired by the mulatto immigrants from the West Indies, began to change the basis of their demands; they recognized the slavery of slaves, but insisted that they themselves were freemen, and sought assimilation and amalgamation with the nation on the same terms with other men. Thus, Forten and Purvis of Philadelphia, Shad of Wilmington, Du Bois of New Haven, Barbadoes of Boston, and others, strove singly and together as men, they said, not as slaves; as "people of color," not as "Negroes." The trend of the times, however, refused them recognition save in individual and exceptional cases, considered them as one with all the despised blacks, and they soon found themselves striving to keep even the rights they formerly had of voting and working and moving as freemen. Schemes of migration and colonization arose among them; but these they refused to entertain, and they eventually turned to the Abolition movement as a final refuge.

Here, led by Remond, Nell, Wells-Brown, and Douglass, a new period of self-assertion and self-development dawned. To be sure, ultimate freedom and assimilation were the ideal before the leaders, but the assertion of the manhood rights of the Negro by himself was the main reliance, and John Brown's raid was the extreme of its logic. After the war and emancipation, the great form of Frederick Douglass, the greatest of American Negro leaders, still led the host. Self-assertion, especially in political lines, was the main programme, and behind Douglass came Elliot, Bruce, and Langston, and the Reconstruction politicians, and, less conspicuous but of greater social significance Alexander Crummell and Bishop Daniel Payne.

Then came the Revolution of 1876, the suppression of the Negro votes, the changing and shifting of ideals, and the seeking of new lights in the great night. Douglass, in his old age, still bravely stood for the ideals of his early manhood—ultimate assimilation *through* self-assertion, and on no other terms. For a time Price arose as a new leader, destined, it seemed, not to give up, but to re-state the old ideals in a form less repugnant to the white South. But he passed away in his prime. Then came the new leader. Nearly all the former ones had become leaders by the silent suffrage of their fellows, had sought to lead their own people alone, and were usually, save Douglass, little known outside their race. But Booker T. Washington arose as essentially the leader not of one race but of two—a compromiser between the South, the North, and the Negro. Naturally the Negroes resented, at first bitterly, signs of compromise which surrendered their civil and political rights, even though this was to be exchanged for larger chances of economic development. The rich and dominating North, however, was not only weary of the race problem, but was investing largely in Southern enterprises, and welcomed any method of peaceful cooperation. Thus, by national opinion, the Negroes began to recognize Mr. Washington's leadership; and the voice of criticism was hushed.

Mr. Washington represents in Negro thought the old attitude of adjustment and submission; but adjustment at such a peculiar time as to make his programme unique. This is an age of unusual economic development, and Mr. Washington's programme naturally takes an economic cast, becoming a gospel of Work and Money to such an extent as apparently almost completely to overshadow the higher aims of life. Moreover, this is an age when the more advanced races are coming in closer contact with the less developed races, and the race-feeling is therefore intensified; and Mr. Washington's programme practically accepts the alleged inferiority of the Negro races. Again, in our own land, the reaction from the sentiment of war-time has given impetus to race-prejudice against Negroes, and Mr. Washington withdraws many of the high demands of Negroes as men and American citizens. In other periods of intensified prejudice all the Negro's tendency to self-assertion has been called forth; at this period a policy of submission is advocated. In the history of nearly all other races and peoples the doctrine preached at such crises has been that manly self-respect is worth more than lands and houses, and that a people who voluntarily surrender such respect, or cease striving for it, are not worth civilizing.

In answer to this, it has been claimed that the Negro can survive only through submission. Mr. Washington distinctly asks that black people give up, at least for the present, three things—

First, political power,

Second, insistence on civil rights,

Third, higher education of Negro youth—

and concentrate all their energies on industrial education, the accumulation of wealth, and the conciliation of the South. This policy has been courageously and insistently advocated for over fifteen years, and has been triumphant for perhaps ten years. As a result of this tender of the palm-branch, what has been the return? In these years there have occurred:

1. The disfranchisement of the Negro.

2. The legal creation of a distinct status of civil inferiority for the Negro.

3. The steady withdrawal of aid from institutions for the higher training of the Negro.

These movements are not, to be sure, direct results of Mr. Washington's teachings; but his propaganda has, without a shadow of doubt, helped their speedier accomplishment. The question then comes: Is it possible, and probable, that nine millions of men can make effective progress in economic lines if they are deprived of political rights, made a servile caste, and allowed only the most meagre chance for developing their exceptional men? If history and reason give any distinct answer to these questions, it is an emphatic No. And Mr. Washington thus faces the triple paradox of his career:

1. He is striving nobly to make Negro artisans businessmen and property owners; but it is utterly impossible, under modern competitive methods, for workingmen and property-owners to defend their rights and exist without the right of suffrage.

2. He insists on thrift and self-respect, but at the same time counsels a silent submission to civic inferiority such as is bound to sap the manhood of any race in the long run.

3. He advocates common school and industrial training, and depreciates institutions of higher learning; but neither the Negro common schools, nor Tuskegee itself, could remain open a day were it not for teachers trained in Negro colleges, or trained by their graduates.

This triple paradox in Mr. Washington's position is the object of criticism by two classes of colored Americans. One class is spiritually descended from Toussaint the Savior, through Gabriel, Vesey, and Turner, and they represent the attitude of revolt and revenge; they hate the white South blindly and distrust the white race generally, and so far as they agree on definite action, think that the Negro's only hope lies in emigration beyond the borders of the United States.

The other class of Negroes who cannot agree with Mr. Washington has hitherto said little aloud. . . . Such men feel in conscience bound to ask of this nation three things:

1. The right to vote.

2. Civic equality.

3. The education of youth according to ability.

They acknowledge Mr. Washington's invaluable service in counselling patience and courtesy in such demands; they do not ask that ignorant black men vote when ignorant whites are debarred, or that any reasonable restrictions in the suffrage should not be applied; they know that the low social level of the mass of the race is responsible for much discrimination against it, but they also know, and the nation knows, that relentless color-prejudice is more often a cause than a result of the

Negro's degradation, they seek the abatement of this relic of barbarism, and not its systematic encouragement and pampering by all agencies of social power from the Associated Press to the Church of Christ. They advocate, with Mr. Washington, a broad system of Negro common schools supplemented by thorough industrial training; but they are surprised that a man of Mr. Washington's insight cannot see that no such educational system ever has rested or can rest on any other basis than that of the well equipped college and university, and they insist that there is a demand for a few such institutions throughout the South to train the best of the Negro youth as teachers, professional men, and leaders.

This group of men honor Mr. Washington for his attitude of conciliation toward the white South; they accept the "Atlanta Compromise" in its broadest interpretation; they recognize, with him, many signs of promise, many men of high purpose and fair judgment, in this section; they know that no easy task has been laid upon a region already tottering under heavy burdens. But, nevertheless, they insist that the way to truth and right lies in straightforward honesty, not in indiscriminate flattery; in praising those of the South who do well and criticising uncompromisingly those who do ill; in taking advantage of the opportunities at hand and urging their fellows to do the same, but at the same time in remembering that only a firm adherence to their higher ideals and aspirations will ever keep those ideals within the realm of possibility. They do not expect that the free right to vote, to enjoy civic rights, and to be educated, will come in a moment; they do not expect to see the bias and prejudices of years disappear at the blast of a trumpet; but they are absolutely certain that the way for a people to gain their reasonable rights is not by voluntarily throwing them away and insisting that they do not want them; that the way for a people to gain respect is not by continually belittling and ridiculing themselves; that, on the contrary, Negroes must insist continually, in season and out of season, that voting is necessary to modern manhood, that color discrimination is barbarism, and that black boys need education as well as white boys.

In failing thus to state plainly and unequivocally the legitimate demands of their people, even at the cost of opposing an honored leader, the thinking classes of American Negroes would shirk a heavy responsibility—a responsibility to themselves, a responsibility to the struggling masses, a responsibility to the darker races of men whose future depends so largely on this American experiment, but especially a responsibility to this nation—this common Fatherland. It is wrong to encourage a man or a people in evil-doing; it is wrong to aid and abet a national crime simply because it is unpopular not to do so. The growing spirit of kindliness and reconciliation between the North and South after the frightful differences of a generation ago ought to be a source of deep congratulation to all, and especially to those whose mistreatment caused the war; but if that reconciliation is to be marked by the industrial slavery and civic death of those same black men, with permanent legislation into a position of inferiority, then those black men, if they are really men, are called upon by every consideration of patriotism and loyalty to oppose such a course by all civilized methods, even though such opposition involves disagreement with Mr. Booker T. Washington. We have no right to sit silently by while the inevitable seeds are sown for a harvest of disaster to our children, black and white.

First, it is the duty of black men to judge the South discriminatingly. The present generation of Southerners are not responsible for the past, and they should not be blindly hated or blamed for it. Furthermore, to no class is the indiscriminate endorsement of the recent course of the South toward Negroes more nauseating than to the best thought of the South. The South is not "solid"; it is a land in the ferment of social change, wherein forces of all kinds are fighting for supremacy; and to praise the ill the South is today perpetrating is just as wrong as to condemn the good. Discriminating and broadminded criticism is what the South needs—needs it for the sake of her own white sons and daughters, and for the insurance of robust, healthy mental and moral development.

Today even the attitude of the Southern whites toward the blacks is not, as so many assume, in all cases the same; the ignorant Southerner hates the Negro, the workingmen fear his competition, the money-makers wish to use him as a laborer, some of the educated see a menace in his upward development, while others—usually the sons of the masters—wish to help him to rise. National opinion has enabled this last class to maintain the Negro common schools, and to protect the Negro partially in property, life, and limb. Through the pressure of the money-makers, the Negro is in danger of being reduced to semi-slavery, especially in the country districts; the workingmen, and those of the educated who fear the Negro, have united to disfranchise him, and some have urged his deportation; while the passions of the ignorant are easily aroused to lynch and abuse any black man. To praise this intricate whirl of thought and prejudice is nonsense; to inveigh indiscriminately against "the South" is unjust; but to use the same breath in praising Governor Aycock, exposing Senator Morgan, arguing with Mr. Thomas Nelson Page, and denouncing Senator Ben Tillman, is not only sane, but the imperative duty of thinking black men.

It would be unjust to Mr. Washington not to acknowledge that in several instances he has opposed movements in the South which were unjust to the Negro; he sent memorials to the Louisiana and Alabama constitutional conventions, he has spoken against lynching, and in other ways has openly or silently set his influence against sinister schemes and unfortunate happenings. Notwithstanding this, it is equally true to assert that on the whole the distinct impression left by Mr. Washington's propaganda is, first, that the South is justified in its present attitude toward the Negro because of the Negro's degradation; secondly, that the prime cause of the Negro's failure to rise more quickly is his wrong education in the past; and, thirdly, that his future rise depends primarily on his own efforts. Each of these propositions is a dangerous half-truth. The supplementary truths must never be lost sight of: first, slavery and race-prejudice are potent if not sufficient causes of the Negro's position; second, industrial and common school training were necessarily slow in planting because they had to await the black teachers trained by higher institutions—it being extremely doubtful if any essentially different development was possible, and certainly a Tuskegee was unthinkable before 1880; and, third, while it is a great truth to say that the Negro must strive and strive mightily to help himself, it is equally true that unless his striving be not simply seconded, but rather aroused and encouraged, by the initiative of the richer and wiser environing group, he cannot hope for great success.

In his failure to realize and impress this last point, Mr. Washington is especially to be criticised. His doctrine has tended to make the whites, North and South, shift the burden of the Negro problem to the Negro's shoulders and stand aside as critical and rather pessimistic spectators; when in fact the burden belongs to the nation, and the hands of none of us are clean if we bend not our energies to righting these great wrongs.

The South ought to be led, by candid and honest criticism, to assert her better self and do her full duty to the race she has cruelly wronged and is still wronging. The North—her co-partner in guilt—cannot salve her conscience by plastering it with gold. We cannot settle this problem by diplomacy and suaveness, by "policy" alone. If worse come to worst, can the moral fibre of this country survive the slow throttling and murder of nine millions of men?

The black men of America have a duty to perform, a duty stern and delicate—a forward movement to oppose a part of the work of their greatest leader. So far as Mr. Washington preaches Thrift, Patience, and Industrial Training for the masses, we must hold up his hands and strive with him, rejoicing in his honors and glorying in the strength of this Joshua called of God and of man to lead the headless host. But so far as Mr. Washington apologizes for injustice, North or South, does not rightly value the privilege and duty of voting, belittles the emasculating effects of caste distinctions, and opposes the higher training and ambition of our brighter minds—so far as he, the South, or the Nation, does this—we must unceasingly and firmly oppose them. By every civilized and peaceful method we must strive for the rights which the world accords to men, clinging unwaveringly to those great words which the sons of the Fathers would fain forget: "We hold these truths to be self-evident: That all men are created equal; that they are endowed by their Creator with certain unalienable rights; that among these are life, liberty, and the pursuit of happiness."

CHAPTER THIRTEEN

Hampton

In 1917, as part of the fiftieth anniversary of Hampton Institute, Du Bois was contacted as part of a history on the school to see if he would be willing to state his reasons for opposing its "industrial education" model. Du Bois responded to the request by writing a scathing critique of the school and its programs in *The Crisis.* This article summarizes as concisely as any of his work his opposition to the Hampton Model and his continuing problems with the school and its policies, long after his formal debates with Washington and his followers had come to an end.

The death of Hollis Burke Frissell, principal of Hampton Institute, brings that institution and its work prominently before the public. It is, therefore, peculiarly fitting that the following correspondence should be made public:

Dear Dr. Du Bois:

In preparation for the Fiftieth Anniversary of Hampton Institute, efforts are being made to collect the necessary material for the history of the school. It is a matter of history that for many years the colored people were opposed to the type of education offered them at Hampton and were consequently also opposed to the school itself. For the sake of learning the facts in regard to this matter I am writing to you and to a number of other prominent colored men to ask for statements in regard to the facts in the case.

I shall be very grateful if you will send me a statement in regard to the attitude (with reasons) of the colored people who were opposed to industrial education during the early days of Hampton and who are still in some cases opposed to it.

Will you kindly say in this connection whether you will object to the use of your name, if that is thought desirable? (Miss) J. E. Davis.

Dear Miss Davis:

I have a wide acquaintance with educated colored folk. My interpretation of their attitude is that they do not oppose and never have opposed Hampton Institute because it teaches industries. On the contrary, they recognize Hampton as probably the best center of trade teaching for Negroes in the United States.

It is true, however, that educated Negroes in the past and at present hold Hampton and some of her methods in grave mistrust. They recognize the worth of her work—the fine spirit of many of her teachers, past and present, and the splendid character of her graduates, but at the same time they cannot forget three important facts:

1. The course at Hampton is so arranged that it cannot be made to fit in with the higher courses of education, as adopted by the leading educational institutions of the United States. Granted that Hampton is and ought to be the finishing school of nine-tenths of her students, the fact remains that Hampton deliberately makes it impossible for her most promising and brilliant students to receive college training or higher technical and professional training or higher technical and professional training save at great disadvantage and a well-nigh fatal loss of time. Friends of Hampton have defended this action by asserting (a) that the Negro does not need college training and (b) that if the colleges do not fit the Hampton course of study, *they* are wrong and not Hampton. Both these assertions educated Negroes regard as preposterous. There are hundreds of Hampton men who deserve and could efficiently use longer and more thorough courses of training than Hampton gives, but who find themselves at the age of nineteen or twenty in an educational blind alley, with further progress barred. They must go out as half educated, partially trained men, when they might be developed to full efficiency. It is, undoubtedly, true that colleges ought to recognize a broader fitting-school [finishing-school] course of study than they do at present, but so long as they do not, it is criminal to make the Negro the peculiar sufferer from their exclusiveness and to deny the undoubted value of the present college curriculum to the finest Negro minds in Virginia.

2. It may be said that Hampton simply specializes in technical training and high school work and that students fitted for higher training can go elsewhere. This brings us to the second indictment against Hampton— her illiberal and seemingly selfish attitude toward other colored schools. She holds little or no fellowship with them; she has repeatedly loaned herself to decrying their work, criticizing and belittling their ideals while her friends continually seek to divert to Hampton the already painfully meager revenues of the colored colleges. Few schools can equal in its own field the efficiency of Hampton, with its millions of endowment, but certainly the splendid work of Atlanta, Fisk, Howard, and other schools, done in poverty and travail and in the face of hostile public opinion, de-

serves better recognition and less criticism than it gets from Hampton and her friends.

Moreover, the students who go to Hampton go for "education." They do not know their own bent and aptitudes. They come from homes where they can hope for little educational guidance. It should be the work of Hampton not simply to train but to sift and to send to colleges or other schools those fitted for work higher or different from that offered by her curriculum. This she never voluntarily does. She feeds no colleges or professional schools; she encourages no artists or musicians; she helps no writers, but apparently proceeds on the assumption that every Negro must be trained to farm, or to be an artisan or a servant. We have no silly illusions as to the number of talented Negroes who deserve higher training, but surely in fifty years it seems that out of tens of thousands of students Hampton might have found a few worthy of the highest training. Small wonder that educated Negroes resent this and demand that Hampton cease to bury talent and deflect genius.

3. The third indictment of educated black folk against Hampton is more difficult to express than the others, and one of which we are less sure, and yet it is a real grievance in our minds. We believe that an institution that professes to teach the Negro self-respect and self-control should give the Negro a larger voice in her government. We do not wish Hampton to be an exclusively Negro institution, but we do think that there should be Negroes on her Board of Trustees; that there should be a larger recognition of Negro achievement, instead of an almost exclusive emphasis of the white philanthropists; and that there should be a closer touch between the school and the body of educated Negro opinion. In fine, we think that Hampton should consider what we want and not simply what she wishes us to want. We do not feel, at present, that Hampton is our school—on the contrary, we feel that she belongs to the white South and to the reactionary North, and we fear that she is a center of that underground and silent intrigue which is determined to perpetuate the American Negro as a docile peasant and peon, without political rights or social standing, working for little wages, and heaping up dividends to be doled out in future charity to his children.

Such a feeling as this may be wrong and ill-founded, but it is real and it easily lies within Hampton's power to disprove it.

These are the reasons why many educated Negroes are and have been "opposed" to Hampton. We have seldom voiced this opposition, and I voice it now only at your invitation. I reiterate my respect for the Institution and my firm belief that it has done great good, but I insist that no school which deliberately curtails the training of the talented, refuses to guide her apter students to their greatest development, save in restricted lines, and not only gives her beneficiaries little or no voice in its control, but seems even to harbor and encourage their enemies—no such school is reaching its greatest usefulness.

CHAPTER FOURTEEN

Education and Work

The following chapter contains a Commencement Address delivered by Du Bois at Howard University, Washington, D.C., on June 6, 1930. Du Bois was sixty-two—seemingly near the end of his career. As he recalled:

> *The Crisis* circulated widely and my word was read and listened to. It occurred to George Crawford, trained at Tuskegee, graduated at Yale, and trustee of Talladega and Howard, that this would be a fit time to crown the marriage of college and industrial education by having Howard confer at once upon me and the president of Tuskegee an honorary degree. (Aptheker 1973, 61)

As David Levering Lewis has pointed out, "the primacy of technical education versus liberal arts was an exhausted debate" (Lewis 2000, 313). In his address Du Bois recalled the progress that had been realized in the years since he engaged in battle with Booker T. Washington, the Hampton Model, and its offspring, the Tuskegee Machine. As he recalled:

> Today all this is past; by the majority of the older of my hearers, it is practically forgotten. By the younger, it appears merely as a vague legend. Thirty-five years, a full generation and more, have elapsed. The increase in Negro education by all measurements has been a little less than marvelous. In 1895, there were not more than 1,000 Negro students of full college grade in the United States. Today, there are over 19,000 in college and nearly 150,000 in high schools. In 1895, 60 per cent of American Negroes, ten years of age or over, were illiterate. Today, perhaps three-fourths can read and write. The increase of Negro students in industrial and land-grant colleges has been equally large. The latter have over 16,000 students and the increasing support of the government of the States; while the great industrial schools, especially Hampton and Tuskegee, are the best endowed institutions for the education of black folk in the world. (page 184 of this book)

Yet despite this fact, Du Bois maintained that the fundamental debate remained—that neither the liberal arts nor the industrial model of education for blacks had succeeded. Perhaps the Depression had led Du Bois to accept the idea that there was a need for both vocational and liberal arts instruction and leadership in the education of college students. Addressing the professorate, he argued that:

> The teacher in a Negro college has got to be something far more than a master of a branch of human knowledge. He has got to be able to impart his knowledge to human beings whose place in the world is today precarious and critical and the possibilities and advancement of that human being in the world where he is to live and earn a living is of just as much importance in the teaching process as the content of the knowledge taught. (pages 194-195 of this book)

Du Bois argues: "The man who teaches blacksmithing must be more than a blacksmith. He must be a man of education and culture, acquainted with the whole present technique and business organization of the modern world, and acquainted too with human beings and their possibilities" (page 195 of this book). Such individuals are difficult to find. Whether a professor of Humanities or an artisan teaching a craft, the teacher in the black college and university needed, according to Du Bois, "to be social statesmen and statesmen of high order" (page 195 of this book).

Du Bois's vision of the black professorate rejected the idea of the detached scholar in his or her ivory tower. Instead, he or she was an individual engaged in the world. As Du Bois explained in the case of a professor teaching mathematics.

> The professor of mathematics in a college has to be more than a counting machine, or proctor of examinations; he must be a living man, acquainted with real human beings, and alive to the relation of his branch of knowledge to the technical problem of living and earning a living. (page 194 of this book)

Significantly, the responsibility for this new model of education lay not only with the professorate, but also with the students who are committed to learning. The goal is to achieve both social improvements for black people as a whole and to give them the necessary skills to be productive working members of the culture.

Apology

Between the time that I was graduated from college and the day of my first experience at earning a living, there was arising in this land, and more especially within the Negro group, a controversy concerning the type of education which American Negroes needed. You, who are graduating today, have heard but echoes of this controversy and more or less vague theories of its meaning and its outcome. Perhaps it has been explained away to you and interpreted as mere misunderstanding and personal bias. If so, the clay of calm review and inquiry is at hand. And I suppose that, of persons living few can realize better than I just what that controversy meant and what the outcome is. I want then today in the short time allotted me, to state, as plainly as I may, the problem of college and industrial education for American Negroes, as it arose in the past; and then to restate it as it appears to me in its present aspect.

Dilemma

First of all, let me insist that the former controversy was no mere misunderstanding; there was real difference of opinion, rooted in deep sincerity on every side and fought out with a tenacity and depth of feeling clue to its great importance and fateful meaning.

It was, in its larger aspects, a problem such as in all ages human beings of all races and nations have faced; but it was new in 1895 as all Time is new; it was concentered and made vivid and present because of the immediate and pressing question of the education of a vast group of the children of former slaves. It was the ever new and age-young problem of Youth, for there had arisen in the South a Joseph which knew not Pharoah,—a black man who was not born in slavery. What was lie to become? Whither was his face set? How should he be trained and educated? His fathers were slaves, for the most part, ignorant and poverty-stricken; emancipated in the main without land, tools, nor capital,—the sport of war, the despair of economists, the grave perplexity of Science. Their children had been born in the midst of controversy, of internecine hatred, and in all the economic dislocation that follows war and civil war. In a peculiar way and under circumstances seldom duplicated, the whole program of popular education became epitomized in the case of these young black folk.

First Efforts

Before men thought or greatly cared, in the midst of the very blood and dust of battle, an educational system for the freedmen had been begun; and with a logic that seemed, at first, quite natural. The night school for adults had become the day school for children. The Negro day school had called for normal teaching and the small New England college had been transplanted and perched on hill and river in Raleigh and Atlanta, Nashville and New Orleans, and half a dozen other towns. This new Negro college was conceived of as the very foundation stone of Negro training. But, meantime, any formal education for slaves or the children of slaves not only awakened widespread and deep-seated doubt, fear and hostility in the South, but it posed, for statesmen and thinkers, the whole question as to what the education of Negroes was really aiming at, and indeed, what was the aim of educating any working class. If it was doubtful as to how far the social and economic classes of any modern state could be essentially transformed and changed by popular education, how much more tremendous was the problem of educating a race whose ability to assimilate modern training was in grave question and whose place in the nation and the world even granted they could be educated, was a matter of baffling, social philosophy. Was the nation making an effort to parallel white civilization in the South with a black civilization? Or was it trying to displace the dominant white master class with new black masters or was it seeking the difficult but surely more reasonable and practical effort of furnishing a trained set of free black laborers who might carry on in place of the violently disrupted slave system? Surely, most men said, this economic and industrial problem of the New South was the first—the central, the insistent problem of the day.

Two Schools of Thought

There can be no doubt of the real dilemma that thus faced the nation, the Northern philanthropists and the black man. The argument for the New England college, which at first seemed to need no apology, grew and developed. The matter of man's earning a living, said the college, is and must be important, but surely it can never be so important as the man himself. Thus the economic adaptation of the Negro to the South must in education be subordinated to the great necessity of teaching life and culture. The South, and more especially the Negro, needed and must have trained and educated leadership if civilization was to survive. More than most, here was land and people who needed to learn the meaning of life. They needed the preparation of gifted persons for the profession of teaching, and for other professions which would in time grow. The object of education was not to make men carpenters, but to make carpenters men.

On the other hand, those practical men who looked at the South after the war said: this is an industrial and business age. We are on the threshold of an economic expansion such as the world never saw before. Whatever human civilization has been or may become, today it is industry. The South because of slavery has lagged behind the world. It must catch up. Its prime necessity after the hate and holocaust of war is a trained reliable laboring class. Assume if you will that Negroes are men with every human capacity, nevertheless, as a flat fact, no rising group of peasants can begin at the top. If poverty and starvation are to be warded off, the children of the freedmen must not be taught to despise the humble work, which the mass of the Negro race must for untold years pursue. The transition period between slavery and freedom is a dangerous and critical one. Fill the heads of these children with Latin and Greek and highfalutin' notions of rights and political power, and hell will be to pay.

On the other hand, in the South, here is land and fertile land, in vast quantities, to be bad at nominal prices. Here are employers who must have skilled and faithful labor, and have it now. There is in the near future an industrial development coming which will bring the South abreast with the new economic development of the nation and the world. Freedom must accelerate this development which slavery so long retarded. Here then is no time for a philosophy of economic or class revolution and race hatred. There must be friendship and good will between employer and employee, between black and white. They have common interests, and the matter of their future relations in politics and society can well be left for future generations and different times to solve. "Cast down your buckets where you are," cried Booker T. Washington; "In all things that are purely social you can be as separate as the fingers, yet one hand in all things essential to mutual progress."

What was needed, then, was that the Negro first should be made the intelligent laborer, the trained farmer, the skilled artisan of the South. Once he had accomplished this step in the economic world and the ladder was set for his climbing, his future would be assured, and assured on an economic foundation which would be immovable. All else in his development, if he proved himself capable of development, even to the highest, would inevitably follow. Let us have, therefore, not colleges but schools to teach the technique of industry and to make men learn by doing.

These were the opposing arguments. They were real arguments. They were set forth by earnest men, white and black, philanthropist and teacher, statesman and seer. The controversy waxed bitter. The disputants came to rival organizations, to severe social pressure, to anger and even to blows. Newspapers were aligned for and against; employment and promotion depended often on a Negro's attitude toward industrial education. The Negro race and their friends were split in twain by the intensity of their feeling and men were labeled and earmarked by their allegiance to one school of thought or to the other.

Present Conditions

Today all this is past; by the majority of the older of my hearers, it is practically forgotten. By the younger, it appears merely as a vague legend. Thirty-five years, a full generation and more, have elapsed. The increase in Negro education by all measurements has been a little less than marvelous. In 1895, there were not more than 1,000 Negro students of full college grade in the United States. Today, there are over 19,000 in college and nearly 150,000 in high schools. In 1895, 60 per cent of American Negroes, ten years of age or over, were illiterate. Today, perhaps three-fourths can read and write. The increase of Negro students in industrial and land-grant colleges has been equally large. The latter have over 16,000 students and the increasing support of the government of the States; while the great industrial schools, especially Hampton and Tuskegee, are the best endowed institutions for the education of black folk in the world.

Was the Controversy Settled

What then has become of this controversy as to college and industrial education for Negroes? Has it been duly settled, and if it lilts, how lilts it been settled? Has it been transmuted into a new program, and if so, what is that program? In other words, what is the present norm of Negro education, represented at once by Howard University, Fisk, and Atlanta on one hand, and by Hampton Institute, Tuskegee, and the land-grant colleges on the other?

I answer once for all, the problem has not been settled. The questions raised in those days of controversy still stand in all their validity and all their pressing insistence on an answer. They have not been answered. They must be answered, and the men and women of this audience and like audiences throughout the land are the ones from whom the world demands final reply. Answers have been offered; and the present status of the problem has enormously changed, for human problems never stand still. But I must insist that the fundamental problem is still here.

What the College has Done

Let us see. The Negro college has done a great work. It has given us leadership and intelligent leadership. Doubtless, without these colleges the American Negro would scarcely have attained his present position. The chief thing that distinguishes the American Negro group from the Negro groups in the West Indies, and in South America, and the mother group in Africa, is the number of men that we have trained in modern education, able to cope with the white world on its own ground and in its own thought, method and language.

On the other hand, there cannot be the slightest doubt but that the Negro college, its teachers, students and graduates, have not yet comprehended the age in which they live: the tremendous organization of industry, commerce, capital, and credit which today forms a super-organization dominating and ruling the universe, subordinating to its ends government, democracy, religion, education and social philosophy; and for the purpose of forcing into the places of power in this organization American black men either to guide or help reform it, either to increase its efficiency or make it a machine to improve our well-being, rather than the merciless mechanism which enslaves us; for this the Negro college has today neither program nor intelligent comprehension.

On the contrary, there is no doubt but that college and university training among us has had largely the exact effect that was predicted; it has turned an increasing number of our people not simply away from manual labor and industry, not simply away from business and economic reform, into a few well-paid professions, but it has turned our attention from any disposition to study or solve our economic problem. A disproportionate number of our college-trained students are crowding into teaching and medicine and beginning to swarm into other professions, and to form at the threshold of these better-paid jobs a white collar proletariat, depending for their support on an economic foundation which does not yet exist.

Moreover, and perhaps for this very reason, the ideals of colored college-bred men have not in the last thirty years been raised an iota.

Rather in the main, they have been lowered. The average Negro undergraduate has swallowed hook, line and sinker, the dead bait of the white undergraduate, who, born in an industrial machine, does not have to think, and does not think. Our college man today, is, on the average, a man untouched by real culture. He deliberately surrenders to selfish and even silly ideals, swarming into semi-professional athletics and Greek letter societies, and affecting to despise scholarship and the hard grind of study and research. The greatest meetings of the Negro college year like those of the white college year have become vulgar exhibitions of liquor, extravagance, and fur coats. We have in our colleges a growing mass of stupidity and indifference.

I am not counseling perfection; as desperately human groups, we must expect our share of mediocrity. But as hitherto a thick and thin defender of the college, it seems to me that we are getting into our Negro colleges considerably more than our share of plain fools.

Acquiring as we do in college no guidance to a broad economic comprehension and a sure industrial foundation, and simultaneously a tendency to live beyond our means, and spend for show, we are graduating young men and women with an intense and overwhelming appetite for wealth and no reasonable way of gratifying it, no philosophy for counteracting it.

Trained more and more to enjoy sexual freedom as undergraduates, we refuse as graduates to found and support even moderate families, because we cannot afford them; and we are beginning to sneer at group organization and race leadership as mere futile gestures.

Why is this? What is wrong with our colleges? The method of the modern college has been proven by a hundred centuries of human experience the imparting or knowledge by the old to the young; the instilling of the conclusions of experience, "line upon line, and precept upon precept." But, of course, with this general and theoretical method must go a definite and detailed object suited to the present age, the present group, the present set of problems. It is not then in its method but in its practical objects that the Negro college has failed. It is handing on knowledge and experience but what knowledge and for what end? Are we to stick to the old habit of wasting time on Latin, Greek, Hebrew and eschatology, or are we to remember that, after all, the object of the Negro college is to place in American life a trained black man who can do what the world today wants done; who can help the world know what it ought to want done and thus by doing the world's work well may invent better work for a better world? This brings us right back to the object of the industrial school.

What the Industrial School Has Done

Negro industrial training in the United States has accomplishments of which it has a right to be proud; but it too has not solved its problem. Its main accomplishment has been an indirect matter of psychology. It has helped bridge the transition period between Negro slavery and freedom. It has taught thousands of white people in the South to accept Negro education, not simply as a necessary evil, but as a possible social good. It has brought state support to a dozen higher institutions of learning, and to some extent, to a system of public schools. On the other hand, it has tempered and rationalized the inner emancipation of American Negroes. It made the Negro patient when impatience would have killed him. If it has not made working with the hands popular, it has at least removed from it much of the stigma of social degradation. It has made many Negroes seek the friendship of their white fellow citizens, even at the cost of insult and caste. And thus through a wide strip of our country it has brought peace and not a sword.

But this has all been its indirect byproduct, rather than its direct teaching. In its direct teaching, the kind of success which it has achieved differs from the success of the college. In the case of the industrial school, the practical object was absolutely right and still is right: that is, the desire of placing in American life a trained black man who could earn a decent living and make that living the foundation stone of his own culture and of the civilization of his group. This was the avowed object of the industrial school. How much has it done toward this? It has established some skilled farmers and among the mass some better farming methods. It has trained and placed some skilled artisans; it has given great impetus to the domestic arts and household economy; it has encouraged Negro business enterprise. And yet we have but to remember these matters to make it patent to all that the results have been pitifully small compared with the need. Our Negro farm population is decreasing; our Negro artisans are not gaining proportionately in industry and Negro business faces today a baffling crisis. Our success in household arts is due not to our effective teaching so much as to the mediaeval minds of our women who have not yet entered the machine age. Most of them seem still to think that washing clothes, scrubbing steps and paring potatoes were among the Ten Commandments.

Why now has the industrial school with all its partial success failed absolutely in its main object when that object of training Negroes for remunerative occupation is more imperative today than thirty-five years ago.

The reason is clear: if the college has failed because with the right general method it has lacked definite objects appropriate to the age and race; the industrial school has failed because with a definite object it lacked appropriate method to gain it. In other words, the lack of success of the industrial education of Negroes has come not because of the absence of desperate and devoted effort, but because of changes in the world which the industrial school did not foresee, and, which even if it had foreseen, it could not have prevented, and to which it had not the ability to adapt itself.

It is easy to illustrate this. The industrial school assumed that the technique of industry in 1895, even if not absolutely fixed and permanent, was at least permanent enough for training children into its pursuit and for use as a basis of broader education. Therefore, school work for farming, carpentry, bricklaying, plastering and painting, metal work and blacksmithing shoemaking, sewing and cooking was introduced and taught. But, meantime, what has happened to these vocations and trades? Machines and new industrial organizations have remade the economic world and ousted these trades either from their old technique or their economic significance. The planing mill does today much of the work of the carpenter and the carpenter is being reduced rapidly to the plane of a mere laborer. The building trades are undergoing all kinds of reconstruction, from the machine-made steel skyscraper, to the cement house cast in molds and the mass-made mail-order bungalow. Painting and masonry still survive, but the machine is after them; while printing and sewing are done increasingly by elaborate machines. Metal is being shaped by stamping mills. Nothing of shoemaking is left for the hands save mending, and in most cases, it is cheaper to buy a new shoe than to have an old one cobbled. When it comes to the farm, a world-wide combination of circumstances is driving the farmer to the wall. Expensive machinery demands increasingly larger capital; excessive taxation of growing land values is eliminating the small owner; monopolized and manipulated markets and carriers make profits of the individual farmer small or nil; and the foreign competition of farms worked by serfs at starvation wages and backed by world-wide aggregations of capital—all this is driving farmers, black and white, from the soil and making the problem of their future existence one of the great problems of the modern world. The industrial school, therefore, found itself in the peculiar position of teaching a technique of industry in certain lines just at the time when that technique was changing into something different, and when the new technique was a matter which the Negro school could not teach. In fact, with the costly machine, with mass production and organized distribution, the teaching of technique becomes increasingly difficult. Any person of average intelligence can take part in the making of a modern automobile, and he is paid, not for his technical training, but for his endurance and steady application.

There were many lines of factory work, like the spinning and weaving of cotton and wool, which the Negro could have successfully been set to learning, but they involved vast expenditures of capital which no school could control, and organized business at that time decreed that only white folk could work in factories. And that decree still stands. New branches of industry, new technique are continually opening—like automobile repairing, electrical installments, and engineering—but these call for changing curricula and adjustments puzzling for a school and a set course of study.

In the attempt to put the Negro into business, so that from the inner seats of power by means of capital and credit he could control industry, we have fallen between two stools, this work being apparently neither the program of the college nor of the industrial school. The college treated it with the most approved academic detachment, while the industrial school fatuously assumed as permanent a business organization which began to change with the Nineteenth Century, and bids fair to disappear with the Twentieth. In 1895 we were preaching individual thrift and saving; the small retail store and the partnership for business and the conduct of industry. Today, we are faced by great aggregations of capital and world-wide credit, which monopolize raw material, carriage and manufacture, distribute their products through cartels, mergers and chain stores, and are in process of eliminating the individual trader, the small manufacturer, and the little job. In this new organization of business the colored man meets two difficulties: First, he is not trained to take part in it; and, secondly, if he gets training, he finds it almost impossible to gain a foothold. Schools cannot teach as an art and trade that which is a philosophy, a government of men, an organization of civilization. They can impart a mass of knowledge about it, but this is the duty of the college of liberal arts and not the shop work of the trade school.

Thus the industrial school increasingly faces a blank wall and its astonishing answer today to the puzzle is slowly but surely to transform the industrial school into a college. The most revolutionary development in Negro education for a quarter-century is illustrated by the fact that Hampton today is one of the largest of Negro colleges and that her trade teaching seems bound to disappear within a few years. Tuskegee is a high school and college, but an unsolved program of the future of its trade schools. And the land-grant colleges, built to foster agriculture and industry, are becoming just like other colleges. And all this, as I said, is not the fault of the industrial school, it comes from this tremendous transformation of business, capital and industry in the Twentieth Century, which few men clearly foresaw and which only a minority of men or of teachers of men today fully comprehend.

The Labor Movement

In one respect, however, the Negro industrial school was seriously at fault. It set its face toward the employer and the capitalist and the man of wealth. It looked upon the worker as one to be adapted to the demands of those who conducted industry. Both in its general program and in its classroom, it neglected almost entirely the modern labor movement. It had little or nothing to teach concerning the rise of trade unions; their present condition, and their future development. It had no conception of any future democracy in industry. That is, the very vehicle which was to train Negroes for modern industry neglected in its teaching the most important part of modern industrial development: namely, the relation of the worker to modern industry and to the modern state.

The reason for this neglect is clear. The Negro industrial school was the gift of capital and wealth. Organized labor was the enemy of the black man in skilled industry. Organized labor in the United States was and is the chief obstacle to keep black folk from earning a living by its determined policy of excluding them from unions just as long as possible and compelling them to become "scabs" in order to live. The political power of Southern white labor disfranchised Negroes, and helped build a caste system. How was the Negro industrial school easily to recognize, in this Devil of its present degradation, the Angel of its future enlightenment? How natural it was to look to white Capital and not to Labor for the emancipation of the black world—how natural and yet how insanely futile!

The Unsolved Problem

Here then are the successes and the failures of both Negro college and industrial school, and we can clearly see that the problem still stands unsolved: How are we going to place the black American on a sure foundation in the modern state? The modern state is primarily business and industry. Its industrial problems must be settled before its cultural problems can really and successfully be attacked. The world must eat before it can think. The Negro has not found a solid foundation in that state as yet. He is mainly the unskilled laborer; the casual employee; the man hired last and fired first; the man who must subsist upon the lowest wage and consequently share an undue burden of poverty, crime, insanity and ignorance. The only alleviation of his economic position has come from what little the industrial school could teach during the revolution of technique and from what the college took up as part of its mission in vocational training for professions.

For the college had to become a trainer of men for vocations. This is as true of the white college as of the colored college. They both tended to change their college curricula into pre-vocational preparation for a professional career. But the effort of the Negro college here was half-hearted. There, persisted the feeling that the college had finished its work when it placed a man of culture in the world, despite the fact that our graduates who are men of culture are exceptional, and if placed in the world without ability to earn a living, what little culture they have does not long survive.

Thus, at the end of the first third of the Twentieth Century, while both college and industrial school can point to something accomplished, neither has reached its main objective, and they are in process of uniting to become one stream of Negro education with their great problem of object and method unsolved. The industrial school has done but little to impart the higher technique of the industrial process or of the business organization and it has done almost nothing toward putting the Negro working man in touch with the great labor movement of the white world.

On the other hand, the Negro college has not succeeded in establishing that great and guiding ideal of group development and leadership, within a dominating and expanding culture, or in establishing the cultural life as the leading motif of the educated Negro. Its vocational work has been confined to the so-called learned professions, with only a scant beginning of the imparting of the higher technique of industry and science.

The New Industrial Revolution

The result which I have outlined is not wholly unexpected. Perhaps we can now say that it was impossible fully to avoid this situation. We have a right to congratulate ourselves that we have come to a place of such stability and such intelligence as now to be ready to grapple with our economic problem. The fact of the matter is, we have up to this time been swept on and into the great maelstrom of the white civilization surrounding us. We have been inevitably made part of that vast modern organization of life where social and political control rests in the hands of those few white folk who control wealth, determine credit and divide income. We are in a system of culture where disparity of income is such that respect for labor as labor cannot endure; where the emphasis and outlook is not what a man does but what he is able to get for doing it; where wealth despises work and the object of wealth is to escape work, and where the ideal is power without toil.

So long as a lawyer can look forward to an income of $100,000 a year while a maid servant is well-paid with $1,000, just so long the lawyer is going to be one hundred times more respectable than the servant and the servant is going to be called by her first name. So long as the determination of a person's income is not only beyond democratic control and public knowledge, but is a matter of autocratic power and secret manipulation, just so long the application of logic and ethics to wealth, industry and income is going to be a difficult if not insoluble problem.

In the modern world only one country is making a frontal attack upon this problem and that is Russia. Other countries are visualizing it and considering it, making some tentative and half-hearted effort but they have not yet attacked the system as a whole, and for the most part they declare the present system inevitable and eternal and incapable of more than minor and stinted improvement.

In the midst of such a world organization we come looking for economic stability and independence. Of course, our situation is baffling and contradictory. And it is made all the more difficult for us because we are by blood and descent and popular opinion an integral part of that vast majority of mankind which is the Victim and not the Beneficiary of present conditions, which is today working at starvation wages and on a level of brute toil and without voice in its own government or education in its ignorance, for the benefit, the enormous profit, and the dazzling luxury of the white rulers of the world.

Here lies the problem and it is the problem of the combined Negro college and vocational school. Without the intellectual leadership of college-bred men, we could not hitherto have held our own in modern American civilization, but must have sunk to the place of the helpless proletariat of the West Indies and of South Africa. But, on the other hand, for what has the college saved us? It has saved us for that very economic defeat which the industrial school was established to ward off and which still stands demanding solution. The industrial school acted as bridge and buffer to lead us out of the bitterness of Reconstruction to the toleration of today. But it did not place our feet upon the sound economic foundation which makes our survival in America or in the modern world certain or probable; and the reason that it did not do this was as much the fault of the college as of the trade school. The industrial school without the college was as helpless yesterday as the college is today helpless without systematic training for modern industry.

Both college and industrial school have made extraordinary and complementary mistakes in their teaching force: the industrial school secured usually as teacher a man of affairs and technical knowledge, without culture or general knowledge. The college took too often as teacher a man of books and brains with no contact with or first-hand knowledge of real every-day life and ordinary human beings, and this was true whether he taught sociology, literature or science. Both types of teacher failed.

The New Educational Program

What then is the unescapable task of the united college and vocational school? It is without shadow of doubt a new broad and widely efficient vocational guidance and education for men and women of ability, selected by the most careful tests and supported by a broad system of free scholarships. Our educational institutions must graduate to the world men fitted to take their place in real life by their knowledge, spirit, and ability to do what the world wants done. This vocational guidance must have for its object the training of men who can think clearly and function normally as physical beings; who have a knowledge of what human life on earth has been, and what it is now; and a knowledge of the constitution of the known universe. All that, and in addition to that, a training which will enable them to take some definite and intelligent part in the production of goods and in the furnishing of human, services and in the democratic distribution of income so as to build civilization, encourage initiative, reward effort and support life. Just as the Negro college course with vision, knowledge and ideal must move toward vocational training, so the industrial courses must ascend from mere hand technique to engineering and industrial planning and the application of scientific and technical knowledge to problems of work and wage.

This higher training and vocational guidance must turn out young men and women who are willing not only to do the work of the world today but to provide for the future world. Here then is the job before us. It is in a sense the same kind of duty that lies before the educated white man but it has an essential and important difference. If we make a place for ourselves in the industrial and business world today, this will be done because of our ability to establish a self-supporting organization sufficiently independent of the white organization to insure its stability and our economic survival and eventual incorporation into world industry. Ours is the double and dynamic function of tuning in with a machine in action so as neither to wreck the machine nor be crushed or maimed by it. Many think this is impossible. But if it is impossible, our future economic survival is impossible. Let there be no misunderstanding about this, no easy-going optimism. We are not going to share modern civilization just by deserving recognition. We are going to force ourselves in by organized far-seeing effort—by out-thinking and out-flanking the owners of the world today who are too drunk with their own arrogance and power successfully to oppose us if we think and learn and do.

It is not the province of this paper to tell in detail just how this problem will be settled. Indeed, I could not tell you if I would. I merely stress the problem and emphasize the possibility of the solution. A generation ago those who doubted our survival said that no alien and separate nation could hope to survive within another nation; that we must be absorbed or perish. Times have changed. Today it is rapidly becoming true that only within some great and all-inclusive empire or league can separate nations and groups find freedom and protection and economic scope for development. The small separate nation is becoming increasingly impossible and the League of Nations as well as Briand's proposed League of Europe shout this from the housetops. And just as loudly, the inevitable disintegration of the British empire shows the impossibility of world-embracing centralized autocracy. This means that the possibility of our development and survival is clear, but clear only as brains and devotion and skilled knowledge point the way.

Teachers

We need then, first, training as human beings in general knowledge and experience; then technical training to guide and do a specific part of the world's work. The broader training should be the heritage and due of all but today it is curtailed by poverty. The technical training of men must be directed by vocational guidance which finds fitness and ability. Then actual and detailed technical training will be done by a combination of school, laboratory and apprenticeship, according to the nature of the work and the changing technique.

The teachers of such a stream of students must be of a high order. College teachers cannot follow the mediaeval tradition of detached withdrawal from the world. The professor of mathematics in a college has to be more than a counting machine, or proctor of examinations; he must be a living man, acquainted with real human beings, and alive to the relation of his branch of knowledge to the technical problem of living and earning a living. The teacher in a Negro college has got to be something far more than a master of a branch of human knowledge. He has got to be able to impart his knowledge to human beings whose place in the world is today precarious and critical and the possibilities and advancement of that human being in the world where he is to live and earn a living is of just as much importance in the teaching process as the content of the knowledge taught.

The man who teaches blacksmithing must be more than a blacksmith. He must be a man of education and culture, acquainted with the whole present technique and business organization of the modern world, and acquainted too with human beings and their possibilities. Such a man is difficult to procure. Because industrial schools did not have in the past stick teachers for their classes and could not get them, their whole program suffered unmerited criticism. The teachers, then, cannot be pedants or dilettantes, they cannot be mere technicians and higher artisans, they have got to be social statesmen and statesmen of high order. The student body of such schools has got to be selected for something more than numbers. We must eliminate those who are here because their parents wish to be rid of them or for the social prestige or for passing the time or for getting as quickly as possible into a position to make money to throw away; and we must concentrate upon young men and women of ability and vision and will.

Ideal

Today there is but one rivalry between culture and vocation, college training and trade and professional training, and that is the rivalry of Time. Some day every human being will have college training. Today some must stop with the grades, and some with high school, and only a few reach college. It is of the utmost importance, then, and the essential condition of our survival and advance that those chosen for college be our best and not simply our richest or most idle.

But even this growth must be led; it must be guided by Ideals. We have lost something, brothers, wandering in strange lands. We have lost our ideals. We have come to a generation which seeks advance without ideals—discovery without stars. It cannot be done. Certain great landmarks and guiding facts must stand eternally before us; and at the risk of moralizing, I must end by emphasizing this matter of the ideals of Negro students and graduates.

The ideal of *Poverty*. This is the direct antithesis of the present American ideal of Wealth. We cannot all be wealthy. We should not all be wealthy. In an ideal industrial organization no person should have an income which he does not personally need; nor wield a power solely for his own whim. If civilization is to turn out millionaires it will also turn out beggars and prostitutes either at home or among the lesser breeds without the law. A simple healthy life on limited income is the only reasonable ideal of civilized folk.

The ideal of *Work*—not idleness, not dawdling, but hard continuous effort at something worth doing, by a man supremely interested in doing it, who knows how it ought to be done and is willing to take infinite pains doing it.

The ideal of *Knowledge*—not guesswork, not mere careless theory; not inherited religious dogma clung to because of fear and inertia and in spite of logic, but critically tested and laboriously gathered fact martialed under scientific law and feeding rather than choking the glorious world of fancy and imagination, of poetry and art, of beauty and deep culture.

Finally, and especially, the ideal of *Sacrifice*. I almost hesitate to mention this—so much sentimental twaddle has been written of it. When I say sacrifice, I mean sacrifice. I mean a real and definite surrender of personal ease and satisfaction. I embellish it with no theological fairy tales of a rewarding God or a milk and honey heaven. I am not trying to scare you into the duty of sacrifice by the fires of a mythical Hell. I am repeating the stark fact of survival of life and culture on this earth: "*Entbehren sollst du—sollst entbehren.*" Thou shalt forego, shalt do without.

The insistent problem of human happiness is still with us. We American Negroes are not a happy people. We feel perhaps as never before the sting and bitterness of our struggle. Our little victories won here and there serve but to reveal the shame of our continuing semi-slavery and social caste. We are torn asunder within our own group because of the rasping pressure of the struggle without. We are as a race not simply dissatisfied, we are embodied Dissatisfaction.

To increase abiding satisfaction for the mass of our people, and for all people, someone must sacrifice something of his own happiness. This is a duty only to those who recognize it as a duty. The larger the number ready to sacrifice, the smaller the total sacrifice necessary. No man of education and culture and training, who proposes to face his problem and solve it can hope for entire happiness. It is silly to tell intelligent human beings: Be good and you will be happy. The truth is today, be good, be decent, be honorable and self-sacrificing and you will not always be happy. You will often be desperately unhappy. You may even be crucified, dead and buried, and the third day you will be just as dead as the first. But with the death of your happiness may easily come increased happiness and satisfaction and fulfilment for other people—strangers, unborn babes, uncreated worlds. If this is not sufficient incentive, never try it—remain hogs.

The present census will show that the American Negro of the educated class and even of the middle industrial class is reproducing himself at an even slower rate than the corresponding classes of whites. To raise a small family today is a sacrifice. It is not romance and adventure. It is giving up something of life and pleasure for a future generation.

If, therefore, real sacrifice for others in your life work appeals to you, here it is. Here is the chance to build an industrial organization on a basis of logic and ethics, such as is almost wholly lacking in the modern world. It is a tremendous task, and it is the task: equally and at once of Howard and Tuskegee, of Hampton and Fisk, of the college and of the industrial school. Our real schools must become centers of this vast Crusade. With the faculty and the student body girding themselves for this new and greater education, the major part of the responsibility will still fall upon those who have already done their school work; and that means upon the alumni who, like you, have become graduates of an institution of learning. Unless the vision comes to you and comes quickly, of the educational and economic problem before the American Negro, that problem will not be solved. You not only enter, therefore, today the worshipful company of that vast body of men upon whom a great center of learning, with ancient ceremony and colorful trappings, has put the accolade of intellectual knighthood, but men who have become the unselfish thinkers and planners of a group of people in whose hands lies the economic and social destiny of the darker peoples of the world, and by that token of the world itself.

PART FIVE

Du Bois and Higher Education

CHAPTER FIFTEEN

Careers Open to College-Bred Negroes

In 1898, a decade following his graduation from Fisk, Du Bois returned to his alma mater to deliver its commencement address. In his speech, he pointed to the careers open to the new graduates. In doing so, he challenged them to address the question of what they could do to help advance the condition of black Americans. As he explained:

> The concrete question, then, that faces you of the class of '98, is: what part can I best take in the striving of the eight million men and women who are bound to me by a common sorrow and a common hope, that through the striving of the Negro people this land of our fathers may live and thrive? (page 207 of this book)

Du Bois concluded his speech invoking three watchwords:

> first, you are Negroes, members of that dark, historic race that from the world's dawn has slept to hear the trumpet summons sound through our ears. Cherish unwavering faith in the blood of your fathers, and make sure this last triumph of humanity. Remember next, that you are gentlemen and ladies, trained in the liberal arts and subjects in that vast kingdom of culture that has lighted the world from its infancy and guided it through bigotry and falsehood and sin. . .finally, remember that you are the sons of Fisk University. (pages 212-213 of this book)

In this speech, Du Bois begins to articulate for the first time what would emerge a few years later as his idea of the "Talented Tenth." Essentially, an elite educated black leadership would provide the direction for the advancement of the Negro people.

To the young ears that hearken behind college walls at the confused murmur of the world beyond, there comes at times a strangely discordant note to mar the music of their lives. Men tell them that college is a play world the mirage of real life; the place where men climb or seek to climb heights whence they must sooner or later sink into the dust of real life. Scarcely a commencement season passes but what, amid congratulation and rejoicing, amid high resolve and lofty sentiment, stalks this pale, half mocking ghost, crying to the newborn bachelor in arts: You have played—now comes work.

And, therefore, students of the class of '98, 1 have thought to take this oft-repeated idea and talk with you in this last hour of your college days about the relation which, in your lives, a liberal education bears to bread-winning.

And first, young men and women, I heartily join in congratulating you to whom has been vouchsafed the vision splendid—you who stand where once I stood,

> When meadow, grove, and stream,
>   The earth, and every common sight,
> To me did seem
>   Apparelled in celestial light,
> The glory and the freshness of a dream.

And yet not a dream, but a mighty reality—a glimpse of the higher life, the broader possibilities of humanity, which is granted to the man who, amid the rush and roar of living, pauses four short years to learn what living means.

The vision of the rich meaning of life, which comes to you as students, as men of culture, comes dimly or not at all to the plodding masses of men, and even to men of high estate it comes too often blurred and distorted by selfishness and greed. But you have seen it in the freshness and sunshine of youth: here you have talked with Aristotle and Shakespeare, have learned of Euclid, have heard the solemn drama of a world, and thought the thoughts of seers and heroes of the world that was. Out of such lore, out of such light and shade, has the vision of the world appeared before you: you have not all comprehended it; you have, many of you but glanced at its brilliant hues, and have missed the speaking splendor of the background.

I remember how once I stood near the ancient cathedral at Berne, looking at the Alps; I heard the rushing waters below and knew their music; I saw the rolling fields beyond and thought them pretty; then I saw the hills and the towering masses of dark mountains; they were beautiful, and yet I saw them with a tinge of disappointment, but even as I turned away, I glanced toward the sky, and then my heart leaped—for there above the meadows and the waters, above the hills and the mountains, blazed in the evening sunshine, the mighty, snow-clad peaks of the high Alps, glistening and glorious with the hues of the rainbow, in spotless purity and awful majesty. And so many a man to whom opportunity has unveiled some revelation of the broader, truer world, has turned away from it, half seen and half known.

But some have seen the vision, have comprehended all the meaning of a liberal education; and now, as you turn away half-regretfully, half gladly, what relation has this day of transfiguration to the hard, cold paths of the world beyond these walls? Is it to be but a memory and a longing, or if more than this, how much more?

I presume that few of you have fully realized that with tomorrow morning you begin to earn your own bread and butter; that today is the commencement of a new life on which you are to find self-support by daily toil. And I am glad if you have not given this matter too much thought or worry, for, surely, if you have done well your college work you have had other things to think of, problems of life and humanity far broader than your own single destiny; not that you have neglected dreams and plans of parts that you might play in life, but that you have scarce thought out its dry details. And, therefore, to most of you the nearness of real life dawned this morning with a certain suddenness; with something of that dark dismay with which the human creator faces his own creature with some thought, too, half of rebellion and an aimless asking: why must I turn from so pleasant a life to one hard and matter of fact? Why must I leave the pleasures of study and dear companionship and high inspiration to "bear the whips and scorns of time, the oppressor's wrong, the proud man's contumely?"

Today the paradox of life rises over you as never before, and you wonder why you, of all men, should not have been born rich and privileged, not to see the vision of the world and all the glory that shall be, fade into some distant future, leaving long paths of dirt and rocks between. All these questions you have asked, I have asked, and all men have asked, who, whether on the college rostrum or with the pick and shovel, have, on a commencement morning, turned from study to deeds, from ideals to realization, from thought to life.

All this I cannot answer plainly, and yet the shadow of answer falls on us all; for why should the sun rise if there be neither noon nor evening, and what is a life that is all beginning? And have not these, your college days, been all the happier for the promise and prophecy of a life to come?

Three universal laws underlie the necessity of earning a living: the law of work, the law of sacrifice, the law of service. The law of work declares that to live one must toil continuously, zealously; the apple may hang ripe upon the tree, but to eat we must pick it; grain will sprout and grow, but not till we plant it; houses will shelter us and clothes cover us only as we build and weave. Sometimes, to be sure, it may seem that enjoyment came without work and sacrifice—but it is not so. Someone toils, someone delves, and though we may shift our burden on the bowed shoulders of others—yet that is the necessity of the sick, or the shame of the lazy, or the crime of the coward.

Blind toil alone, however, will not satisfy the wants of aught but the lowest and simplest culture; the greater satisfaction comes from the sacrifice of today's enjoyment that tomorrow's may be greater; of this year's consumption to increase next year's production; of the indulgence of youth to the vigor of old age, of the pleasure of one life to the richer heritage of humanity; this is the law of sacrifice, and we see it everywhere: in the fruit we save to ripen, in the fields that lie fallow, in the years given to training and education, and in the self-sacrifice of a Socrates, a Darwin, or a David Livingstone.

Even this does not complete the laws of life as we find it in the twilight of the nineteenth century. We must not only work and sacrifice for ourselves and others, but also render each other mutual service. The physician must heal not himself, but all men; the tailor must mend the whole village; the farmer must plant for all. Thus in the civilized world each serves all, and all serve each, and the binding force is faith and skill, and the skill is bounded only by human possibility and genius, and the faith is faithful even to the untrue.

Such are the laws of that life, young people, which you enter today. And upon these laws have been built through the ages, in sweat of brow and sorrow of soul, all that fair world whose darkly glorious vision has made its study sweet to you, and its knowledge precious.

While these be the laws of universal life, their application differs in each age, and an equipment in life suitable to one century may be fatally unsuited to another. Therefore, you must not make the mistake of misunderstanding the age in which you live; and I especially warn you here, because as American Negroes, in the strange environment and unusual conditions of life which surround you, it will be peculiarly easy for you to fail to catch the spirit of the times; to distort the proportions of life, to seek to do what others have done better, and to seek quickly to undo what cannot legally be undone. I have often feared that the failure of many a promising young Negro was due largely to this natural ignorance.

Young Negroes are born in a social system of caste that belongs to the middle ages; they inherit the moral looseness of a sixteenth century; they learn to lisp the religious controversies of the seventeenth century; they are stirred by discussions of the rights of man that belong to the eighteenth century, and it is not wonderful if they hardly realize that they live upon the threshold of the twentieth century. You, men of Fisk, must not misunderstand your age; you must know that the world does not feel the injustice of caste as it once did, but rather sees in it some antidote for a vulgar democracy; you must remember that there are central elementary moral precepts which the world utterly refuses to excuse or palliate; you must realize that the controversies of Methodists and Baptists chiefly interest antiquarians and not active Christians of today; that we insist today on men's duties rather than their rights, and that the spirit of the century in which you will work is service not indulgence.

And surely no century more richly deserves understanding than the nineteenth. It has not the romantic interest of the fifteenth, when the world rose in a dream and wandered in the sunshine of its new discovered self, and poetry and art and tales from over seas; it has not the rugged might of that sixteenth century, when the dark monk faced the emperor of all the world, daring to be honest rather than orthodox, and crying, "Here I stand. God help me! I cannot waver."

But whatever the nineteenth century may lack in romantic or striking interest, it repays and more than repays in human opportunity, in the broadness of its conception of humanity, in the wonderful organization of effort to serve humanity. Never before have work and sacrifice and service meant so much, never before were there so many workers, such widespread sacrifice, such world-service. In the business of governing men, never before did so many take part. The issue is not altogether successful, and yet its measure of success far exceeds the wildest dreams of the world of long ago.

Never before have so many hands and heads joined to make the earth yield her increase, to make glad the waste places of the earth, to ply the loom, and whirl the spindle, and transform the useless and the worthless. On our breakfast table lies each morning the toil of Europe, Asia, and Africa, and the isles of the sea; we sow and spin for unseen millions, and countless myriads weave and plant for us; we have made the earth smaller and life broader by annihilating distance, magnifying the human voice and the stars, binding nation to nation, until today, for the first time in history, there is one standard of human culture as well in New York as in London, in Cape Town as in Paris, in Bombay as in Berlin.

Is not this, then, a century worth living in—a day worth serving? And though toil, hard, heavy toil, be the price of life, shall we not, young men and women, gladly work and sacrifice and serve "That one, far off, divine event,/ Toward which the whole creation moves"?

And we serve first for the sake of serving—to develop our own powers, gain the mastery of this human machine, and come to the broadest, deepest self-realization. And then we serve for real end of service, to make life no narrow, selfish thing, but to let it sweep as sweeps the morning broad and full and free for all men and all time, that you and I and all may earn a living and earn, too, much more than that— a life worth living.

This, fellow workers, is the veil of toil that hangs before the vision glorious. And yet, when on commencement morning, we leave behind the vivid hues of this, our inspiration, believe me, it is not easy to guard the sacred image, to keep alive the holy fire that lights and lightens life; to hold amid the toil and turmoil of living those old ideals fixed and tranquil before the soul. How often do we see young collegians enter life with high resolve and lofty purpose and then watch them shrink and shrink and shrink to sordid, selfish, shrewd plodders, full of distrust and sneers. Woe to the man, who, with the revelation of the world once before him, as it stands before you now, has let it fade and whiten into common day—life is death.

But you who, firm and inspired, turn toward the work of living, undismayed, knowing the world that was, loving that world that is, and believing in the world that is to be, just what can you do—what careers may you follow to realize the ideals and hopes of this day?

You cannot surely be knights and kings and magicians, but you can choose careers fully as wonderful and much more useful. You look about you in the world and see servants, they whose function it is to help the helpless, the weak and the busy to cook, that Washington may command armies; to sweep, that Edison may have time to think. You see the laborer, that wizard who places his weak shoulders against the physical world and overturns mountains and pushes away forests, and guides the rivers, and garners the harvests. You see the manufacturer guiding the laborer with brains and with capital: he is the alchemist in whose alembic dirt turns to houses, grass to coats, and stones to food. The merchant you see standing beside him, the prophet who enables us to laugh at famine, and want, and waste, by bringing together buyer and seller, maker and user, reader and writer. There is the teacher, the giver of immortal life, the one who makes the child to start where his fathers left off, that the world may think on with one mind. Yonder stands the physician with the long sought elixir of life, the lawyer clothed in justice, the minister who seeks to add to justice righteousness, and to life ideals higher than life. Your restless eye may easily overlook the corner where sits the scientist seeking the truth that shall make us free, or the other, where the artist dies that there may live a poem or painting or a thought.

All these ways of earning a living you may see in the world, and many more. But it does not follow that you may idly or thoughtlessly choose one as you pick a flower on a summer's day. To choose a life calling is a serious thing: first, you must consider not so much what you want to do as what wants to be done; secondly, you cannot wander at will over all the world of work that wants workers, but duty and privilege and special advantage calls to the work that lies nearest your hands. The German works for Germany, the Englishman serves England, and it is the duty of the Negro to serve his blood and lineage, and so working, each for each, and all for each, we realize; the goal of each for all.

The concrete question, then, that faces you of the class of '98, is: what part can I best take in the striving of the eight million men and women who are bound to me by a common sorrow and a common hope, that through the striving of the Negro people this land of our fathers may live and thrive?

The most useful and universal work, and the type of all other work, is that of the servant and common laborer. The ordinary, unskilled part of this work I pass over it is useful, it is honorable, but you have been trained for skilled work, and it is throwing away the money of this institution if its college graduates are to become Pullman porters. Even the higher branches of house-service, as cooking and nursing, and the great field of skilled labor, are rather for different training, and you will rightly leave them to the skilled graduates of our great industrial schools, with the sincere hope that so useful and promising avenues will soon be filled by able and honest artisans.

The first field that opens itself to you is the calling of the farmer. I do not mean the farmhand or the milkmaid, nor even the agricultural scientist. I mean the man who, by rational methods and business sense, with a knowledge of the world market, the methods of transportation, and the possibilities of the soil, will make this land of the South to bloom and blossom like Belgium and Holland, France and Germany; who will transform the slipshod, wasteful, happy-go-lucky farming of the South into the scientific business methods of New England and the West. There is little more reason for leaving farming to people without brains or culture than there would be in thus abandoning the other great fields of industry.

Especially, however, do the Negro people need the country gentleman—the man of air and health and home and morals; and today we have an unparalleled chance to supply such an aristocracy. Throughout Tennessee and Georgia and Virginia, where the young people are hurrying to the industries of the cities, stand the fine old abandoned farms and decaying mansions of a gentry that has passed. You are the ones to buy these farms at a nominal price, start a new agriculture, and a balance for the sickly crowding of cities and to furnish the food and material which these cities increasingly demand, and thus help to solve some of the most intricate of our social problems.

The next great field open to you is that of the merchant, where again there is among Negroes no discouraging competition, and a broad field for development.

Those Negroes who urge the blight of color prejudice as a barrier to their entering mercantile pursuits, quite forget that they have before them an undeveloped market of eight million souls, and that these millions spend every year $150,000,000 to $300,000,000, and that a part of this expenditure, at least, could be made through Negro merchants, if well-trained, educated, active men would only enter this field and cultivate it. Of course, the training of slavery was most unfortunate for business qualities. There linger among the freedmen's sons habits of laziness, of being perpetually five minutes behind time, of inattention to detail, which are fatal to modern business methods. All this can and must be unlearned, and the college man who, making himself familiar with the best business methods of a business age, starts in to open this field will not only earn and deserve a living for himself, but will make it easier for thousands to follow his example.

And this brings me to a thought that I want especially to impress upon college men: the time has come when the American Negro is being expected to take care of himself, and not much longer to depend on alms and charity; he must become self-supporting—a source of strength and power instead of a menace and a burden to the nation; the hindrance that today prevents him from fulfilling this expectation with reasonable quickness is his anomalous economic condition—his lack of remunerative employment. And you, young men and women, are the ones to supply this lack. We have workers enough, brawny and willing; we have some skill, and the industrial schools are furnishing more; moreover, a people that have today more than $26,000,000 invested in church property alone, and who spend at least $10,000,000 each year in those churches, have capital enough to collect in savings banks and put into industrial enterprises. But what we do lack, and what schools like this must begin to supply in increasing numbers is the captain of industry, the man who can marshal and guide workers in industrial enterprises, who can foresee the demand and supply it—note the special aptitude of laborers and turn it to advantage—so guide with eye and brain the work of these black millions, that, instead of adding to the poverty of the nation and subtracting from its wealth, we may add to the wealth of the land and make Negro poverty no longer a byword.

Here is a field for development such as few ages offer a body of willing workers such as few nations furnish. And this field calls not for mere money-makers, or those who would ape the silly display and ostentation of certain classes of Americans; nor does it call for men narrowed and shrunk by the soul-destroying commercialism of the hour, that philosophy which imagines men made for industry and not industry for men; but rather here is a chance to set a nation working, to make their work more effective, to build and fortify Negro homes, to educate Negro children, to establish institutions of protection, reform, and rescue, and to make the Negro people able to help others even as others have helped us.

Let us turn now to the professional class and ask about the openings there for college-bred men. As to the demand in one department there can be no doubt. If ever a nation needed the gospel of health presented to them, it is the Negro race, with its alarming death rate, its careless habits, its widows and orphans, and its sick and maimed. For the well-trained physician, as distinguished from the quack and the man who is too hurried to learn, there is large and important work. The remuneration which a poor people can pay will not be large, but the chance for usefulness and far-reaching influence on the future of our race and country can scarcely be overestimated. Especially is the calling open to young women, who ought to find here congenial, useful employment, and employment, perhaps, next in nobility to that of the noblest and best-motherhood.

When we come to the profession of law we have a narrower and less obvious field, one in which there is plenty of room for success, but against the peculiar difficulties of which young people need warning and advice. These difficulties arise from the fact that, first, the Negro himself furnishes little important or lucrative law business, and secondly, even among the whites, the profession is overcrowded and only men of ability or some wealth and much influence can expect much success. Thus, many changes must come before the handicap of color prejudice will allow Negroes to start in this profession with an even chance. Yet, here as elsewhere, blood will tell.

For thirty years the chief function of the Negro college has been that of furnishing teachers for the Negro schools, and the extraordinary success and value of this work has not yet been adequately recognized. Nevertheless, it is evident that this work has already passed through many phases and is about to pass through others. Fisk University at first furnished common school teachers, then teachers of schools that teach common school teachers; finally, teachers of men who teach the teachers; with each of these steps comes, to be sure, a demand for better quality, but also for a smaller quantity. The field for teaching, therefore, open to the class of '98 is smaller than that open to former classes and more exacting in its demands.

What is true now is apt to be emphasized in the future; specially trained teachers of high attainments will ever find some demand for their services. On the other hand, most college graduates will slowly turn to other work. Hereafter, when Negro education is more firmly founded, the better-trained college men will be more in demand. This, then, is a field still open—of broad usefulness and demanding the very best in character, and the better in training and knowledge, only the competition is sharp and is destined to be sharper.

I now turn to the Christian ministry with something of diffidence. The development of the Negro church has been so extraordinary, and of such deep sociological interest that its future course is a matter of great concern. As it is now, churches organized among Negroes are, for the most part, curiously composite institutions, which combine the work of churches, theaters, newspapers, homes, schools, and lodges. As a social and business institution the church has had marvelous success and has done much for the Negro people. As a religious institution, also, it has played some part, but it is needless to say that its many other activities have not increased the efficiency of its function as a teacher of morals and inspirer to the high ideals of Christianity.

An institution so popular that there is now in the United States one organization for every sixty Negro families, has, naturally, already attracted to its leadership a vast army of men. Moreover, the severest charge that can be brought against the Christian education of the Negro in the South during the last thirty years is the reckless way in which sap-headed young fellows, without ability, and in some cases without character, have been urged and pushed into the ministry. It is time now to halt. It is time to say to young men like you: qualifications that would be of no service elsewhere are not needed in the church; a general desire to be good, joined to a glib tongue, is not the sort of combination that is going to make the Negro people stop stealing and committing adultery. And, instead of aimless, wholesale invitations to enter this calling of life, we need to put our hands kindly on the shoulders of some young candidates, and tell them firmly that they are not fitted to be heads of the church of Christ.

What we need is not more but fewer ministers, but in that lesser number we certainly need earnest, broad, and cultured men; men who do a good deal more than they say; men of broad plans and far-seeing thought; men who will extend the charitable and rescue work of the churches, encourage home-getting, guard the children of the flock, not on Sundays, but on weekdays, make the people use savings banks, and, in fine, men who will really be active agents of social and moral reform in their communities. There, and there only, is the soil which will transform the mysticism of Negro religion into the righteousness of Christianity.

There is then an opening for college men in this field, but it is a field to be entered with more care than others, not with less; to be chosen by men of more stable character than others, not of less; and it is the one field where the man who doubts his fitness had best give the world the benefit of the doubt. But to those consecrated men who can and will place themselves today at the head of Negro religious life and guide this wavering people to a Christianity pure and holy and true—to those men in the day of reckoning shall surely come the benediction of a useful life, and the "Well done!" of the Master.

Finally, I come to the field of the scientist and the artist—of the men who seek to know and create. And here little can be said of openings or of hindrances—for the way of such men is the dim and unfenced moor that wends its path beyond the world into the unknown: the man who enters here must expect long journeys, poor and unknown and often discouraged. To do in science and literature today anything worth the doing, anything that is really good and lasting, is hard to anyone, impossible to many. And here the young Negro so often forgets that "art is long and time is fleeting." The first applause of his good-natured race too often turns his head; lets him rest on his oars, and instead of pursuing more doggedly the faint chance of doing some little masterpiece, he lingers upon his notoriety and puts his picture and biography in the papers.

For the man who will work and dig and starve there is a chance to do here incalculable good for the Negro race; for the woman in whose soul the divine music of our fathers has touched some answering chord of genius, there is a chance to do more than follow the masters; to all of you in whom the tragedy of life, or its fitful comedy, has created a tale worth the telling, there is a chance to gain listeners who will know no color line. Everywhere there is work to be done; in physical and social science, in literature, painting and architecture, in music and sculpture, in every place where genius and toil will unite and strive.

Let me now briefly review these fields of work:

A broad field of scientific, businesslike farming.

The uncultivated but promising field of the Negro merchant, with a constituency of eight millions.

The pressing demands for captains of industry to employ the labor, to direct the work, and develop the capacity of Negro workmen by industrial enterprise.

The large field for well-trained physicians.

Some small demand for lawyers.

A considerable field for specially-trained teachers.

The pressing necessity for fewer ministers of better type and more thorough devotion.

An ever open field for talent and application in literature, science, and art.

Such are some of the paths that open before you, class of '98, and along these you go toward the goal you have set for yourselves. Which path you will take you must choose, and the choice is difficult. Nevertheless, it cannot be long put off—for no choice is a choice. And when you have chosen, stand by it, for the man who is ever wavering and choosing again is wasting God's time. Choose, then, remembering that failure is the lot of many men, and that no success will be so marvelous but what it beckons to greater goals beyond.

And with the lifework chosen, remember that it can become, as you will it, drudgery or heroism, prosaic or romantic, brutal or divine. Who of the world today cares whether Washington was a farmer or a merchant? Who thinks of Lincoln as a country lawyer, or reads of St. Peter, the fisherman, prays to Jesus Christ, the carpenter? If you make the object of your life—calling food and drink, food and drink it will yield you grudgingly; but if above and beyond mere existence you seek to play well your part because it is worth playing—to do your duty because the world thirsts for your service, to perform clean, honest, thorough work, not for cheap applause, but because the work needs to be done—then is all your toil and drudgery transfigured into divine service and joins the mighty lives that have swept beyond time into the everlasting world. In this sense is it, young men and women, that the vision of life you have gained here is truer and holier and more real than the narrow, sordid views of life which you meet on the streets and in the homes of smaller souls. Cling to those ideals, cherish them, and in travail and sorrow, if need be, make them more true.

It is now ten years since I stood amid these walls on my commencement morning, ten years full of toil and happiness and sorrow, and the full delight of hard work. And as I look back on that youthful gleam, and see the vision splendid, the trailing clouds of glory that lighted then the wide way of life, I am ever glad that I stepped into the world guided of strong faith in its promises, and inspired by no sordid aims. And from that world I come back to welcome you, my brothers and my sisters. I cannot promise you happiness always, but I can promise you divine discontent with the imperfect. I cannot promise you success—'tis not in mortals to command success.

But as you step into life I can give you three watchwords: first, you are Negroes, members of that dark, historic race that from the world's dawn has slept to hear the trumpet summons sound through our ears. Cherish unwavering faith in the blood of your fathers, and make sure this last triumph of humanity. Remember next, that you are gentlemen and ladies, trained in the liberal arts and subjects in that vast kingdom of culture that has lighted the world from its infancy and guided it through bigotry and falsehood and sin. As such, let us see in you an unfaltering honesty wedded to that finer courtesy and breeding which is the heritage of the well-trained and the well-born. And, finally, remember that you are the sons of Fisk University, that venerable mother who rose out of the blood and dust of battle to work the triumphs of the Prince of Peace. The mighty blessing of all her sons and daughters encompass you, and the sad sacrifice of every pure soul, living and dead, that has made her what she is, bend its dark wings about you and make you brave and good! And then through the weary striving and disappointment of life, fear not for the end, even though you fail:

> Truth forever on the scaffold,
>   Wrong forever on the throne.
> Yet that scaffold sways the future,
>   And behind the dim unknown
> Standeth God within the shadow,
>   Keeping watch above his own.

CHAPTER SIXTEEN

Atlanta University

This essay was first published in 1905 in *From Servitude to Service: Being the Old South Lectures on the History and Work of Southern Institutions for the Education of the Negro*. Du Bois had come to Atlanta University in 1897. Besides teaching, his purpose was to establish a line of social science research on the condition of Negro life and culture in the United States.

The Atlanta University studies were to continue for over a decade. They represent the most comprehensive and systematic study of black social and cultural issues to come from the beginning of the twentieth century. As Du Bois explained in the following essay:

> Atlanta University seeks to become a centre for the careful, earnest and minute study of the Negro problems, through the experience and active cooperation of other graduates scattered all over the South. For this purpose we have established a department of social inquiry and an Annual Conference to study the Negro problem; we have been careful not to let the size of the field or the intricacy and delicacy of the subject tempt us into superficial or hasty work. Each year some definite phase of the problem is taken, the inquiry is limited in extent, and every effort is made to get thorough unbiased returns. (page 231 of this book)

Du Bois had limited funds and largely untrained students to help him in the collection of his data. The studies were established on a ten-year repetitive cycle for the purposes of comparative data. They included: *Mortality among Negroes in Cities*, 1896; *Social and Physical Condition of Negroes in Cities,* 1897; *Some Efforts of Negroes for Social Betterment,* 1898; *The Negro in Business,* 1899; *The College-bred Negro,* 1900; *The Negro Common School*, 1901; *The Negro Artisan*, 1902; *The Negro Church*, 1903; *Crime Among Negroes,* 1904; and *Methods and Results of Ten Years' Study*, 1905. The cycle started again in 1906 with *Morality among Negroes in Cities* and continued until 1910, when Du Bois left Atlanta University to work for the National Association for the Advancement of Colored People.

As one reads Du Bois's description of Atlanta University and its work, it is clear that the school's purpose was consistent with his vision of the Talented Tenth and the social uplift of African-Americans through the leadership of its most talented and educated citizens. Describing the founders of Atlanta University, he explained:

> They did not establish simply a primary school, or a grammar school, or a high school. On the contrary they established all these schools and in addition to this a college, and made the college the centre and norm of all their work. They did this, first for the development of individual Negro talent, second for inspiration and leadership of Negro communities, and third, for the supplying of teachers. Their primary idea was stated in perfectly plain language; they proposed to train men; they believed that a black boy with the capacity to learn, was worth teaching and that the only limitations to the development of an individual human soul were that soul's capacity and its obligations to its fellow men—its duty to society. In the case of the emancipated and enfranchised Negro this duty to his fellow men revealed itself most pressingly and imperatively as a call for enlightenment and inspiration for the mass from leaders. Much as the Negro race needed to know in agriculture, they needed to know still more as to life. (page 217 of this book)

As a controversial figure, Du Bois considered his presence at Atlanta University problematic and leading to the school losing endowment and support. By 1910 Du Bois had come to believe that carefully calculated scholarship—no matter how thorough or carefully done—would not be sufficient to address the problem of race in American culture. In *Dusk of Dawn*, he recalled that a poor Negro in central Georgia, named Sam Hose had supposedly killed his landlord's wife. Du Bois wrote an editorial piece, "evident facts," on the case. He gave it to Joel Chandler Harris, the editor of the *Atlanta Constitution*, only to discover that Hose had been lynched and that his knuckles were on display in a grocery store on Mitchell Street (602-3).

As a result of this, and similar events, Du Bois came to the conclusion that "one could not be a calm, cool, and detached scientist while Negroes were lynched, mired and starved," and that "there was no such definite demand for scientific work of the sort I was doing, as I confidently assumed would be easily forthcoming" (603).

So Du Bois left the relatively quiet and protected environment of the Academy to take up the cause of American blacks as an editor and propagandist. Eventually, he came to the conclusion that unless theory was linked to practice, it was of relatively little value. As he explained: "the ordered knowledge which research and tireless observations must give must be sought in the midst of action" (Quoted by Foner 1970, 7).

Most men in this world are colored. A faith in humanity, therefore, a belief in the gradual growth and perfectability of men must, if honest, be primarily a belief in colored men. Atlanta University was founded as an expression of the same faith in humanity within, as in humanity without the color line. That faith in men meant a firm belief that the great mass of human beings of all races and nations, withal their differences and peculiarities, were capable of essentially similar development and that the method of bringing about that development was by the education of youth. The founders of Atlanta University did not wait until this thesis was absolutely proven beyond peradventure—they held it to be a perfectly valid assumption to make, and to work on, immediately, and therefore they established Atlanta University, two years after Lee surrendered.

They did not establish simply a primary school, or a grammar school, or a high school. On the contrary they established all these schools and in addition to this a college, and made the college the centre and norm of all their work. They did this, first for the development of individual Negro talent,— for inspiration and leadership of Negro communities, and third, for the supplying of teachers. Their primary idea was stated in perfectly plain language; they proposed to train men; they believed that a black boy with the capacity to learn, was worth teaching and that the only limitations to the development of an individual human soul were that soul's capacity and its obligations to its fellow men—its duty to society. In the case of the emancipated and enfranchised Negro this duty to his fellow men revealed itself most pressingly and imperatively as a call for enlightenment and inspiration for the mass from leaders. Much as the Negro race needed to know in agriculture, they needed to know still more as to life. They were poor carpenters, but they were still poorer fathers and mothers; they did not understand the methods of modern industry, but they knew even less of the aims of that civilization which industry serves. Sad it was that the slave was an undeveloped hand, it was far sadder that he was an undeveloped man. This, then, was the second problem to which the founders of Atlanta University addressed themselves, and it was no small one. There are many ways of developing manhood and inspiring men. All ways this institution did not try, but it did try one which the experience of four thousand years of civilized life on this earth has proven of foremost value—and that is the sending of missionaries of culture among the masses. This is not the only teaching a mass of untaught people need—they need teaching in the technique of industry, in methods of business, in the science of agriculture. But they need especially in their halting, hesitating beginnings the guidance of men who know what civilization means—who stand before them as guides not simply to teach them how to walk, but to teach them whither to go, and while logically we may argue that learning to walk ought to precede preparations for a great journey, yet as a matter of fact and history, it is the inspiration of some goal to be reached that has ever led men to learn how to get there.

The third object of Atlanta University was to train teachers. Everybody, both in Reconstruction days and now, agrees that some amount of elementary training is necessary for the Freedmen's sons. Missionaries, government agents and army officers all agreed from the first that schools were needed. But schools call for teachers and, therefore Normal schools were needed. Nor was this all. A Normal school in Massachusetts trains an educated person in the art of teaching. In the South, among Negroes after the war, there was no such educated class to train. A Normal school then in the South must be primarily a high school and college; it must first educate its teachers and then train them to teach.

And, moreover, in case it cannot do both these things well, surely it is far better to send out among the masses educated persons who lack technical training in methods of teaching rather than to send persons who have technique without education. So that in these three ways Atlanta University was demanded: to train talented Negro youth, to disseminate civilization among the untaught masses, and to educate teachers.

It is, however, one thing to conceive a great human need and quite another thing to realize this in deeds and sacrifices, in bricks and stone. And when in the world's history struggling human beings have in doubt and travail, in weariness and anxiety, established a great engine of human betterment, it behooves us who sit and see and hope in God's good time to help—to ask what they did and how they did it and who were the men that did these things. These questions it is my task to answer and to show how there to the southward, where the great Blue Ridge first bows and crumbles before the far-off sea, twelve men in 1867 founded an institution of learning which has meant so much to the higher aspirations and untrammelled development of two hundred million black men on this earth. These men created on the barren red mud of North

Georgia a little cluster of brick buildings, now six in number, which have mothered five thousand sons and daughters in thirty-five years and which first, last and ever have stood for one unwavering ideal. They created this institution out of poverty and distrust in the midst of enmity and danger, in the face of ignorance and crime. Dying, they left their legacy to us—their legacy and their burden.

What sort of men established and carried on the work of Atlanta University? They were not all visionaries and dreamers, and yet among them were men who saw the vision and dreamed the dream. Two of the original founders represented the American Missionary Association, that great movement born at the slave ship that wandered into Connecticut and coming to the fullness of manhood just as the nation needed it in the reconstruction crisis. One was a tall and dark-haired man, who afterward carried the idea of equal opportunity for black men to Nashville and founded Fisk University there; three were northern business men, resident in Atlanta; two were Negroes, new clothed with authority, and one was Edmund Ware. These men are nearly all dead today, but around the work of their hands have clustered many and diverse helpers. A bishop like Atticus G. Haygood, Southern bred, but emancipated and honest; a justice of the Georgia Supreme Court like McKay; a president of one of Atlanta's greatest banks; and men like Charles Cuthbert Hall, of New York, and Samuel M. Crothers, of Cambridge. Today Atlanta University is directed by four of its own graduates and by members of the governing boards or faculties of Harvard and Yale Universities, Williams and Dartmouth Colleges, Union Theological Seminary, and Tuskegee Institute.

But, after all, the founder of Atlanta University was Edmund Ware, and Edmund Ware was a man of faith. We are not dealing in faith these days. We are discounting it, and sometimes half sneering at it. Because in the past a certain type of simple-hearted enthusiast has believed so piteously in things absurd, impossible and false, we have come to discount the whole proceeding, striving to know even where knowledge is yet impossible, and pitying loftily that old-fashioned goodness that believed in men, that glorified in sacrifice, and had an unwavering faith that somewhere beyond the mists was a good God, and that the world was as good as the God that made it. Edmund Asa Ware was born in North Wrentham, now Norfolk, Mass., a few miles from Boston, in 1837. He fitted for college at the Norwich Free Academy, Connecticut, and was graduated from Yale University in 1863. After his graduation, he taught for a time in the school in which he had fitted for college, and then was principal of a public school in Nashville, Tenn. Soon the way opened for him to enter a field of labor of which he had dreamed and planned in his schoolboy days, and he began the life work for which he believed he had a divine commission and from which he could not be diverted by his alluring offers of money, comfort and position. His friend has written of him:

"He was conscientious. His mother had no recollection of his ever being untruthful. His village teachers all commended him for his unvarying conformity to the right in school. It is said that when fifteen years old, he had never been absent a day, nor had a mark for tardiness. One morning as the bell stopped, writes one, his seat was observed to be vacant. Those near the windows, looking out, saw him running at full speed, trying to gain his seat before his name should be called. The teacher was seen to cast an eye to the window and then to linger a moment before he called the roll. Thus he was seated to respond when the W's were reached."

What sort of a man did such a boy make? Certainly not a good business man in the modern sense; not a leader in literature or polite society; not a member of Congress; nor even a promising pillar of the State Legislature. And yet, after this man had lived less than fifty years and lay white, thin and dead in the darkened halls of Atlanta University, there came a stream of men who had known him, black and white, student and teacher, Northerner and Southerner, and this is the picture they painted:

The Superintendent of the Freedmen's Bureau for Georgia, said: "It was he who counseled and advised with the colored and other members of the constitution convention and secured the wise provision in the constitution for the establishment of a public school system, and afterwards, with members of the first Legislature, by which it was established and put into operation. He was in thorough sympathy with the religious work carried on at the same time by the Christian teachers and church organizations, but found oftentimes his greatest difficulties in overcoming the sectarian differences which interfered with the harmonious operation of the school work. This he had always in view, and, by his gentleness and forbearance and generous catholic spirit, he removed many ignorant prejudices that stood in the way."

A student said: "His manner of speech was terse, laconic, forceful, animated, in perfect harmony with the fervency of soul, with that restless activity which was so peculiarly manifest in all his doings. On leaving him I felt that I had been talking with a man who was living a higher life, living above the ordinary aims and petty ambitions of this world, a man who, though toiling in a field obscure and unpopular, nevertheless was entirely devoted to the cause he had espoused, and showed in every look and word a faith which rose sublimely above the mists and shadows of the present.". . . "This spirit of work which so completely possessed Mr. Ware, he naturally endeavored to transfuse into his pupils. I shall never forget those talks he used to give to the students every year just before the closing of school for the summer vacation. With what emphasis he used to say to the young men: 'Now, if you can get schools to teach, it is well. Teach them. Do all the good you can. But if you can't get schools to teach, don't hesitate a minute to work with your hands. Go into the field. Dig, hoe, pick cotton. Labor is honorable.' "

Another graduate said: "After that interview with him alone, after feeling his tender caresses as he sat near me, and after listening to the mild tones of his voice, and seeing, face to face, those eyes, not now indignantly flashing, but full of sweetness and tenderness, after this, there never was any terror in that face or those eyes for me during all the following years that I knew him. During the last eighteen or nineteen years I have seen many a student quail before that steady, withering gaze, which Mr. Ware knew so well how to use. But for me there ever remained that same soft expression, first seen during our first interview, in the little library upstairs at Storrs' School in 1867. That look has, in a great measure, influenced my course of life; has often kept me in the right path, when temptation was strong to go otherwise."

A friend added: "I think I never knew a man so strong of will who was so free from the lower self. If ordinary ambition entered into his calculations, it strengthened by the reaction it aroused, the very virtue it assailed. It was preeminently as moral teacher and quickener that he excelled. True as steel himself, he felt a lie as men feel a personal insult. He did not like even an insincere or merely conventional tone."

And finally Bishop Atticus G. Haygood, of the Methodist Episcopal Church, South, and author of the "Brother in Black," and who was at one time a trustee of the University, in speaking of the "Man who can wait," said: "Only those who began with Mr. Ware nearly twenty years ago this new and difficult work of trying to educate in a rational and Christian manner the enfranchised people of this country, and so to help in introducing into the family of Christian and civilized nations a new race, can understand how much Edmund Ware, when he first began work in this city, needed to be a man who could do his work and wait. The conditions under which this work is carried on are different now; very small encouragement do workers in this field get from us of the white race in the Southern States, although next to the Negro race, we are, of all men on earth, most concerned in the success of your work and most concerned because we have most at stake in this work. The social environments are not inspiring now; but let me assure you 1885 is very far from 1865. To have gone on as President Ware did during those early years there must have been in his heart deathless love and pity for men who needed what he could give them,—a faith in the gospel and eternal righteousness that never wavered, and a love for God that made work easy and suffering joy."

I have dwelt upon the character of this man because, in some places, it is the fashion of the day to represent those who went south after the war to help the freedmen as officious busy-bodies, goody-goody sort of folk, with heads very nearly as soft as their hearts. And yet that wonderful call which sounded in the ears of the sons and daughters of the North in the later sixties was a call to far greater heroism and self-sacrifice than that which called them earlier through the smoke of Sumter. They could not, like the soldiers, expect monuments, the notice of historians, or even (shall I write it?) pensions, but they could expect work, danger, contempt, and forgetfulness, and those who dared this, at least deserve the respect and reverence of thinking men!

I said that Edmund Ware was a man of faith. As early as 1867 he was writing North in his capacity as state superintendent of education; he said:

> "The Education Association will meet in Macon on the 9th of October, and then will come the demand for teachers. Please let me know before the time, how many teachers (board paid by colored people) you can give me, besides those at the points you already hold. Make a rough estimate, only make it large enough. You must do something on faith. I know the people of the North will do much more than they have yet done, if the matter is only presented in the right way to them. Get young ladies in each town to agree to carry round a paper, and get all the people to subscribe from ten cents to ten dollars per month, and then go round and collect it monthly. All that is wanted is a few workers in each city and town and it will all be done."

After he became president of an institution on paper, then this wonderful unwavering faith, slowly, surely became transmuted. The first building came from the American Missionary Association; the second from the State of Georgia, with its growing number of black legislators. The Recitation hall and the Manual Training building came from two Massachusetts women, the Housekeeping Cottage from circles of the King's Daughters and Rev. Dr. D. L. Furber, the Training School from the General Educational Board and other friends, and now a Library from Andrew Carnegie. This has been the material growth. But that which Western colleges call the "plant" of Atlanta University, is the least of its real being. Our buildings are simple and small, not unpleasing in appearance, neat and substantial, but nothing calculated especially to impress the beholder. The peculiar spiritual growth which this institution typifies is on the other hand the object of our especial pride. Not even the heavy loss caused by President Ware's premature death checked for a moment this inner growth, for a leader and successor stood ready trained in heart and mind for the work.

Atlanta University is fortunate in having but two presidents in her thirty-five years of existence. The successor of President Ware was the son of a man who, at one time, furnished many of the textbooks which were used in the schools of Boston, and a nephew of Nathaniel P. Willis.

President Bumstead was born in Boston in 1841, was graduated at the Boston Latin School, and in 1863 at Yale. He was major of the Forty-third United States Colored troops in the civil war and afterward graduated at Andover and entered the ministry. He joined Atlanta University as teacher of Science in 1875, and since that time as teacher and president has given to that institution the best years of a singularly devoted life. His name will go down in history as that of the Apostle of the Higher Education of the American Negro.

Many men and women of energy and devotion have built their lives into this work. Every stone on that broad campus has meant the pulse of some man's life blood and the sacrifice of some woman's heart. There sits tonight within those Southern walls a woman bent and bowed, old with years, and yet ever young in the hearts of a thousand black men to whom, for thirty years, she was more than mother; there sounds within those halls today the voice of a white-haired man who, thirty-five years ago, sacrificed a government position and a good salary and brought his young wife down to live with black people. Not all the money that you and yours could give for a hundred years would do half as much to convince dark and outcast millions of the South that they have some friends in this world, as the sacrifice of such lives as these to the cause.

I have said that the founder of this institution planned a college-even a university. How far has that plan honestly been carried out? There are in name today numerous universities in the South for colored men, and this is often brought as an argument against Negro colleges—their absurdly overwhelming number. This is, in reality, untrue. There are very few institutions in the United States really doing college work for Negroes. Many institutions called colleges represent an ambition or an ideal, while as a matter of present fact such schools are higher institutions simply in name; in reality they are great primary and grammar schools with a score of high school students and a few or none of college grade. They represent, in many cases, high hopes and laudable ambition, but in some cases they have no present prospect or design of developing into real colleges, and in some other cases they have been tempted to be content with calling a high school a college, possibly after the venerable example of Harvard in its early days. This practice, however, has led to the suspicion that all Negro colleges are of low rank and parading more or less under false pretenses.

There are in the United States today about five institutions which, by reason of the number of students and grade of work done, deserve to rank as Negro colleges. How far, now, is the work done at an institution like Atlanta University deserving of the respect due to liberal training?

If there is one thing at Atlanta University upon which we pride ourselves it is that we have never succumbed to the temptation of mere numbers. We have today seventy-five students of a rank above the high school—fifty in the regular college course, and twenty-five in the teacher's college. It is fair to say that we might, by a general lowering of standard, easily have a college of one hundred to one hundred and fifty. This we have steadily refused to do. On the contrary, we have sought unceasingly, year by year, to raise and fix a fair standard, and I think it is perfectly just to say that so far as our work goes in Atlanta University, the standard equals that of any New England school. We have a high school of two hundred and twenty-five pupils, divided into two parallel courses of three years, an English and classical. This gives one year less than the New England high schools with their four-year courses. Above the high school there are two courses of study offered: a regular college course of four years, leading to the bachelor's degree and a teacher's training course of two years, leading to a normal diploma. Our college rank is thus one year behind the smaller New England colleges, and this rank has been proven in case of several of our graduates, who have afterward taken the A.B. degree in leading Northern colleges after one year's study.

In maintaining this standard we have, of course, our peculiar troubles. In New England there is difficulty in articulating the high school and college courses. In the South the almost total absence of high schools for Negroes makes a preparatory department necessary to a college like ours. All other Negro colleges in the South have grammar grades in addition, but we have simply the high school and the college, and consequently find our great difficulty in fitting our Junior high school year to the eighth grade of the public schools. The varying quality of work done in the public schools makes it necessary that our first year should be one of sifting and examination. About one-half of our public school candidates do the work of this class in a year; a fourth more do the work in something over a year, and are given electives so as to start even with the regular second year class. The other fourth, from poor preparation or lack of ability and other reasons, drop out.

For admission to the high school we require eight grades of common school work. If the pupil proposes to take the full college course, he has before him about 2,800 recitation periods of forty-five minutes each, or, in laboratory work, of twice that length. Three-tenths of these are given to ancient languages, three-tenths evenly divided between science and mathematics, two-tenths to English and modern languages at the rate of English seven and German two, and two-tenths to history, sociology, philosophy and pedagogy at the rate of history and sociology nine and other studies two. In addition to this there are 384 hours of manual training. By electives the proportion of modern languages can be increased.

The length of the entire normal course is five years, and the total number of recitation periods, of forty-five minutes each, is 2,028. Three-tenths of these are given to pedagogy, three-tenths to mathematics and science, two and a half tenths to English, one-tenth to philosophy and history, etc.

How far is the charge true that old-fashioned studies and out-of-date methods are being used in Negro colleges to fit black boys for a world which prides itself on being rather ahead of time than even up with it? We willingly plead guilty to a persistent clinging to many of the older forms of discipline. We still count the teacher as of considerably more importance than the thing taught. This explains considerable amount of Latin in our curriculum. We have one of the most successful Latin teachers in the South, a man not only learned in method, but of great and peculiar personal influence. We are willing and anxious for our college men to have four or five years' contact with this man, and we seriously doubt if a greater course in engineering under a lesser man would be a real gain for the development of manhood among us. On the other hand, our teachers and instructors have been drawn from Yale, Harvard, Dartmouth, Wellesley, Boston University, Worcester Polytechnic, Fisk, and our own institution. Our dean ranked his class at Dartmouth; a former dean was the DeForest medal man at Yale; the head of our normal department is from Bridgewater, and for sixteen years has done some of the most successful normal work in the South; two classmates of President Ware at Yale joined him in his work, and now his two children, from Yale and Columbia, are taking up their father's mantle.

There are five full professors and ten instructors. The library has 11,500 volumes, classified by the Dewey system and well selected. There is a physical laboratory 50 x 22 feet, in which all class work is carried on by individual experiments and measurements. Adjoining this is a science lecture room with considerable apparatus. The chemical laboratory is 50 x 25 feet, with individual desks and chemicals. There are small geological and mineralogical cabinets, and the beginning of a zoological cabinet in the lower orders. The astronomy class has a small telescope, and in the mathematical department there are surveying and engineering instruments. The department of Sociology and History has sets of modern and ancient maps and a class room library with reference works, duplicate text-books and statistical treatises. The recitation rooms are large and light, and nearly all furnished with the tablet chairs.

Manual training is an integral part of our work, and is carried on in two buildings, one for the girls and one for the boys. Manual training is required of all high school students. The boys' building has a floor devoted to wood working, with power saws, planers, etc., a lumber storage room and a paint room. Another floor is occupied by the turning lathes, twenty individual benches with tools, and a drawing room with eighteen sets of instruments. In the basement, iron-working is carried on with forges and lathes. The printing office has a full equipment, includeing a power press.

Manual training for girls is carried on at the Housekeeping Cottage, and consists in cooking, sewing, dressmaking, drawing and general housekeeping.

When we enumerate these facilities for manual training, people are usually surprised, and say, "Why, you have, then, an industrial school after all!" This we disclaim. We do not have an industrial department for the important work of teaching trades. Our equipment, almost without exception, is an integral part of our educational work, and is designed for its educational effect alone. Just as the boy works with his own hands in the chemical laboratory or the laboratory in sociology, so he works in the manual training shop, and the object in all three cases is the same, viz.: to develop the boy to the full capacity of his powers, mental and physical. With the education thus gained, the boy might use his chemistry in the study of medicine, or his sociology in the ministry, or his manual dexterity at a trade school, but we do not pretend to train either physicians, clergymen or carpenters. I speak of this because there is so much confusion of ideas on the point, especially so far as Southern schools are concerned. Schools of higher training in the South are often supposed to be places without manual training, despising and ridiculing it, and knowing nothing of its great educative power, while an industrial school is supposed to be necessarily and always a centre of education.

If you should visit Atlanta University you would see little evidence of student manual work in finished products of wood, or iron, or stone. Our furniture is from the factory, our buildings erected by hired labor, and our important repairs largely done by outside workmen. Nevertheless, the influence of our manual training of the students is easily traceable in their after life.

When the Conference for Southern Education, popularly associated with the Ogden parties, met in Athens, Ga., they especially admired the industrial exhibit of the Negro schools. "That is the sort of work that is needed," they said repeatedly, "where was the Principal trained?" And then they found out that he and all his teachers came from Atlanta University. They had never learned basket making or clay modelling there, but they had received a far more fundamental training in human power. With this as a basis, it took them but a short time to master the technique.

The work of teacher training is also carried on by the laboratory method—that is it is centred in the model school containing a kindergarten and four grades (to be extended to eight grades eventually) with all the equipment of a modern school. Here, under instructors, the normal students teach, observe and experiment.

I have indicated the formal curriculum of Atlanta University and the facilities for carrying it out. But this is not all of our educational work with our students. A centre of education with us is our school Home; among the earliest ideals entertained by the University is one that may be designated as home-building. In its first days, officers and teachers kept before the minds of students and their parents the desirability of securing land and homes, and many a cottage in Atlanta owes its existence to the personal counsel and pecuniary assistance of some teacher in the University; and when, at the beginning of a summer vacation, some three or four hundred were sent out to teach school in the smaller towns and rural districts, among other injunctions it was impressed upon them to encourage and assist the people among whom they were to labor, to buy land and make themselves homes, and specific items of information with reference to accomplishing this were given them. And when these student teachers returned from their summer's work they were asked to report what they had done in this line and also to give facts they had gathered as to the amount of land the people owned or were buying.

The effect of this policy is shown in the statistics of Negro property in Georgia. Of course it would not be fair to claim that Atlanta University is solely responsible for this record, but certainly the influence of this institution has been a potent factor in the increase of property from nearly nothing in 1860 to a real value of nearly thirty-five millions in 1905.

Atlanta University is more than a school, it is a home. The dormitories are not simply a collection of rooms where students may study and lodge and care for themselves, but each of them is under the supervision of a competent woman, who takes the place of a mother and sees that the students are regular in their habits, tidy in dress, neat in the care of rooms, attentive to study, polite in manners, careful in regard to health, and made comfortable in illness. The dining room, too, where teachers and students assemble for meals, is not merely a commons, where simply a sufficient quantity of food is furnished, but is a place where teachers and students eat together, talk and learn to know each other; where the etiquette of family life is carefully observed—indeed this is one of the few places in America where black and white people meet as simple, friendly human souls, unveiled from light and unguarded from feared contagion; bound in human sympathy and help.

And so, in these ways, is carried out the intention expressed in the first catalogue of 1868-70, and in the latest 1903-04, in these words: "It is designed to make the school as far as possible a home for those who attend," and it may be added that in thus making it a home it becomes a home builder.

With the home life go the home chores and duties—the care of the rooms, the sweeping of the halls, the washing of the dishes, and the little errands here and there. The comparatively small number of our students makes the home life peculiarly cheerful and cozy. Teachers and students know each other intimately, and in a way impossible in large institutions, and always the graduate looks back upon the home life as the greatest and best gift of the Alma Mater.

Not only is Atlanta University a school and a home; it is in the larger sense of the word, a church. I do not mean by that anything narrow or sectarian, but I do mean that we whose work it is to train youth in the South have to face some patent facts: first, the religious conditions among both whites and blacks are such that the differences between Methodists and Baptists sometimes overshadow the differences between heaven and hell; that particularly among young educated Negroes this is a day of rapid religious evolution which might easily end anywhere or nowhere; consequently it will not do in the South to leave moral training to individual homes, since their homes are just recovering from the debauchery of slavery, and only in a minority of instances are they capable of the necessary teaching. As the larger home, then, of its sons and daughters, Atlanta University is, and always has been, a teacher of religion and morality. Our chaplain, the son of the late president, and a graduate of Union Theological Seminary, is a young man of clear-hearted devotion, and both his work and example are of great influence. A part of our religious exercises are voluntary and all of them are maintained at a level of high earnestness with a minimum of cant and empty form.

Such is our course of training. The great question, however, which men of right may ask of Atlanta University is, "What has this training resulted in? How far has this institution justified its existence? How far has it trained men of talent, civilized communities, and given real teachers to the black South?"

It is in the answer to this question that Atlanta University makes its greatest claim to public attention; and yet it is a very difficult thing to exhibit a process of education to the eye.

The experience in this line with which every teacher is so familiar is exaggerated in our case, for we and the whole Negro race are often judged for time and eternity by a fifteen-minute visitor.

On the other hand, when in the towns and country districts of the South the work of the graduates and former students of this institution is carefully studied, the verdict is always unanimous; that there is not in the country an institution which, in thirty-five years of work, has sent into the world a set of men and women stronger in character and attainment, and more useful in their fields of labor. The General Educational Board, after investigation, came to its endorsement on this ground particularly. Southern born men who still oppose Negro colleges have repeatedly acknowledged the remarkable character of our graduates. The School Board of Atlanta has put the Negro public schools of the city under the almost complete control of teachers whom we have trained; the state of Georgia, while it gave us aid repeatedly, bore testimony through its committees of the high quality of work done, and when afterwards that aid was taken from us and given to a new institution at Savannah, the institution was largely manned with our graduates, from its president down.

Atlanta University has taught some five thousand students. Of these 677 have finished a full high school course, and 487 of them have received a degree or normal diploma:

Occupations of Graduates	College	Normal	Total
Total	124	367	*489
Male	101	15	116
Female	23	352	*373
Living	108	311	*417
Dead	16	41	57
Teachers	62	78	240

Ministers	13	...	13
Physicians	4	...	4
Lawyers	2	...	2
Dentists	1	...	1
U.S. Service	12	2	14
Business	7	8	15
Students	4	3	7
Wives	1	#101	111
Others	2	10	12

*Two graduated in two departments.
44 other wives are classed as teachers.

In its work of training teachers, Atlanta University has rendered its greatest service to the country. Sixty per cent of our graduates teach; they teach in city and county, in public and private schools, in primary, secondary and higher schools, and the schools of all religious denominations; five are presidents of colleges and normal schools, fourteen are principals of high and secondary schools, twenty are connected with industrial schools. I presume it is no exaggeration to say that our graduates and former students are reaching 20,000 black boys and girls each year, and handing on the light which they have received.

The work done by these men as students has been honest and fair. Our graduates have made good records at Harvard, Dartmouth, and the University of Chicago, University of Michigan, and Northern professsional schools like Andover and Hartford theological seminaries, and the University of Pennsylvania Medical School. Research work done at our institution has been, in several cases, published by the United States government, and even recognized abroad. We have not, so far as we know, graduated any men of very exceptional genius, but we have sent out a score of men of unusual ability, measured by any standard, and we have trained a few who, by ability and forceful personality, are above the average of the trained men of any race.

Our great work, however, has been the sending of missionaries of culture throughout the South, and in this work Atlanta University has had conspicuous success. Of course such an influence is difficult to measure.

Considering the intimate connection of Atlanta University with the State of Georgia, we may, perhaps, best measure its influence by studying that state; in a sense Atlanta University founded the public school system of the state, since its first president was the first state superintendent of education. Of the thirteen leading Negro institutions in the state outside of Atlanta University, seven have presidents trained at this school, and two or three others have some of our graduates as teachers; and all of them have students trained by our graduates. The public schools of all the leading cities, Atlanta, Savannah, Athens, Columbus, and Macon, are very largely manned by our former students, and in all walks of life the influence of our graduates and former students is felt.

A recent study of Georgia shows that Negro population, property and literacy in Georgia are increasing, while serious crime has begun to decrease. This record is not due to any one single cause, but certainly the influence of Atlanta University has been a most potent factor. In the work of Negro uplift throughout the land our graduates are not alone nor altogether singular graduates of a score of other worthy institutions are working with them, but the long, thorough courses of study in our work, the unbending mental discipline as a foundation for all work, whether manual or intellectual, has left its enduring mark on the Atlanta University man. The work of these college trained men from this and other institutions is not to be judged simply by what they have done, but still more from what they have prevented. I am persuaded that Americans do not dwell enough on this side of the case. You complain of crime and vagrancy among Negroes, and both are large and threatening, as it is perfectly natural they should be, but consider what they might have been if this race had been left without leaders—not leaders who could simply read and write and hoe, but real thinkers, men of vision, men who realized the tremendous import of this vast social movement and could stand ever ready within the veil to calm passion and direct energy and say to the turbulent waters, "Peace be still."

The peculiar character of work, however, makes Atlanta University more than a simple college—it is a social settlement where, for six or seven years, the best we can find of the growing generation of Negroes is brought into contact with the standards of modern culture in school and home and campus. Nor do we wish to stop here—the Social Settlement aims to do more than teach the slums; it seeks also by studying slums to teach the world what slums mean. And Atlanta University seeks to become a centre for the careful, earnest and minute study of the Negro problems, through the experience and active cooperation of other graduates scattered all over the South. For this purpose we have established a department of social inquiry and an Annual Conference to study the Negro problem; we have been careful not to let the size of the field or the intricacy and delicacy of the subject tempt us into superficial or hasty work. Each year some definite phase of the problem is taken, the inquiry is limited in extent, and every effort is made to get thorough unbiased returns. To establish such a work with few funds, and untrained investigators was difficult, but today, after nine years of work, we feel as though the department was permanently organized for efficient work, and that interesting and instructive results will follow its further prosecution. The nine investigations already accomplished make a fairly well rounded study of human life as lived by the American Negro.

They consist of the following studies:

1. Mortality among Negroes in Cities, 1896.
2. Social and Physical Condition of Negroes in Cities, 1897.
3. Some Efforts of Negroes for Social Betterment, 1898.
4. The Negro in Business, 1899.
5. The College-bred Negro, 1900.
6. The Negro Common School, 1901.
7. The Negro Artisan, 1902.
8. The Negro Church, 1903.
9. Crime Among Negroes, 1904.
10. Methods and Results of Ten Years' Study, 1905.

Our present plan is to begin a second cycle of studies similar to these beginning with a study of Negro Mortality in 1906.

The results of these studies have been widely used; they are in the chief libraries of the world and have been commended by the *London Times, The Spectator, The Manchester Guardian, The Outlook, The Nation, The Dial, The Independent,* and leading daily papers. While we believe that social inquiry of this sort is fully justified if it seeks merely to know and publish that knowledge, we have also sought in addition to this to inspire our graduates in various communities to use the information we collect as a basis of concrete efforts in social betterment, and we can already point to some results of this policy.

CHAPTER SEVENTEEN

Gifts and Education

This brief editorial, published in the February 1925 issue of *The Crisis*, was part of a series of pieces that Du Bois wrote that called for adequate and appropriate funding for black colleges, as well as the elimination of their dependency upon philanthropic sources such as the General Education Board, the Rockefeller Foundation and the Phelps Stokes Fund. The article points to the extent to which battles Du Bois had engaged in concerning black higher education—in particular its dependency on Northern philanthropic funding—still had not been reconciled twenty-five years later.

The recent gifts of Duke and Eastman to Negro education, together with the former benefactions of Rockefeller, Carnegie, Peabody and others, must call for gratitude from black folk. Under present conditions, the only hope for Negro education lies in the gifts of the rich and without these ignorance and caste will be the continued lot of American Negroes.

Nevertheless, it is a shame that present conditions make this necessary. It is a shame that the white laborers of the South will not allow the states to support decent common schools and high schools for Negroes, and compel the race to go begging up and down the land, hat in hand, crawling to the door steps of the rich and powerful for the dole of knowledge. And then these same laborers, backed by organized labor in the North, sneer and yell and curse at black labor because it is not intelligent and underbids them.

It is a shame that the rotten boroughs of the South, voting without intelligence or conscience, wielding from two to seven times the political power of the East and Middle West, can send to Congress big-mouthed demagogues who oppose appropriations to Howard, our only university supported by national taxation, and starve it and hamper it and curtail its growth.

It is a shame that our dependence on the rich for donations to absolutely necessary causes makes intelligent, free and self-respecting manhood and frank, open and honest criticism increasingly difficult among us. If someone starts to tell the truth or disclose incompetency or rebel at injustice, a chorus of "Sh!" arises from the whole black race. "Sh!" You're opposing the General Education Board! "Hush!" You're making enemies in the Rockefeller Foundation! "Keep still!" or the

Phelps Stokes Fund will get you. "Stop!" or the rich Mr. This and the affluent Mrs. That will dam the flow of funds to Fisk or Talladega, to hospital or home.

Whether the fear be true or not—whether these organizations or persons would be influenced or not by honest criticism, the fear of the thing is sapping the manhood of the race. It is breeding cowards and sycophants. It is lifting fools and flatterers to place and power and crucifying honest men. We thank the givers for priceless gifts but we eternally damn the system that makes education depend upon charity.

CHAPTER EIGHTEEN

Negroes in College

In this article, first published in the *Nation* in March of 1926, Du Bois described the unrest among students at Fisk and other leading black colleges throughout the South. Du Bois described himself as being largely out of touch with education since 1910 when he began to work for the NAACP, until 1924 when he visited his daughter Yolande at Fisk University where she was completing her senior year.

While he was at the school, George Streator, a junior, contacted him and explained to Du Bois that "The student discipline at Fisk had retrograded so as to resemble in some respects a reform school. The administration of the school seemed based on organized gossip" (Aptheker 1973, 41). According to Du Bois, the desperate attempt to get funds had led the administration to surrender to Southern conservatism.

Du Bois spoke to the alumni at Fisk on June 1, 1924, in a speech given in Memorial Chapel. He had graduated from the school thirty-five years earlier. In his speech, Du Bois blasted the school's administration:

> What now is Fisk doing to uphold and to spread the spirit of freedom in this institution? It is not doing what it should. In Fisk today, discipline is choking freedom; threats are almost universal. A favorite expression is, "if you don't like Fisk University get out!" If you do not agree with the policies of the institution go elsewhere. Students are made to promise not simply to obey the rules of the institution but to obey *all future rules that may be made.* (Aptheker 1973, 45)

Du Bois's speech, titled "Diuturni Silenti," was a bombshell. Like his 1908 speech, "Galileo Galilei," which precipitated the resignation of the school's president, James G. Merrill, this speech also ignited a controversy that eventually led to the resignation of the school's white president, Fayette A. McKenzie.

The trouble at Fisk University last year opened the eyes of many people. They realized that the problems of higher education were by no means confined to white students. Here was a Negro college where the students not only had no voice in their own government but could not edit a college paper, could not have an athletic association, and could not have any organization without faculty participation. And when the students openly rebelled, they were expelled and some of them put in jail. Since then Fisk University has cleaned house. The former president and most of the faculty have gone and the trustees are trying to rebuild the institution on broader and better lines.

But the sort of difficulty that culminated in the trouble at Fisk is found in many other institutions and this is true notwithstanding the fact that the American Negro is striving for higher education as never before. In the school year 1924-1925, 752 Negroes received their first degree in arts, 44 were made masters in arts, 4 received their doctorates in philosophy and science, and 6 were elected to the Phi Beta Kappa; while 395 received professional degrees. But this represents a minimum, accomplished through great difficulty and discouragement and is not half or perhaps a third of what the American Negro could and would do today if properly encouraged.

We may divide the institutions which educate Negroes into three classes: those which are taught mainly by whites but attended only by Negro students; those which are taught mainly by Negroes and are attended by Negroes; and the general educational institutions of the land. In all these there is today more or less ferment concerning policies and objects as far as Negroes are concerned.

The largest Negro university in the United States is Howard at Washington. The board of trustees of Howard held a special meeting December 10. Representatives of the General Alumni Association appeared before them and demanded the dismissal of J. Stanley Durkee, the white president of the institution. The trustees refused to dismiss him and bore testimony "to our confidence in President Durkee's character and purpose." The charges against Dr. Durkee as voiced by the General Alumni Association fall under the following heads: First, almost total lack of social contact between the white president on the one hand and colored professors and colored students on the other. Second, the attempted dismissal or forced resignation of the leading colored professors including Kelly Miller, the best-known Howard alumnus; George William Cook, who has been with the institution fifty years; C. G. Woodson, a Harvard doctor of philosophy; T. W. Turner, a Cornell doctor of philosophy, and many others. Third, personal disrespect toward colored professors; calling one "a contemptible puppy," kicking another out of his office. Fourth, as the Howard Welfare League has written: "The spirit of education has departed from Howard. Visiting the institution today, the investigator discovers a system of espionage. This is operated to defend an administrative corps which, having no fixed policy, is subject to frequent attacks by the instructors disposed to preserve the traditions of education. The system is financed by personal preferment chiefly in the form of university patronage."

The board of trustees and the friends of the president declare that the alumni have not proved their allegations; of this the public is not in a position to judge. But certain it is that there is violent unrest at Howard and has been for the last five years. It culminated last year in a student strike and in a special meeting of the alumni during the summer at which the president was violently denounced.

Turning now from Howard, we find trouble at Lincoln in the southeastern part of Pennsylvania, an old Presbyterian school which has trained an unusually large number of colored men. Lincoln has never had a colored professor and never had a colored member on its board of trustees. For a long time it had no colored teachers. Then it began to appoint colored tutors and assistants and it even promised to allow representation of the alumni on the board of trustees. This has never taken place; and while the alumni from time to time have protested, they did not want to make trouble as long as the old regime of teachers stayed. When a new president was to be appointed, the alumni insisted upon a voice. And then came the kind of thing which faces Negro education whenever it demands freedom. The white Presbyterians practically said: "We are furnishing the money for this school and we are going to run it as we see fit. It is none of your business whom we make president. If you don't like this kind of thing, support your own education." Not, of course, that they put the matter as bluntly as this but this is what they meant and it was this attitude which made the alumni hesitate. The trustees have nominated two successive candidates for the presidency. The first refused to accept when he heard of the opposition of the alumni. The second is considering the matter.

It is extraordinary that in schools like Howard and Lincoln it should be assumed that the parents of the students and the graduates of the school have no right to a voice in the policies of the school. Imagine such a standard at Harvard or at Yale! And does the fact that Harvard and Yale graduates are rich and able largely to support their colleges while Howard and Lincoln graduates are poor, create the wide difference in the attitude of the universities?

That the threat of withdrawal of support is no idle threat is shown by the situation at Atlanta University. Atlanta University has a distinguished past. It has had white teachers of eminence and learning. But because it was furthest down on the color-line frontier, it was compelled to take, from the beginning, a strong hand. It refused to close its doors to white students, it early gave the alumni representation on its board of trustees, it insisted upon social equality between the races within the walls of the institution. On the other hand, it held up high standards of scholarship, has always furnished a large proportion of the teachers in the higher public and private schools of the South, and was the first institution in this country to begin a scientific study of the Negro problem.

Despite this it has had a most difficult time in raising funds, and when recently Edward T. Ware, a young progressive Yale man, became president of the institution he was given to understand by philanthropic agencies in the North, such as the General Education Board, that if Atlanta University would surrender some of its radicalism and continued to their notions of what a Negro institution should be they would support it. But the institution has continued to have a free atmosphere and the voice of the alumni in its conduct has been influential. The result is today that Atlanta University is starving to death. Unless liberal Americans come to its rescue it cannot continue to do the work which it has done so well in the past. And it is this kind of fate that deters the insurgents at Howard and at Lincoln.

On the other hand, at Hampton the opposite policy has been pursued. Hampton has prided itself on its friendliness to the South. It has yielded in the past to practically every demand that the South has made, and while the demands of Virginia have not been as impossible to comply with as those of Georgia yet they have made Hampton decry the higher education of Negroes, admit colored men to the faculty with some reluctance, and carry out a system of racial segregation upon its own campus which brought annoying problems.

Despite all this and in curious contradiction Hampton has been compelled to establish a college department. The Hampton graduates, who have been in great demand in Southern public schools because the South has assumed they will be more tractable than others, were often unable under the old Hampton curriculum to pass the examinations. As a result Hampton has not only enriched her high school but established certain college courses and now offers a bachelor's degree. At the same time the demands upon her on the part of the Bourbon South have increased, and during the days when she and Tuskegee are trying to raise adequate endowment the "Anglo-Saxon" clubs of Virginia are demanding more complete racial segregation and separation on the Hampton campus. This cannot be granted without stirring up trouble with the students and alumni.

Most people hearing of these difficulties in colored institutions with white teachers immediately leap to the conclusion that the cure for all this is colored teachers and colored presidents. There are cases where the substitution of a colored president for a white president has brought happy results. But a colored president is no certain panacea. If we look at the matter carefully we will see that it is the character of the man and not the color of the skin that makes for success or lack of success. As a general thing, in colored colleges with colored presidents there is also unrest and protest because, for the most part, such presidents have not had the opportunity of broad education and contact and they are peculiarly cramped in their activities mad growth either by the white philanthropists who are "helping their institutions or the white churches that are supporting them or the white State officials under whom they work."

At Wilberforce, for instance, we have a church school dominated by the resident African Methodist bishop on the one hand and by State politics on the other. The bishop is a man of limited education and his idea of an institution of learning is quite as narrow as the idea of any bigoted white bishop. He has made his son president and the result that through political manipulation and church domination Wilberforce has never become a real seat of liberal education. It is provincial, narrow, and vindictive, without discipline or ideal; and no man of broad learning and forward-looking plans is able to stay there long.

Nor is this situation confined to Wilberforce. A young colored graduate of one of our great Northern institutions went to teach economics at a Southern Negro school with Negro teachers. He stayed a little over a year and resigned. He writes:

You know the superstitions and orthodoxies by which even the so-called higher institutions among us are bound; and how skeptical administrators—white and black—view liberal thought among the faculty. A liberal on the faculty of the average Negro college usually succumbs to his orthodox environment or leaves the class in disgust. Were the liberal individual the only victim, the situation would not be worth such serious attention as some of us think necessary. The fact of the matter is that the cultural development of the Negro people is bound up inextricably with the life or death of liberalism in the various universities and colleges.

In Missouri an attempt was made to reorganize on broader lines Lincoln University, an institution founded by colored soldiers after the Civil War. A graduate of Atlanta University was made president and began the rebuilding. He had hardly started, however, when the politicians, colored and white, camped on his trail and but for the vote of the white State superintendent of education he would have been summarily dismissed this year without a hearing. The action of the State superintendent delayed the matter and black Missouri protested so vehemently that Nathan Young is still working at his difficult job.

Let us turn now from the Negro colleges to the white colleges. Throughout the South and, with one or two exceptions, in the border States, no Negro can be admitted to a white college. This means not separation; it means depriving Negroes of the best advantages of higher training. The State of Georgia, for instance, spends $655,135 for the higher training of its white youth and $10,000 for the higher training of its colored youth.

In Northern institutions for the most part Negroes are not denied admission. Princeton, while it shuffles and refuses to make a clear statement, has never admitted a Negro to its college department although it has had Negroes in the theological school. Yale has never encouraged their attendance. Harvard used to encourage them until their number began to grow. Vassar has graduated but one Negro student and did not know it at the time. Bryn Mawr and Barnard have tried desperately to exclude them. Radcliffe, Wellesley, and Smith have treated them with tolerance and even cordiality. Many small institutions or institutions with one or two Negro students have been gracious and kindly toward them, particularly in the Middle West. But on the whole, the attitude of the Northern institution toward the Negro student is one which varies from tolerance to active hostility.

In later years the tendency toward hostility has increased. This is because of the overcrowding of colleges, which has made them seek for pretexts to exclude prospective students, and because of the increase in the number of Negro applicants. In cases where colored students are received, effort is often made to segregate and insult them in various ways. They have been forced to establish their own fraternities, and even when their fraternities are established, are of national scope and of good standing certain universities the University of Michigan for instance, refuse representation of colored fraternities on the Interfraternity Council.

Almost all Catholic institutions refuse to accept Negro students. There is not, I am told, a single colored candidate for the priesthood in a regular Catholic theological seminary and of the Catholic colleges only Fordham and Detroit admit Negroes.

In social affairs within white colleges discrimination has naturally been rife; for, first of all, what is a social affair? And what is social equality? Is it social equality for Negro and white students to sit in the same classrooms; or to eat in the college commons; or to room in the same dormitories; or to join the same clubs or fraternities; or to attend the class and college dances? Different institutions have drawn the line at different places. Williams has recently tried to force a colored boy out of its college dining room. Harvard tried to keep colored boys out of its freshman dormitories. Michigan asked colored students to leave a university dance.

But it was left for Johns Hopkins to carry segregation to its furthest extent. Johns Hopkins gives extension courses and one of the courses was chosen by the teachers of Wilmington, Delaware. Among these teachers were twenty-four colored teachers. Immediately they were notified by the authorities of Johns Hopkins that these colored teachers could not be admitted to the extension courses. All of the teachers, both colored and white, thereupon refused to take the course!

The whole problem resolves itself to this fundamental question: Do we want Negroes educated according to their ability and with the aim of making them independent, self-directing, modern men or are we determined still to educate them as a subordinate caste? Upon the way in which we answer this question depends our interpretation of the problems presented above.

CHAPTER NINETEEN

The Negro College

In 1933, Thomas E. Jones was appointed president of Fisk University. Du Bois came back to Fisk to speak. Jones must have viewed his coming with a certain degree of nervousness since the two previous times Du Bois had spoken at Fisk had led to the resignation of the school's presidents. Du Bois explained to Jones that he had no desire to prolong his career as a "Fisk kingmaker" (Aptheker 1973, 82). Instead, he wanted an opportunity to "guide in general" the direction of Negro colleges and universities.

Both Carter Woodson, a Howard University historian, and Du Bois had come to the conclusion during the 1930s that blacks had been systematically "miseducated" in the United States of America. As a solution to this problem, Du Bois laid out a culturally based and "Afro-centric" educational model, one in which the black or Negro school:

> seeks from a beginning of the history of the Negro in America and in Africa to interpret all history; from a beginning of social development among Negro slaves and freedmen in America and Negro tribes and kingdoms in Africa, to interpret and understand the social development of all mankind in all ages. It seeks to reach modern science of matter and life from the surroundings and habits and aptitudes of American Negroes and thus lead up to understanding of life and matter in the universe. (page 247 of this book)

Du Bois argued that the universal, and seemingly neutral, university of the type proposed by Abraham Flexner earlier in the century was not appropriate for blacks. Instead, he maintained that the Negro college or university was uniquely shaped by the black experience. As he explained:

> a Negro university in the United States of America begins with Negroes. It uses that variety of the English idiom which they understand; and above all, it is founded or it should be founded on a knowledge of the history of their people in Africa and in the United States, and their present condition. Without whitewashing or translating wish into fact, it begins with that; and then it asks how shall these young men and women be trained to earn a

living and live a life under the circumstances in which they find themselves or with such changing of those circumstances as time and work and determination will permit. (page 246 of this book)

Du Bois was highly pragmatic in his approach. He believed that segregation was the reality of life in the United States.

We are segregated; we are a caste. This is our given and at present unalterable fact. Our problem is how far and in what way can we consciously and scientifically guide our future so as to ensure our physical survival, our spiritual freedom and our social growth? Either we do this or we die.There is no alternative. (page 251 of this book)

In the end, the Negro college and university would be the command center for the war against American racism.

It has been said many times that a Negro University is nothing more and nothing less than a university. Quite recently one of the great leaders of education in the United States, Abraham Flexner, said something of that sort concerning Howard. As President of the Board of Trustees, he said he was seeking to build not a Negro university, but a University. And by those words he brought again before our eyes the ideal of a great institution of learning which becomes a center of universal culture. With all good will toward them that say such words— it is the object of this paper to insist that there can be no college for Negroes which is not a Negro college and that while an American Negro university, just like a German or Swiss university may rightly aspire to a universal culture unhampered by limitations of race and culture, yet it must start on the earth where we sit and not in the skies whither we aspire. May I develop this thought.

In the first place, we have got to remember that here in America, in the year 1933, we have a situation which cannot be ignored. There was a time when it seemed as though we might best attack the Negro problem by ignoring its most unpleasant features. It was not and is not yet in good taste to speak generally about certain facts which characterize our situation in America. We are politically hamstrung. We have the greatest difficulty in getting suitable and remunerative work. Our education is more and more not only being confined to our own schools but to a segregated public school system far below the average of the nation with one-third of our children continuously out of school. And above all, and this we like least to mention, we suffer social ostracism which is so deadening and discouraging that we are compelled either to lie about it or to turn our faces to the red flag of revolution. It consists of studied and repeated and emphasized public insult of the sort which during all the long history of the world has led men to kill or be killed. And in the full face of any effort which any black man may make to escape this ostracism for himself, stands this flaming sword of racial doctrine which will distract his effort and energy if it does not lead him to spiritual suicide.

We boast and have right to boast of our accomplishment between the days that I studied here and this forty-fifth anniversary of my graduation. It is a calm appraisal of fact to say that the history of modern civilization cannot surpass if it can parallel the advance of American Negroes in every essential line of culture in these years. And yet, when we have said this we must have the common courage honestly to admit that every step we have made forward has been greeted by a step backward on the part of the American public in caste intolerance, mob law, and racial hatred.

I need but remind you that when I graduated from Fisk there was no "Jim Crow" car in Tennessee and I saw Hunter of '89 once sweep a brakeman aside at the Union Station and escort a crowd of Fisk students into the first-class seats for which they had paid. There was no legal disfranchisement and a black Fiskite sat in the Legislature; and while the Chancellor of the Vanderbilt University had annually to be reintroduced to the President of Fisk, yet no white Southern group presumed to dictate the internal social life of this institution.

Manifestly with all that can be said, pro and con, and in extenuation, and by way of excuse and hope, this is the situation and we know it. There is no human way by which these facts can be ignored. We cannot do our daily work, sing a song or write a book or carry on a university and act as though these things were not.

If this is true, then no matter how much we may dislike the statement, the American Negro problem is and must be the center of the Negro American university. It has got to be. You are teaching Negroes. There is no use pretending that you are teaching Chinese, or that you are teaching white Americans or that you are teaching citizens of the world. You are teaching American Negroes in 1933, and they are the subjects of a caste system in the Republic of the United States of America and their life problem is primarily this problem of caste.

Upon these foundations, therefore, your university must start and build. Nor is the thing so entirely unusual or unheard of as it sounds. A university in Spain is not simply a university. It is a Spanish university. It is a university located in Spain. It uses the Spanish language. It starts with Spanish history and makes conditions in Spain the starting point of its teaching. Its education is for Spaniards—not for them as they may be or ought to be, but as they are with their present problems and disadvantages and opportunities.

In other words, the Spanish university is founded and grounded in Spain, just as surely as a French university is French. There are some people who have difficulty in apprehending this very clear truth. They assume, for instance, that the French university is in a singular sense universal, and is based on a comprehension and inclusion of all mankind and of their problems. But it is not so, and the assumption that it is arises simply because so much of French culture has been built into universal civilization. A French university is founded in France; it uses the French language and assumes a knowledge of French history. The present problems of the French people are its major problems and it becomes universal only so far as other peoples of the world comprehend and are at one with France in its mighty and beautiful history.

In the same way, a Negro university in the United States of America begins with Negroes. It uses that variety of the English idiom which they understand; and above all, it is founded or it should be founded on a knowledge of the history of their people in Africa and in the United States, and their present condition. Without whitewashing or translating wish into fact, it begins with that; and then it asks how shall these young men and women be trained to earn a living and live a life under the circumstances in which they find themselves or with such changing of those circumstances as time and work and determination will permit.

Is this statement of the field of a Negro university a denial of aspiration or a change from older ideals? I do not think it is, although I admit in my own mind some change of thought and modification of method. The system of learning which bases itself upon the actual condition of certain classes and groups of human beings is tempted to suppress a minor premise of fatal menace. It proposes that the knowledge given and the methods pursued in such institutions of learning shall be for the definite object of perpetuating present conditions or of leaving their amelioration in the hands of and at the initiative of other forces and other folk. This was the great criticism that those of us who fought for higher education of Negroes thirty years ago, brought against the industrial school.

The industrial school founded itself and rightly upon the actual situation of American Negroes and said: "What can be done to change this situation?" And its answer was: "A training in technique and method such as would incorporate the disadvantaged group into the industrial organization of the country," and in that organization the leaders of the Negro had perfect faith. Since that day the industrial machine has cracked and groaned. Its technique has changed faster than any school could teach; the relations of capital and labor have increased in complication and it has become so clear that Negro poverty is not primarily caused by ignorance of technical knowledge that the industrial school has almost surrendered its program.

In opposition to that, the opponents of college training in those earlier years said: "What black men need is the broader and more universal training so that they can apply the general principle of knowledge to the particular circumstances of their condition."

Here again was the indubitable truth but incomplete truth. The technical problem lay in the method of teaching this broader and more universal truth and here just as in the industrial program, we must start where we are and not where we wish to be. As I said a few years ago at Howard University, both these positions had thus something of truth and right. Because of the peculiar economic situation in our country the program of the industrial school came to grief first and has practically been given up. Starting even though we may with the actual condition of the Negro peasant and artisan, we cannot ameliorate his condition simply by learning a trade which is the technique of a passing era. More vision and knowledge are needed than that. But on the other hand, while the Negro college of a generation ago set down a defensible and true program of applying knowledge to facts, it unfortunately could not completely carry it out, and it did not carry it out, because the one thing that the industrial philosophy gave to education, the Negro college did not take and that was that the university education of black men in the United States must be grounded in the condition and work of those black men!

On the other hand, it would be of course idiotic to say, as the former industrial philosophy almost said, that so far as most black men are concerned education must stop with this. No, starting with present conditions and using the facts and the knowledge of the present situation of American Negroes, the Negro university expands toward the possession and the conquest of all knowledge. It seeks from a beginning of the history of the Negro in America and in Africa to interpret all history; from a beginning of social development among Negro slaves and freedmen in America and Negro tribes and kingdoms in Africa, to interpret and understand the social development of all mankind in all ages. It seeks to reach modern science of matter and life from the surroundings and habits and aptitudes of American Negroes and thus lead up to understanding of life and matter in the universe.

And this is a different program than a similar function would be in a white university or in a Russian university or in an English university, because it starts from a different point. It is a matter of beginnings and integrations of one group which sweep instinctive knowledge and inheritance and current reactions into a universal world of science, sociology, and art. In no other way can the American Negro college function. It cannot begin with history and lead to Negro history. It cannot start with sociology and lead to Negro sociology.

Why was it that the Renaissance of literature which began among Negroes ten years ago has never taken real and lasting root? It was because it was a transplanted and exotic thing. It was a literature written for the benefit of white people and at the behest of white readers, and starting out privately from the white point of view. It never had a real Negro constituency and it did not grow out of the inmost heart and frank experience of Negroes; on such an artificial basis no real literature can grow.

On the other hand, if starting in a great Negro university you have knowledge, beginning with the particular, and going out to universal comprehension and unhampered expression, you are going to begin to realize for the American Negro the full life which is denied him now. And then after that comes a realization of the older object of our college—to bring this universal culture down and apply it to the individual life and individual conditions of living Negroes.

The university must become not simply a center of knowledge but a center of applied knowledge and guide of action. And this is all the more necessary now since we easily see that planned action especially in economic life, is going to be the watchword of civilization. If the college does not thus root itself in the group life and afterward apply its knowledge and culture to actual living, other social organs must replace the college in this function. A strong, intelligent family life may adjust the student to higher culture; and, too, a social clan may receive the graduate and induct him into life. This has happened and is happening among a minority of privileged people. But it costs society a fatal price. It tends to hinder progress and hamper change; it makes education propaganda for things as they are. It leaves the mass of those without family training and without social standing misfits and rebels who despite their education are uneducated in its meaning and application. The only college which stands for the progress of all, mass as well as aristocracy, functions in root and blossom as well as in the overshadowing and heaven-filling tree. No system of learning—no university can be universal before it is German, French, Negro. Grounded in inexorable fact and condition, in Poland, Italy, or elsewhere, it may seek the universal and happily it may find it—and finding it, bring it down to earth and us.

We have imbibed from the surrounding white world a childish idea of progress. Progress means bigger and better results always and forever. But there is no such rule of life. In six thousand years of human culture, the losses and retrogressions have been enormous. We have no assurance this twentieth century civilization will survive. We do not know that American Negroes will survive. There are sinister signs about us, antecedent to and unconnected with the Great Depression. The organized might of industry North and South is relegating the Negro to the edge of survival and using him as a labor reservoir on starvation wage. No secure professional class, no science, literature, nor art can live on such a subsoil. It is an insistent, deep-throated cry for rescue, guidance, and organized advance that greets the black leader today, and the college that trains him has got to let him know at least as much about the great black miners' strike in Alabama as about the age of Pericles.

We are on the threshold of a new era. Let us not deceive ourselves with outworn ideals of wealth and servants and luxuries, reared on a foundation of ignorance, starvation, and want. Instinctively, we have absorbed these ideals from our twisted white American environment. This new economic planning is not for us unless we do it. Unless the American Negro today, led by trained university men of broad vision, sits down to work out by economics and mathematics, by physics and chemistry, by history and sociology, exactly how and where he is to earn a living and how he is to establish a reasonable Life in the United States or elsewhere—unless this is done, the university has missed its field and function and the American Negro is doomed to be a suppressed and inferior caste in the United States for incalculable time.

Here, then, is a job for the American Negro university. It cannot be successfully ignored or dodged without the growing menace of disaster. I lay the problem before you as one which you must not ignore.

To carry out this plan, two things and only two things are necessary—teachers and students. Buildings and endowments may help, but they are not indispensable. It is necessary first to have teachers who comprehend this program and know how to make it live among their students. This is calling for a good deal, because it asks that teachers teach that which they have learned in no American school and which they never will learn until we have a Negro university of the sort that I am envisioning. No teacher, black or white, who comes to a university like Fisk, filled simply with general ideas of human culture or general knowledge of disembodied science, is going to make a university of this school. Because a university is made of human beings, learning of the things they do not know from the things they do know in their own lives.

And secondly, we must have students. They must be chosen for their ability to learn. There is always the temptation to assume that the children of the privileged classes—the rich, the noble, the white—are those who can best take education. One has but to express this to realize its utter futility. But perhaps the most dangerous thing among us is for us, without thought, to imitate the white world and assume that we can choose students at Fisk because of the amount of money which their parents have happened to get hold of. That basis of selection is going to give us an extraordinary aggregation. We want, by the nicest methods possible, to seek out the talented and the gifted among our constituency, quite regardless of their wealth or position, and to fill this university and similar institutions with persons who have got brains enough to take fullest advantage of what the university offers. There is no other way. With teachers who know what they are teaching and whom they are teaching, and the life that surrounds both the knowledge and the knower, and with students who have the capacity and the will to absorb this knowledge, we can build the sort of Negro university which will emancipate not simply the black folk of the United States, but those white folk who in their effort to suppress Negroes have killed their own culture.

Men in their desperate effort to replace equality with caste and to build inordinate wealth on a foundation of abject poverty have succeeded in killing democracy, art, and religion.

Only a universal system of learning rooted in the will and condition of the masses and blossoming from that manure up toward the stars is worth the name. Once built it can only grow as it brings down sunlight and starshine and impregnates the mud.

The chief obstacle in this rich land endowed with every national resource and with the abilities of a hundred different peoples—the chief and only obstacle to the coming of that kingdom of economic equality which is the only logical end of work, is the determination of the white world to keep the black world poor and make themselves rich. The disaster which this selfish and shortsighted policy has brought lies at the bottom of this present depression, and too, its cure lies beside it. Your clear vision of a world without wealth, of capital without profit, of income based on work alone, is the path out not only for you but for all men.

Is not this a program of segregation, emphasis of race, and particularism as against national unity and universal humanity? It is and it is not by choice but by force; you do not get humanity by wishing it nor do you become American citizens simply because you want to. A Negro university, from its high ground of unfaltering facing of the truth, from its unblinking stare at hard facts does not advocate segregation by race; it simply accepts the bald fact that we are segregated, apart, hammered into a separate unity by spiritual intolerance and legal sanction backed by mob law, and that this separation is growing in strength and fixation; that it is worse today than a half century ago and that no character, address, culture, or desert is going to change it in our day or for centuries to come. Recognizing this brute fact, groups of cultured, trained and devoted men gathering in great institutions of learning proceed to ask, What are we going to do about it? It is silly to ignore the gloss of truth; it is idiotic to proceed as though we were white or yellow, English or Russian. Here we stand. We are American Negroes. It is beside the point to ask whether we form a real race. Biologically we are mingled of all conceivable elements, but race is psychology, not biology; and psychologically we are a unified race with one history, one red memory, and one revolt. It is not ours to argue whether we will be segregated or whether we ought to be a caste. We are segregated; we are a caste. This is our given and at present unalterable fact. Our problem is how far and in what way can we consciously and scientifically guide our future so as to ensure our physical survival, our spiritual freedom and our social growth? Either we do this or we die. There is no alternative. If America proposed the murder of this group, its moral descent into imbecility and crime and its utter loss of manhood, self-assertion, and courage, the sooner we realize this the better. By that great line of McKay:

"If we must die, let it not be like hogs."

But the alternative of not dying like hogs is not that of dying or killing like snarling dogs. It is rather conquering the world by thought and brain and plan; by expression and organized cultural ideals. Therefore let us not beat futile wings in impotent frenzy, but carefully plan and guide our segregated life, organize in industry and politics to protect it and expand it and above all to give it unhampered spiritual expression in art and literature. It is the counsel of fear and cowardice to say this cannot be done. What must be can be and it is only a question of science and sacrifice to bring the great consummation.

What that will be, no one knows. It may be a great physical segregation of the world along the color line; it may be an economic rebirth which ensures spiritual and group integrity amid physical diversity. It may be utter annihilation of class and race and color barriers in one ultimate mankind differentiated by talent, susceptibility and gift— but any of these ends are matters of long centuries and not years. We live in years, swift-flying, transient years. We hold the possible future in our hands but not by wish and will, only by thought, plan, knowledge, and organization. If the college can pour into the coming age an American Negro who knows himself and his plight and how to protect himself and fight race prejudice, then the world of our dream will come and not otherwise.

CHAPTER TWENTY

The Future of Wilberforce University

Du Bois delivered the following commencement address at Wilberforce University in 1940. The speech was subsequently published later in the year in the *Journal of Negro Education*.

Du Bois had taught for two years at Wilberforce at the beginning of his career. He met his wife, Nina Gomer, there. His appointment was to teach Latin and Greek. He was replacing the distinguished classicist William Sander Scarborough, who had been fired by the school for his outspokenness. Du Bois had thought that he would assist Scarborough in his work—not suddenly be made head of the department. The school, which was devoutly religious (A. M. E. Church), was clearly a bad fit for someone of Du Bois's temperament and interests. As indicated in the speech that follows, he did not conform to the school's conservative philosophy, or to its expectation that he would actively participate in its religious life.

As was the case in 1908 and 1924 speeches at Fisk, Du Bois was merciless in his criticism of Wilberforce. Summarizing the situation at the school, he explained how, in his opinion:

> The quality of educational work done here for more than half a century has never until recently received recognition as being in accord with the standards of the nation. You have not so established yourself in this country as to make it unnecessary for a first-class student to apologize for attending Wilberforce University rather than Ohio State or the University of Chicago. You have been content for a half century to do second-grade work and to make voluminous and frequent excuses therefore. (page 256 of this book)

Du Bois argued that the school should be a center of academic excellence and leadership—a focal point for the advancement of blacks in the region and the nation.

In this context, Du Bois's speech echoes his earlier call for Negro colleges and universities to be centers for black studies and advancement. While this is an obvious role for such schools in our own time, Du Bois's position flew in the face of conservative educational practice in his era.

I first saw Wilberforce University in September, 1894. Only two months previously I had returned from the University of Berlin and had finished here and there a continuous education which lasted from my sixth to my twenty-sixth birthday. I was at the time full of ideals, quick and arrogant in judgment, with many personal idiosyncrasies. I walked on to this campus, carrying my gloves in one hand and my cane in the other, according to the best fashion of the German student of that day. Yet I was not altogether impossible; I was comparatively indifferent, for instance, to the matter of money. This was the first salaried job that I had ever held and yet I refused an offer of $1,050 at another institution for the $800 offered here, because Wilberforce meant something to my imagination. I had heard its name since I was a child. On May 24, 1856, one of the midnight endorsers who made the purchase of Wilberforce possible, was John DuBois a member of a family from which I descend.

I taught at Wilberforce two years: Greek, Latin, German, and English and begged in vain to add Sociology to the load; I married a Wilberforce girl; I made here life-long friends like Paul Laurence Dunbar and Charles Young; and for the forty-six years since my first coming, I have known every president of Wilberforce University and visited the campus at least once during their administrations and in some cases many times. At one of the sessions of the older Board of Trustees I was elected an honorary alumnus.

Notwithstanding all this, I was from the moment I stepped on this campus until today, an outspoken critic of Wilberforce. This was true not because I disbelieved in Wilberforce or underrated its work, but for exactly the opposite reason. From the first, I had for Wilberforce the very highest ideals: I wanted for it nothing cheap, second hand, or inferior; I pictured growing up here a great university, not simply Negro, not simply American, but a university in the full sense of those famous institutions of learning with which I had been connected for six years in the United States and in Europe. With all the impetuosity of youth, I had not the slightest doubt of the possibility of building up such an institution. I can imagine the astonishment with which persons heard my first lecture here. It was a sort of inaugural address after the German fashion, attending my advent as professor, in which I outlined with perfect confidence the plan of an institution, unlimited in breadth and efficiency.

My dreams were not wholly built on air. I took into account the extraordinary geographical situation of Wilberforce: practically in the longitudinal center of the Negro population of the United States, and yet in latitude North of Mason and Dixon's line. I was thrilled by the natural beauty of this place and uplifted by the romantic history of its founding. Because of this very dream and high ideal, I was from the first bitter and uncompromising at every act which did not agree with, and every plan that did not lead toward, the sort of institution I had in mind.

I Leave Wilberforce

The result was that after only two years' experiment I left Wilberforce. I was not kicked out, but that was only because I moved before the inevitable swing of the boot. Eventual dismissal was certain and I had sense enough to see it. But notwithstanding that, my interest in this school instead of waning, if anything, increased; my criticism of its shortcomings has never ceased and equally I have never lost my belief in its possibilities.

I come, therefore, again, in my role of open and frank critic of Wilberforce University and in an attempt to guide its possible future. I would have you believe that there lurks in what I am going to say, nothing of personal pique or disappointment. There is nothing that I desire of Wilberforce University. I have no scores to settle. For the most part those with whom I was intimately associated while here are long since dead. Some few of the teachers I do know but for the most part I have not seen or heard from them for near a decade. In a sense then I come both as an old friend and yet to most of you as a stranger; but to all as one who knows the history of Wilberforce University, who has followed this history with intense and vivid interest and who speaks with only one idea in mind that, rising out of the muddle and dispute, failure and promise of the present situation, there should eventually arise a Wilberforce which would be recognized by any standard as one of the great institutions of learning in the United States.

The Present Plight

As you know quite as well as I, this is not the case today. I am deeply disappointed that it is not. Even as I left here as a teacher in the summer of 1896, I firmly believed that a half century would see the institution established in accord with some of the ideals that I had and had expressed. This has not happened. I come back forty-six years after to find the institution still desperately lacking in most things that a great university demands.

The scientific output of this institution in books and articles, in literature and art, in technical efficiency and economic organization falls so far below the standard of great schools that one searches almost in vain for tangible evidence of scientific work done by Wilberforce professors and graduates. There are some to be sure but they stand out in the midst of a great desert. You have not produced great scholars or scientists, great technicians nor great thinkers, and yet there is no earthly reason why you should not have done this. Let me illustrate by the case of one of the smaller colored colleges. In two decades of work between 1919 and 1939 the teachers and graduates of West Virginia State College published thirty-three books and monographs, one hundred fifty-five articles and prepared thirty-one unpublished manuscripts, a total of two hundred nineteen pieces of scientific work which is, if I mistake not, at least ten times the output of Wilberforce. One encouraging effort in recent days, the *Wilberforce University Quarterly*, I hailed with new hope, but I fear now this will be a casualty of the late war. The quality of educational work done here for more than half a century has never until recently received recognition as being in accord with the standards of the nation. You have not so established yourself in this country as to make it unnecessary for a first-class student to apologize for attending Wilberforce University rather than Ohio State or the University of Chicago. You have been content for a half century to do second-grade work and to make voluminous and frequent excuses therefore.

In addition to this, and perhaps in a sense even more significant, is the situation of this surrounding community. Forty years ago, Xenia was an important manufacturing and commercial center. Wilberforce was a prosperous farming district. One had a right to believe in 1895 that the middle of the twentieth century would see here in Southern Ohio, a thriving economic center with prosperous manufactures and commercial enterprises and with a large and growing colored community here of home owners, farmers, merchants, scientists, and technicians; not only comfortable and self-supporting but a respected and integral part of the economic and social organization of the Middle West. I know the blighting effect of war and depression and the difficulties of economic maladjustment and race prejudice; and yet it seems to me that it apparently has not occurred to this community that any development of the sort was possible under Wilberforce leadership. In appearance and character, in occupation and ambition, the Wilberforce community looks like a center of stagnation, lack of ambition, and, in a certain chilling sense, lack of hope. The surrounding country and Xenia have deteriorated; and when a few weeks ago I wanted to get a through-train from Chicago to Xenia the nearest I could get was Dayton. That would have been a joke in 1900. On the other hand, the physical expansion of Wilberforce as a school has been great in the amount of land controlled, in the number of buildings, in the size of its student body. Buildings like this hall, like the library, and like several of the dormitories are striking evidence of growth; and yet even here you who have seen the marvelous physical expansion that has taken place in other Negro institutions throughout this country know that Wilberforce is behind. In the growth of its faculty, in the caliber of its teaching and facilities for teaching Wilberforce has also grown but here it has lagged far behind similar institutions.

The Ravine

There is one other thing that may seem to you unimportant and aside but it looms to vast size in my thought; and that is, the way in which you have conceived and the way in which you have treated, the natural beauty of your surroundings. Here is a lovely undulating land with beautiful trees, grass and wild flowers, with roads winding naturally between the hills and with little brooks and rivers murmuring day and night through broad meadows. As it seems to me you have looked upon this beauty as a thing to be leveled, flattened, and scarred. That your ideal would be something slick and square, with brooks hushed, rivers put underground and hills pressed down into the earth. Consider, for instance, the ravine, one of the loveliest natural possibilities of Greene County. It begins with the old main road of Wilberforce and stretches down, widening and deepening to the green meadows and river below. It is a God-created center of natural beauty and development, a potential amphitheatre, a focus around which a university could be ranged, set in the very midst of this community. It was this murmuring vale of healing waters that back in the early nineteenth century attracted people of leisure to Tawawa Springs to drink in its crystal clarity and loll in leisure under the great branches of its oaks and elms. Since then this community has done everything that it could to shame and obliterate the ravine. In my day already they were using it as a refuse dump. Later they made it the center of a sewage disposal area; but recently they have piled mud in its center to make an extra road. I can remember how once as young teachers protesting against the beginning of profanation of this marvelous beauty spot, we planned to give Shakespeare's "Midsummer Night's Dream" in the ravine, ranging the auditors upon its sloping sides and playing in its flower-covered depths. We wanted to raise money for a library. The library in 1896 occupied a room half the size of this rostrum. It was kept locked. I chased Professor Scott over this campus for a week to get the key. We determined to transfer the library to the little-used double parlors and to raise funds for this by this pageant in the ravine. The way our plan was stopped was prophetic a powerful bishop in 1896 had decided to appoint his good-for-nothing son as a professor in this school. We stopped our midsummer night's dream to stage a strike and protest. In the end we won temporarily; the eventual loss of our jobs became merely a matter of time.

Reasons for Failure

Why now has Wilberforce failed as an institution of learning to reach the heights toward which it must eventually climb if it survives, and why as a community has it failed to become neat, prosperous, beautiful, and self-supporting? You know the answer which the average white citizen of Ohio gives to this question: he simply says "Negroes!" That would not disturb me so much in itself, were it not for the fact that the average colored citizen of the nation is coming to say the same thing. Literally dozens among the best Negroes of Ohio with whom in recent years I have talked concerning Wilberforce have all come to the fatalistic conclusion that you cannot expect an ideal development in education or community life here simply because colored people are in control. If I believed that I would not be here. But I do not believe it. And I do not believe it, because I have had opportunity in the last quarter century to see at first hand the kind of development which is taking place in Negro institutions of learning where the same problems that you face here are being attacked and solved.

I have already told you that when I was offered work at Wilberforce University, a position at what was then Lincoln Institute in Jefferson City, Missouri, was open for me. I refused the larger salary offered there because Lincoln Institute at the time was the well-known plaything of graft and petty politics. The president of the Institute could only hold his job by handing over to members of the Trustee Board a part of the money which the Institute was overcharged by the merchants who sold it supplies. Appointments to positions in the Institute were matters of petty political deals, personal likes and dislikes, and pool-room politics. There were no standards of instruction or educational accomplishment, and there were cheap buildings with a small enrollment of students who came because they could go nowhere else. Today Lincoln University of Missouri is not yet reborn but its birth pains are distinctly audible. It has driven partisan politics out of the institution. It has killed several presidents in the process but the deed is about done. It has secured a steadily increasing income, more adequately paid professors, new buildings, and better prepared students.

I saw last year the Florida A. and M. College at Tallahassee after an interval of twenty-five years. I was astonished. From a ramshackle agglomeration of few buildings, few teachers, and indifferent students it has today magnificent buildings and a thousand college students; and while its salaries are still too low and its standards of scholarship not as high as they must be, it is a growing and developing college. The same can be said of Virginia State College at Petersburg; the thoughtful planning of that campus, the disappearance of the eye-sore which was long its main building, and the number of well-trained men who have regularly and consistently been appointed to the faculty and given security of tenure and encouragement for graduate study and scientific work, is one of the finest pieces of academic accomplishment in the South.

The possible relation of a college to its community is illustrated at Prairie View, Texas. So astonishing has been this development that when recently a white president of a great Northwestern state wanted to know how his institution could best get into helpful touch with its community, the trustees of the General Education Board referred him to the Texas Colored State College at Prairie View. The president of that college is in close connection with every secondary school in the state; he has records of every Negro student about to be graduated from every high school in Texas; he is continuously studying the economic condition of colored folk in every part of the state; he is bringing them regularly to Prairie View for conference and discussion at the rate of over ten thousand actual visitors a year. Adjoining the campus is today being developed a settlement of a score of one hundred forty-acre farms, financed by the Federal Government, and for that settlement, industry and occupations outside of farming and teaching are already being carefully planned and carried out.

Or suppose we turn to some of the older institutions: Fisk, Howard, and Atlanta University. A record of the books and articles published by professors and graduates of these institutions in the last year form a contribution to American literature recognized over the whole country. These books are reviewed in the leading periodicals of the nation; the research of their laboratories is recognized even in Europe; the standards of scholarly accomplishment are being set just as high as those in white institutions. In other words, what can be done at Wilberforce is already being done by colored folk in all parts of the nation and in no case have these people had the natural and geographical advantages, the social freedom, and the political power that you have here.

The History of Wilberforce

Not in race nor character, not in ability nor power do the failures of Wilberforce find root. What are then the main reasons of the difficulties which have beset your path? We ourselves in moments of depression are prone to blame our blood for every failure and misfortune, but to know the truth we must address ourselves first to the historical rise of this institution and see what obstacles it has encountered and how it has tried to surmount them and what the results of these efforts in our day have been.

Looking into the historical threads that were woven into the web of this institution I can descry three sets of human beings whose efforts have made Wilberforce and who have been responsible in large part for its successes and its failures. First came three extraordinary figures: Daniel Payne, John Mitchell, and Benjamin Lee. If ever three saints strove without thought of self and with utter devotion to the highest ideals which they could conceive to build here a worthy monument for your worship, these were the men. Two of them I knew personally and one died but the year before I came to Wilberforce, leaving a memory singularly vivid and green. It is not often that it is given any group of human beings to command the services of three such men. Daniel Payne, the little bishop, short, slight, shriveled, was a man of plodding learning, of austere personal morality, of unflinching firmness and indefatigable energy; no thought of himself or of his own interest ever stood for a moment between him and what he thought best for Wilberforce University, for the African Methodist Church, and for the Negro race. John G. Mitchell, large, calm and placid, starved for thirty-seven years to make a real theological seminary here, living always serenely above the clouds, with a firm and unshakeable belief in a higher world and in its intimate causal relations with this earth. Benjamin Lee came later. He was a more practical man who knew evil, looked it squarely in the face, and fought it doggedly; he was intensely earnest; solemn in soul and action, impatient of dishonesty, greed and sensuality, and always striving desperately to do and make others do what seemed to him exactly the right thing. With these three men, this college started on a high and ideal plane with little money but with great and unselfish hopes.

There came afterward, connected in various ways with this institution and with the church, three hammers: powerful, ambitious but ruthless men who represented force and driving power unhampered by ideals; who had no inhibitions of learning or social standards but drove a way through all sorts of obstacles; and under their leadership both the church and the school lurched now forward and now back. Contemporaneous with these and later were three politicians, who represented compromise and adjustment. They were victims rather than leaders; they were the buffers between Ideals and Power, Good and Evil, Theory and Practice. They handled the Church and the State, the public and the school, the teachers and the students. Some were gifted men who had to do unpleasant things and devise devious paths in a crooked world. One man, who belonged to this class of leaders was president of this school when I came, Samuel T. Mitchell.

Samuel Mitchell

Samuel Mitchell faced a most difficult problem. Another sort of man, a man like Payne, John Mitchell, or Lee, would have handled his problem differently. But Samuel Mitchell was more subtle and faced a more complex modern world. He was a small, handsome man with captivating manners. He influenced men; he was extraordinarily successful in conference and personal meeting; he stooped to conquer. He came to the presidency of Wilberforce in 1884 and remained until the last year of the nineteenth century. I once blamed Samuel Mitchell severely for his course of action. But time and experience have explained much if not all. He faced the same problem that you face: how can the church of a poor working people support an increasingly costly system of education? Mitchell worked hard to increase income, and in his administration it rose fifty per cent higher than ever before. But at that it was miserably inadequate. He must get more, but how?

During his day the problem of the church and education was apparently settled but in fact was beginning momentous change. It went without saying, before 1900, that churches should promote education, establish colleges, and conduct universities. The union of church and education seemed in that day logical and almost inevitable. Already, however, the burden of supporting education with limited church funds and expanding church programs was beginning to be felt and the alternative had long seemed to be the accumulation of endowments. Thus most of our greater universities like Harvard, Yale, and Princeton starting as denominational schools gradually accumulated endowment funds sufficient to make them independent of the churches and the connection was gradually severed.

Wilberforce had long kept before her this ideal of endowments but there was no precedent then of rich white folk amply endowing a colored institution and there were no rich Negroes. But poor Negroes tried to relieve this situation by heroic efforts to increase its gifts to education. With the appointment of a secretary of education in 1884, the A. M. E.

Church responded so that in 1900 it was raising $20,000 a year. This was a notable effort. If all the money raised for education in the Church could have been concentered upon Wilberforce, which was Payne's original idea, the situation would have been well in hand. But in 1904, the church educational fund was being distributed among twenty-five institutions, including ten colleges which averaged less than $3,000 a school. Particularism was too strong: every bishop, each district, each state wanted and in a sense needed its school. The cost of raising funds for Wilberforce both in actual money and effort became prohibitive.

Moreover, at this time throughout the nation the state was coming in and beginning to support higher education. This support was not altogether effective because it involved a great deal of petty politics and selfish bargaining and consequently low standards in teaching appointments and in scholarship. No one then could have foreseen that in the course of less than a half century, higher education would be very largely in the hands of the state with the prospect that before long the privately endowed or church supported institution will have largely disappeared.

The Bargain of 1889

Samuel T. Mitchell finding increasing difficulty in raising funds and yet the educational demand expanding, conceived the shrewd bargain of 1889. With his inimitable charm and ability to fascinate and convince, he succeeded in the face of the prohibitions of the state constitution and in spite of the just fears of church leaders, in bringing about a certain sort of union between the State of Ohio and the African Methodist Episcopal Church for the support of Wilberforce. As we can now see, it was a dangerous compromise and the time may come when we will look back upon this as the cause of the eventual collapse of this institution. But that will only be if in the face of the continued friction and upheavals that have followed the bargain, we throw up our hands, refuse to look facts in the face, and fail to grasp the plow that is before us and the real furrow that can yet be run.

What have been the results of this consolidation of the A. M. E. school, Wilberforce University, and the State of Ohio as owner of the combined normal and industrial department at Wilberforce? First of all there has been a serious combination of the church and politics. From 1856 to 1889, Wilberforce had become the political capital of the A. M. E. Church and its nation-wide membership. Here the little Bishop, Daniel Payne, as senior prelate of the church ruled. Power became concentrated in his hands, through his extraordinary moral purity, his unselfish ideals, and his indomitable energy. All of the rulers of the Church came to Wilberforce to consult him; bishops' councils were held here; general officers and general policies were decided upon. The senior bishop knew the characters of everybody in the church: when this man aspired to the bishopric—No, said the little bishop, he is not an honest man! No, he is not a moral man! No, he is lazy and selfish and will not work!

When Bishop Payne died, it meant that what had been an ecclesiastical dictatorship in strong, honest, and unwavering hands became a matter of wide intrigue, manipulation, and political arrangement. The well-being and interests of Wilberforce became inextricably intermingled with the interests, and often the selfish personal interests, of the church leaders. The so-called Board of Trustees of Wilberforce University was a body of hundreds of men distributed all over the United States, only a minority of whom ever came to any meeting and came then, most of them, because of church politics and not because of their interest in Wilberforce.

I remember vividly the first meeting of the Trustees while I was here. As they began to swarm in I took my cane and gloves and went to the woods for a long walk.

"Where have you been?" asked my colleagues.

"To the woods," I answered, innocently.

They threw up their hands. "That's not the thing to do when trustees come to Wilberforce," they said. And they were right.

When now President Mitchell in his effort to raise funds projected this politically-minded Wilberforce into state politics and thus more than doubled the available income of the school, it was natural for ministers, bishops, and presidents of Wilberforce to dabble further in partisan politics until they have helped emphasize that very interference of politics with education which it has been the desperate effort of state universities all over America for fifty years to avoid.

This situation did not however develop immediately in the case of Wilberforce. As Mitchell conceived the consolidation there was to be one head of the combined institutions; the state institution was to be in fact a department of Wilberforce University, although the legal phrase had it "at Wilberforce University."

Politics and Wilberforce

The policy which has developed concerning the relation of the State Department and the University is interesting to review: first came the logical action, back to which the state and the University must revert if this institution is to grow and develop properly; that is, the president of the university was also superintendent of the combined normal and industrial department. This is the only way in which one institution with a single policy can be built up. President Mitchell was at the head of both departments from the beginning of state aid until 1896—seven years.

Such a combination, however, presupposes that the interests of the state as well as the university not only be combined but carefully looked after by the single head, so that neither party to the combination would feel under-rated or cheated. The feeling arose under President Mitchell that the State was being used simply for its money and as an unimportant adjunct to the University.

The next step of the State was characteristic but not radical. It appointed a separate head for the State Department, but chose for the position a man long connected with Wilberforce University, the son of one of its founders and absolutely loyal to its ideals, J. P. Shorter. Shorter was a strict administrator and careful business man, and he supplemented President Mitchell's ability to handle persons and compose differences by his own accuracy and executive methods. This went on for fourteen years, and the two parts of the institution worked in considerable, if not perfect, harmony. The main difficulty which now began to show itself and later was emphasized was that the combined normal and industrial department had more money than the University, and yet was the subordinate partner.

Then, soon after the advent of President Scarborough, there came a momentous change: the State appointed as superintendent a young man well-trained as an educator and also experienced as executive and business man. President Scarborough, on the other hand, was a scholar and a theorist in no way designed for the details of administration and with little liking for it. The inevitable happened; the real presidency of Wilberforce was gradually transferred to the State side. The normal department went forward by leaps and bounds. It bought lands and built buildings; it arranged teachers' homes; it introduced electricity; it organized its curriculum; it paid its teachers good salaries; it developed other far-sighted plans; while the University hung on as a sort of poor relative of the dominant owner and was really largely supported by state charity. When the administrations changed in 1920, and Gregg came as president, while Joyner retired, there came a third policy, irregularly and less clearly developed: the head of the normal department became more and more a mere fiscal officer and neither a trained educator nor a conspicuous executive. This tended to separate the two institutions and friction arose and multiplied. Almost, it can be said, two separate and rival institutions appeared here—one with power and no money, the other with money and no clear policy.

It was almost inevitable during the years from 1900 to 1940 that into this situation petty state politics should begin to intrude, and this was in no small part the fault of the A. M. E. Church and of Wilberforce University itself. From the time that Samuel T. Mitchell found that political manipulation could bring funds to Wilberforce, from that time on the temptation on the part of the Church to work this source was difficult to withstand. Bishops, presiding elders, ministers, and presidents of the institution became politicians and worked for what they thought was either their own advantage or the advantage of Wilberforce. Other colored people in the State not connected with the A. M. E. Church saw no reason why they should not share the spoils. The caliber of the persons appointed to the board by the State gradually decreased. In earlier years, some of the best known people of the State, white and black, served upon the board of the normal and industrial department. They were replaced as time went on by persons who, whatever their other qualifications were, had often never attended college, knew little about college problems, and certainly had not been trained or experienced in the technical work of administering an institution of education.

Throughout the United States it has been found that in state universities, this tendency has had to be met and fought and stopped. In the University of Wisconsin the University of Michigan, the University of Illinois, Indiana University, in all the Negro land-grant colleges, and in other institutions, it has taken the voters a quarter of a century to learn that appointments in an institution of learning cannot be used to reward political support or to give jobs to friends or as matters of personal sympathy.

Educational Ideals

Education is a great and serious end. It has to do primarily not with soils and crops, not with stone and iron, but with the souls of your own children and thus with the future of the Negro race in America. It is becoming one of the greatest functions of government. If it is seduced and cheapened and ruined by putting in charge of it people, who, however worthy they may be personally, are ignorant of the difficult technique of carrying on the training of youth, the whole program is ruined. This is the sort of thing that has happened and is happening to Wilberforce University. Perverted standards have come in. In the eyes of many quite honest people it seems to be natural that the teaching jobs at Wilberforce should be handed around to people whom they like and taken away from people they don't like. The question as to what sort of man one is whether truthful or a liar; dignified or a clown; an earnest worker or a lazy wastrel does not concern them. They do not inquire whether the candidate knows his subject and knows how to teach it. They assume without reflection that there should be appointed to the faculty and upon the trustee board anybody who is a friend to the governor; that if there is a person at Wilberforce or elsewhere who has been unfortunate, who has suffered, who has not received the consideration that he ought to, that a perfectly legitimate way to settle this difficulty is to appoint him professor or dean even though everybody knows he cannot perform his duties because of congenital unfitness or crass ignorance.

Nor do these perverted standards stop here. Indeed they did not begin here. In the case of the Church and the University, it has become a sort of unwritten law that the bishop of this district should be a sort of super-president; that he should rule the University and at the same time dictate to the board of trustees and also enter into political understanding with the State. I remember vividly when Bishop Arnett laid down law and gospel for President Mitchell. This puts the president in an impossible position: he must placate the bishop of Wilberforce; he must be on good terms with bishops of other districts, who are furnishing funds for Wilberforce; he must keep in touch with the officials of the State; he must try to bring into line the man whom the State for any reason, political or personal, appoints at the head of the normal and industrial department; and then incidentally he must keep a faculty and a body of students at their proper tasks. No human being can successfully occupy such a place.

The Path of Progress

Here then is the situation that confronts us. What is to be done about it? When some years ago a talented professor of history in Howard University, Charles Wesley, was considering accepting the presidency of Wilberforce University, I wrote him hurriedly and said: Under no circumstances accept the presidency of Wilberforce unless at the same time you are made head of the combined normal and industrial department.

The path of progress before Wilberforce is clear and inevitable: first there must be one head to this institution. Anything else spells friction, lost effort, and eventual disaster. It will be difficult to bring this about. There will have to be a rearrangement of trustee boards and a new understanding with State officials. This can only be done by a determined effort on the part of the colored people of Ohio, the A. M. E. Church, and Wilberforce University to convince the world that what they want here is not jobs for their friends or religious bigotry or the settlement of personal grudges, but a great institution of learning primarily for the Negro race and eventually for the nation; that to this end they propose to subordinate every selfish interest; that they plan to work in accordance with the best advice of the most influential people of Ohio, white and black; that they will consider no political bargain on the part of either Church or State, but with high and unselfish ends unite to rebuild Wilberforce.

There must be, I repeat, as the beginning of reorganization one head to this combined institution, appointed after thorough consultation and understanding between State and Church and the best educational advice of Ohio. That man must undertake this work as a life-time job and not as a mere stepping-stone on his way to the bishopric. As the best guarantee for this, he would best not be a clergyman at all. But minister or layman, he must hold the scales of perfect justice between the Church on the one hand and the State on the other, handling all funds in method and intent with absolute and unswerving honesty. His controlling board of trustees should be nominated by the Church and appointed by the governor and should represent fairly the interests of the colored people of Ohio and the interests of education in the whole state. In accordance with the best and only rule of administration, this board should confine itself to settling general policy and should leave the appointment and dismissal of teachers to the president and then hold him alone responsible for the good conduct and efficiency of this University.

This calls for a union of high effort. Can you make it? You, the school, the community, the State?

Christianity and Wilberforce

I have noted in your president's report the insistence that Wilberforce University is a Christian institution. This is an old note. It has been sounded again and again with all kinds of variations for nearly a hundred years. It was a matter of emphasis when I was here near a half century ago and it did not impress me. It did not impress me because it was all too evident that what most people at Wilberforce called Christianity was a childish belief in Biblical fairy tales, a word-of-mouth adherence to dogma, and a certain sectarian exclusiveness. It often seemed to me when I lived here a miserable misapprehension of the teaching of Christ. I do not attempt in the slightest way to interfere with anyone's sincere and deep-seated belief. If a man believes that faith in Jonah and the whale is necessary to his soul's salvation, I shall not gainsay him. But I do believe that the generation of young folk before me and the world-at-large have some clear and definite ideas of what real religion calls for and I believe that the citizens of Ohio want tangible proof of certain matters before they will continue to support Wilberforce.

Today, in plain English, if Christianity means anything, it means honesty, unselfishness, and hard work. It means honesty in the handling of funds whether they are the pennies of black washerwomen or the thousands of the State appropriation. It means the absolute wiping out of petty graft, of waste and of stupid carelessness. In addition to this, Christianity means sympathy; the realization of what it costs a human being to live and support a family in decency; the realization that a man cannot do scientific research and scholarly work on a $1,000 a year; the realization that teachers and students are human beings who suffer and strive and fail. Above all, Christianity means unselfishness; the willingness to forego in part one's personal advantage and give up some personal desires for the sake of a larger end which will be for the advantage of a greater number of people. And finally, Love is God and Work is His Prophet.

Frankly, I have never found at Wilberforce University any outstanding evidence of this kind of Christianity. Once upon a time it was here, and that is why I recall the role of the Three Saints who put their lives into this institution. It has since then, time and time again, been openly, crassly, and impudently contradicted by dishonesty, cruelty, and utter selfishness.

May I illustrate: when I was asked to come to Wilberforce in 1894, it was to teach Latin and Greek. I did not know much about them, but I knew that Scarborough was head of the department and I was glad and willing to work under his tutelage. Imagine my astonishment, when I arrived at Wilberforce, to find that I was head of the department; that one of your periodical quarrels had taken place, and the president had transferred Scarborough to the Theological Department to teach nobody for nothing; while I, a student of sociology, was the whole department of Latin and Greek in the University! This illustrates better than anything I can say the utter stupidity of such action. Scarborough may have been a difficult man to get along with. I do not know. But he knew Latin and Greek better than most American teachers. Laying aside all personal likes and dislikes he should have been kept at that job. And the opposite is also true: if he had known no Greek and been a poor teacher and an unworthy man, he certainly did not belong in a theological seminary. To appoint a man to position because of sympathy is just as wrong as to dismiss him from the work he is best fitted to do.

Unless, therefore, the Christianity which you vaunt here is going to be the sort I have described you will have endless difficulty in extricating Wilberforce from its plight. On the other hand, if this institution handles its funds honestly, is sympathetic and decent in the treatment of its teachers and unselfish in the establishment of high aims, and if it can do real scientific work in education; then with one head to the combined institution you have begun reconstruction. But here you cannot sit still. Eventually this preliminary treaty of peace between State and Church must go forward toward a complete and definitive consolidation.

Two Paths to the Future

The first possible path is that the Church gradually withdraw from its present dependence upon the State and establish an independent, self-controlled, and self-supported institution. This appeals to many of you. It is in many respects a great and fine ideal. The difficulty with this program—and the inevitable difficulty—is its cost and the preliminary change in machinery which it involves. Such an institution must become first independent not of but in the Church. The local bishop must loose his stranglehold upon the president. The General Conference and board of bishops must likewise stand aside content with general oversight and refraining from continual interference. The school must cease to be a mere stepping-stone to the bishopric. It must exist for itself. Its own board of trustees must be in supreme control and they must in accordance with universal practice in modern education put the actual executive responsibility upon the president. At the same time that the Church thus withdraws from intermeddling with the institution and that the trustees put on its executive officer responsibility and the power at the same time the Church must furnish vastly increased funds; arid here is the rub. Can the Church do it and will it?

There was once a legend that Mark Hopkins, a log and a boy could constitute a college. That legend is no longer valid. The boy needs today a library and a large and costly library with a competent and well-trained staff—not three over-worked slaves. Without it, he cannot get a modern education. The boy needs laboratories carefully planned, systematically conducted, with materials and tools; and laboratories cost a lot of money. The boy must have not one but a dozen instructors; they must be not merely good men who can read and write, but good men with long, thorough training in the accumulating and widening knowledge of their fields of instruction. For these and a dozen other different reasons the cost of conducting a first class college today as compared with fifty years ago has risen enormously. Ignoring for the moment the millions of dollars a year that are spent at Harvard and Columbia, let us turn our attention to colored colleges remembering that the A. M. E. Church has never been able to raise for education as much as $50,000 in a single year and usually it has raised much less.

As compared with that let us remember that it costs $275,000 a year to run Fisk University; over $300,000 a year to run the Atlanta University system; $365,000 a year to run Virginia State College, while Prairie View College costs $420,000; Southern University of Louisiana cost $650,000 last year; and Howard University costs $1,000,000 a year. It costs huge sums of money to conduct universities today and there is no reason to believe that the cost is going to be less in the future; rather if anything, more.

With the demands upon them today nearly all churches are giving up their attempts to run colleges and universities. The great reunited Methodist Church is practically giving notice to all its institutions that they must prepare to stand alone. The Baptists are following. The Presbyterian Church has taken the same path. An institution like Wilberforce could hardly get from the A.M.E. Church adequate funds, even if the church gave up the other smaller institutions and concentrated upon Wilberforce. Today even that looks impossible. Loyalties have been built around Morris Brown College and Edward Waters College and in most of twenty-five institutions, which makes their closing unthinkable.

Wilberforce will start too late to get much from the distribution of funds now going on under the great foundations, and in addition to that the whole attempt to support higher education even by endowment is made today exceedingly uncertain by the industrial changes brought about partly by world war and partly by far-reaching economic revolution. Millions of dollars of former endowment funds are today worthless from these causes and the future of the endowed college, as I have said before, looks very uncertain.

Wilberforce as a State School

The second possibility is one from which Wilberforce and its constituency has always recoiled but I think you will have to look it straight in the face and that is for Wilberforce University to become a full-fledged state school. There is an example before you of a state colored college to which I beg your careful attention. In 1832, Richard Humphries, a white Quaker, who was once a West Indian slave-owner was living in Philadelphia. On his death he left $10,000 to found an institution for Negroes. Negroes were at that time excluded from the public schools and colleges of that State. His money went to found the Institute for Colored Youth and from that time until after the Civil War, that Institute was one of the best colored high schools of the United States and trained some of our most distinguished leaders The wife of a bishop of this church was long its honored principal.

After the Civil War, however, Negroes were gradually admitted to all the schools and colleges of Pennsylvania. The endowment of the Colored Institute was too small to support it and the attendance not large. The trustees finally moved the school out into the country to Cheyney and established it on an excellent site. Then came the question of support. The new principal, Leslie P. Hill, struggled for years, passing the hat to colored people and white in order to support this school which was now a teacher-training school. He could not get enough money. But the number of his students, attracted by good teaching and pleasant surroundings and repelled from other schools by social ostracism, increased. At last it was clear that either the school must close or the state must support it. Hill, therefore, asked that Cheyney become a recognized state teacher-training school and college.

The colored people of Pennsylvania literally raised hell. They accused Hill of deliberate encouragement of segregation and of an attempt to lower the standard of Negro education. I once went down to Philadelphia to argue in support of Hill's proposition. I shall not soon forget the bitterness with which I was assailed. Nevertheless, Cheyney today is a state college adequately supported from public taxes and perhaps the most beautifully housed of any of our schools with an excellent group of well-paid teachers. Colored students still attend the University of Pennsylvania, the University of Pittsburgh, and the other state normal schools; but in addition to that they attend Cheyney; and the net result of making Cheyney a state school is to my mind thoroughly vindicated.

If Wilberforce should become a state university, it need not and indeed according to the letter of its charter it cannot ever become an exclusively colored school. The charter of Wilberforce University said from the beginning in 1863 "There shall never be any distinction among the trustees, faculty, or students on account of race or color." Added to this comes the constitution of the State of Ohio which prohibits the establishment of a purely racial school.

But there is no reason why an institution of higher learning like Wilberforce University should not be established here depending entirely upon State and Federal appropriations and student fees; that these appropriations instead of being as they are today too small for the establishment of a first-class educational institution become larger and larger, as there is developed here the will and ability to use them in the right way.

There is no reason why a predominantly colored faculty and colored student body should not constitute Wilberforce University and yet gradually raise itself to be the equal in every respect of any institution in this State or in the United States; thus proving to a skeptical generation that color is not connected with ability or honesty. When the time comes in the future, as it may well come, that white persons would be appointed now and then to the teaching force here and white students appear in the student body, it might also happen that colored men would be appointed to the faculty of Ohio State University and colored students continue to be received there, but not as mere outsiders, not as pariahs, but as integral and welcome members of the institution.

I believe that this is the logical and right way to settle the difficulties and recurring upheavals at Wilberforce University. And I believe this because recently in spite of all the difficulties which have faced the university administration it has received from an independent and not over-friendly authority gratifying testimony as to what can be done at this institution, if the institution is organized and can function as a university should.

Educational Recognition

I do not think that the A. M. E. Church and the Wilberforce constituency realize what it has meant that for eighty-four years Wilberforce University has had no recognized standing in the United States as an educational institution. It has had sympathy; it has been commended for hard effort but its standing has not been officially recognized. The bachelor's degree of Wilberforce University has never been sufficient to admit its possessor to recognized standing in a single institution of the world. Now this is serious. How serious it is can only be known by those acquainted with the present standards and methods of education. In Europe such an institution would not be allowed to confer degrees at all and in the United States until 1939 the Wilberforce degree was nationally discounted. Today for the first time in its history Wilberforce has received recognition, conditional to be sure, but official recognition that its degrees are reaching the national standard. Educationally this is the greatest accomplishment in the history of Wilberforce University.

In 1935, the officials of the North Central Association of Colleges and Secondary Schools made a careful investigation; they noted particularly this difficulty which I have stressed of two institutions with double control; with clashes of personalities, political interference and lack of funds. Four years later they came back. They generously recorded the fact that great improvement had been made; that through the efforts of the president who had made vital changes in the faculty, the clash of personalities had been abated; the teaching force had been strengthened; the library had been strikingly improved; and the general business administration was better. They said that while this pronounced progress had been accomplished that they could not at present recommend the admission of Wilberforce to the North Central Association.

Despite this, however, the Board of Review of the Commission on Higher Education, while recognizing that Wilberforce was still confronted with the same difficult problems, decided nevertheless to accredit the institution subject to the supervision of a committee which was to make annual reports in 1940, 1941 and 1942.

The University, therefore, for the first time in its history has received conditional recognition as a standard institution.[*]

Following this, a special committee report for the first of the trial years, 1940, records still continued improvement and "tangible evidence of an increased unity of purpose within the institution." It believes that Wilberforce is making reasonable progress in general and looks forward to the permanent accrediting of the institution after 1942; but the committee is still apprehensive because of threatened political interference. The interference has taken place. Through new legislation, a new state board comes into control. The balance of power swings toward the State, while the Presidency is still in the hands of the Church. The new board, over the president's recommendations, appoints and

---

[*]The committee of examiners of March, 1939, "despite the pronounced development which has taken place at Wilberforce University during the three years of President Walker's administration," nevertheless "find themselves constrained regretfully to recommend to the Board of Review that Wilberforce University be not present included in the membership list of the North Central Association of Colleges and Secondary Schools."

However the Board of Review of the Commission on Institutions of Higher Education decided to "accredit the institution subject to the guidance of a committee which will make an annual report in 1940, and in 1941, and a final report in 1942." Unless conditions improved, the Board of Review will then "find it necessary to give further consideration to the retention of Wilberforce University on the list of accredited institutions."

dismisses teachers. This throws the institution back again to the fundamental problem of putting a permanent end to this double control and of ceasing to make Wilberforce the football of partisan politics, whether this situation arises from dabbling in politics by Wilberforce officials or from outside politicians muscling in.

In either and both cases, an aroused public opinion, with stern rebuke of this cheapening and frustration of the great objects of an old and respected institution can set the present muddle straight and start the program which I have indicated.

The Wilberforce Community

But Wilberforce is more than a school and its problems transcend the Church. It is not simply a community; it is not simply the educational capital of three-quarters of a million people united in a great and powerful organization; it is, or ought to be, one of the main centers out of which trained and scientific guidance for twelve million people could come. Now the chief present problem of these twelve millions today is the matter of employment at a wage which will allow them to live like civilized human beings. In the present increasing turmoil of the world, there must eventually come, on the part of leading nations, a wide and fundamental readjustment of economic organization and industrial life and work and wage. Some of you assume that when this reorganization comes you are going automatically to inherit what belongs to you; but this will not happen unless you plan for yourselves in accordance with the best thought and training of the day.

That means that around Wilberforce as a community there should begin to grow a thriving self-supporting body of citizens, well-trained in science and art, abreast with the world in thought, raising their own food, building their own homes and beginning to manufacture the clothes and other articles that they use; and that this independent economy, separate from the school and yet nourishing it, racial and yet broadly interracial, should spread out through Greene County and Ohio and the Nation.

There should begin here that necessary and fateful organization of consumer power which once rescued Denmark and Sweden and is the only way out for the economic independence and physical survival of the Negro.

This program which you should organize and plan today was begun for you more than a century ago when the colored people of Cincinnati rose up against their impossible surroundings called the first national convention of the Negroes in 1831 and began that mass migration to Canada which was the greatest movement among Negroes before the

Civil War. Wilberforce University arose on the echo of the Cincinnati effort and if it ever finally succeeds, it will be because building upon that past it goes forward into an economic future starting here and developing into a community life high in thought, scientific in planning, and unselfish in deed.

Envoi

Gentlemen and ladies of the graduating classes: I have said little today directly to you, whose day of celebration this is. I have talked to your elders and to those set in authority over you. But every word I have uttered is indirectly for you. For yours is the kingdom and the power and the glory, forever. Your fathers will tell you that what I advise and plan is impossible. They are right. It is impossible. But The Impossible is just what you have got to do to save Wilberforce; and believe me when I say, out of the depth of years and the lore of centuries: This is a world where many times, the Impossible has been triumphantly achieved.

"Awake, awake, put on thy strength; 0, Zion, put on thy beautiful robes."

CHAPTER TWENTY-ONE

The Future and Function of
the Private Negro College

Among the very last speeches made by Du Bois on higher education, he revisits in this piece themes going back to the beginning of the century, as well as looking toward the future.

We all know the main lines of the rise of Negro education in the United States: after a desperate and sporadic struggle to finance and maintain Negro schools, resulting in several schools among free Negroes north and south and in two schools of higher training before the Civil War, there came after emancipation, a mass demand for popular education unequalled by any other group in world history. Of how that demand was met I wrote forty years ago in *The Souls of Black Folk*:

Through the shining trees that whisper before me as I write, I catch glimpses of a boulder of New England granite, covering a grave, which graduates of Atlanta University have placed there, with this inscription:

> In grateful memory of their former teacher and friend and of the unselfish life he lived, and the noble work he wrought; that they, their children, and their children's children might be blessed.

This was the gift of New England to the freed Negro; not alms, but a friend; not cash, but character. It was not and is not money these seething millions want, but love and sympathy, the pulse of hearts beating with red blood;—a gift which today only their own kindred anti race can bring to the masses, but which once saintly souls brought to their favored children in the crusade of the sixties, that finest thing in American history, and one of the few things untainted by sordid greed and cheap vainglory. The teachers in these institutions came not to keep the Negroes in their place, but to raise them out of the defilement of the places where slavery had wallowed them. The colleges they founded were social settlements; homes where the best of the sons of the freedmen came in close and sympathetic touch with the best traditions of New England. They lived and ate together, studied and worked, hoped and harkened in the dawning light. In actual formal content their curriculum was doubtless old-fashioned, but in educational power it was supreme, for it was the contact of living souls.

Since those days these colleges have gone through various transitions. For a while they had to support themselves by contributions chiefly from the missionary funds of Northern churches and from federal funds which Negroes provided. Then for twenty-five years they tried to raise larger sums from philanthropists, often from prosperous sons of the original teachers and founders. Later the colored colleges turned toward the state for aid. Today the private institutions are facing the fact that unless they receive increased contributions, not now in sight, and these funds reach large figures, they must either close or become fully state schools.

I have in many cases urged that the state must in the future support and control higher education because of its large and increasing cost. The church today carries, or should carry, too heavy a burden of social duties to permit it to continue to support large and increasingly expensive colleges. With almost unanimous action, they are shifting this burden to public appropriation or private philanthropy. This means of course less religious influence in colleges, which has both its good and bad side. I said at Wilberforce only a few years ago that the only visible future for that first of Negro colleges was to become a state school. Private philanthropy as a support of higher education is undesirable, as I shall point out later.

There are in the United States today one hundred and eighteen Negro colleges giving from one to four years of college work. Thirty-six of these are supported by government funds, chiefly from the United States and the states. Eighty-two are supported by private organizations. In 1940 these colleges were attended by about 45,000 students and 28,000 of these were in schools of A or B grading, meaning that they were doing fairly efficient college work.

Source of Income

These colleges receive considerably more than $15 million a year in income of which $9 million goes at least to the private colleges. But the source of this income has been varying in instructive ways during the generation from 1910 to 1940. In 1910, for instance, private institutions received less than a fifth of their income from student fees while today they receive nearly a third from fees; indicating the marked economic progress of Negroes which enables them today to pay a considerable share of the expense of educating their children. When I was at Fisk in the years from 1884 to 1888, there was not a single college student who was able to pay ten per cent of the fees.

The contribution from endowment funds, furnished chiefly by philanthropists has not varied much, ranging from 38 to 46 per cent. There are indications that this source may dwindle in the near future because endowments are not eternal and can only be depended upon for relatively short periods. This is a reversal of our economic beliefs in the nineteenth century. Led on by British capitalism, founded on Negro slavery, we assumed that income from a given batch of invested capital would if rightly administered continue forever. This we now realize is false and evil. Wealth for consumption or future use is no more eternal than the muscle or brain which created it and can only last forever by continuing to take from wages and giving to profit an absolutely unjustifiable share. It is on this fact that the whole argument for more equitable distribution of production rests. Consequently we see endowments of all sorts dwindling, and richly endowed institutions continually appealing for more funds. Three-fourths of my communications from Harvard since my graduation in 1890, have been appeals for contributions.

But the most serious fact is that while the private institutions got nearly one-half their support from gifts in 1910, they got only a fifth of that support from gifts in 1940. What now are these institutions going to do? Some of them have begun to turn and are turning increasingly to state aid. Of the sixteen leading private Negro colleges Tuskegee, Wilberforce, and probably Lincoln (Pennsylvania) are doubtless going to get their income increasingly from the state. Certain of the smaller church schools such as Clark, Paine, Morris Brown and Shaw, cannot hope for larger contributions from the church and must, therefore, explore other methods of support.

Atlanta University, as a graduate school, has adequate funds from endowment just now to meet its present needs but it will not have twenty years from now for an expanding future. There are certain other schools such as Talladega, Morehouse, Dillard, Fisk, Knoxville and Virginia Union which were formerly church schools, but have already outgrown that support and the problem of their future is serious. Xavier will, of course, continue to be supported by the Catholic Church for reasons not entirely educational.

Are Institutions Worth Saving?

Two questions, therefore, present themselves: are these institutions worth saving? Especially, is this last group of six private institutions without adequate or any church suport worth saving or is this their fate either to become state schools or disappear?

First it is clear that they cannot hope for support from miscellaneous and philanthropic gifts and this would be undesirable even if it were possible. Education is not and should not be a private philanthropy; it is a public service and whenever it becomes merely a gift of the rich it is in danger. Probably the greatest threat to American education today is the fact that its great and justly celebrated private institutions are supported mainly by their rich graduates: Harvard, Yale, Columbia, Princeton together with smaller institutions like Amherst and Williams are increasingly looked upon as belonging to a certain class in American society: the class of the rich, well-to-do employers, whose interests are more or less openly opposed to those of the laboring millions. It is because of this unfortunate situation that the clear unhampered study of the industrial process and of economic science has made so little progress in the United States at a time when the critical situation of the modern world calls desperately for such knowledge and teaching.

In the same way and for something of the same reasons the state institutions are often inhibited from development of the economic and social sciences because of political influence and because of wealth and class working through politics. But here is the hope of the democratic process; as democracy replaces oligarchy in industry, concurrently, the social and educational work of the state will improve in object and method. We can see evidence of this in state universities like Wisconsin and Michigan. On the other hand in southern states like Texas, the State University has been the football of the oil interests. Negro state colleges were a generation ago hot-beds of graft for white politicians; only in the last ten years have they been able to begin to develop a decent educational program.

In the long interim, while the state is gathering strength and democratic authority for its educational duties, and perhaps long after that, may not there be a field in the private college for a certain educational leadership and individuality? And particularly in a distinct social group, like that of the American Negro, may there not be a peculiar function for the Negro private colleges which no other social organ could fill? There would certainly seem to be a distinct place in the educational world for some private institutions whose support is such that they would be free to teach what they thought ought to be taught, particularly in the critical and developing field of social investigation.

If this is true of colleges in general, it is equally true for the same and additional reasons in the Negro college. We American Negroes are not simply Americans, or simply Negroes. We form a minority group in a great vast conglomerated land and a minority group which by reason of its efforts during the last two generations has made extraordinary and gratifying progress. But in the making of this progress, in the working together of peoples belonging to this group, in the patterns of thinking which they have had to follow and the memories which they shared, they have built-up a distinct and unique culture, a body of habit, thought and adjustment which they cannot escape because it is in the marrow of their bones and which they ought not to ignore because it is the only path to a successful future.

Definition of Culture

What is a culture? It is a careful Knowledge of the Past out of which the group as such has emerged: in our case a knowledge of African history and social development—one of the richest and most intriguing which the world has known. Our history in America, north, south and Caribbean, has been an extraordinary one which we must know to understand ourselves and our world. The experience through which our ancestors have gone for four hundred years is part of our bone and sinew whether we know it or not. The methods which we evolved for opposing slavery and fighting prejudice are not to be forgotten, but learned for our own and others' instruction. We must understand the differences in social problems between Africa, the West Indies, South and Central America, not only among the Negroes but those affecting Indians and other minority groups. Plans for the future of our group must be built on a base of our problems, our dreams and frustrations; they cannot stem from empty air or successfully be based on the experiences of others alone. The problem of our children is distinctive: when shall a colored child learn of the color line? At home, at school or suddenly on the street? What shall we do in art and literature? Shall we seek to ignore our background and graft ourselves orb a culture which does not wholly admit us, or build anew on that marvelous African art heritage, one of the world's greatest as all critics now admit? Whence shall our drama come, from ourselves today or from Shakespeare in the English seventeenth century.

Many Negroes do not realize this. In their haste to become Americans, their desire not to be peculiar or segregated in mind or body, they try to escape their cultural heritage and the body of experience which they themselves have built-up. This is the reason that there is always a certain risk in taking a colored student from his native environment and transplanting him suddenly to a northern school. He may adjust himself, he may through the help of his own social group in the neighborhood of this school successfully achieve an education through the facilities offered. On the other hand he may meet peculiar frustration and in the end be unable to achieve success in the new environment or fit into the old.

For these and analogous reasons I am convinced that there is a place and a continuing function for the small Negro college. This is additional reason that this college should have a certain kind of independent support. If a number of small colleges with one or less than two hundred students with a carefully selected faculty and clearly conceived methods and ideals could survive in America, they might have unusual opportunity to fill a great need and to do a work which no other agency could do so well. They would not be subservient to the dominant wealth of the country; they would not be under the control of politics in, a state now directed for the most part at present by prejudiced persons guided by a definite ideal of racial discrimination.

Method of Support

The question then comes: how can such schools be supported and what would their program be? It was estimated in that very excellent National Survey of Higher Education of Negroes made by the United States Office of Education in 1940 that the cost of educating a student in a small private college was about $452 a year in addition to housing and board. If we put this total cost at $900, it would probably be true that Negro students could pay from one-fourth to a third of this cost. At $600 a student a small college then would cost $120,000 a year to which must be added something for buildings, grounds, a broad program of free scholarships and other items of administration which might bring the total cost to $150,000. Extra gifts for buildings, emergencies, and scholarships might still come from church, liberal donors or even the state; the main source of current maintenance must be the organized alumni.

How now could a small college raise $150,000 outside of what the students pay? There is, of course, but one method and that is for the alumni and the local constituency of the college to tax themselves for this amount. A college with two thousand graduates could raise this sum rather easily if each graduate gave $100 a year not as a pledge but as an actual payment. This amounts to two dollars a week. If the college had only one thousand graduates it would amount to four dollars a week, I say "tax" and I mean tax: a payment as regular and recognized as just as compulsory as any tax.

The question comes, therefore, could the graduates of such colleges be made to see vividly enough the necessity of their continued existence so that they would be willing to tax themselves to this considerable amount. I believe it would be possible but only possible if this kind of contribution was lifted out of the class of ordinary miscellaneous giving to which we are so used and stressed throughout the college course as an absolute necessity for the maintenance of independent methods of education. This would be an innovation. I am not sure that we have in our student body today and our body of graduates the guts for any such real sacrifice. We are used to being educated for nothing and expecting praise for giving our valuable time. We pay on the nail for spring clothes, automobiles, and golf clubs, but for a college training? I do not know.

Aims and Program

What now should such a college be and what should it do? It should in the first place be small. We should get rid of the idea of bigness which permeates American ideals. A college of two thousand students is an entirely different kind of institution from a college of one hundred students. The success and marked success of Fisk and Talladega and Atlanta and similar institutions in earlier years was the fact that their college department consisted of a small number of students brought into direct contact for long periods with able teachers. When I first went to Atlanta University to teach there were only twenty-five students in college and the whole college department at Fisk during my undergraduate days consisted of less than twenty persons. What is needed for efficient education of youth is individual attention, close acquaintanceship with their fellows and that skilled guidance that only can be gotten in the small college.

Secondly, this college must have a carefully selected faculty; its president must be not a financier and collector of funds but an educational administrator capable of laying down an educational program and selecting the people who can carry it out. The teachers in such a college must be scholars and gentlemen; scholars in the sense of having direct and careful acquaintanceship with modern science and gentlemen in the sense of knowing and practicing the highest canons of good taste and conduct. The curriculum of a college of this sort would be comparatively simple: the idea of acquainting growing youth with what the world has known in science and art and what it is doing today; and in making that acquaintanceship as complete and thorough as time allows: the idea of knowing thoroughly the lives of people today, comparing them with the people of the past and evolving through science a guide and prophet for the future.

For this reason the college should be equipped with library, laboratories, a museum and an art gallery. The library should contain the body of human life and experience in such quantity and number as to be easily and quickly accessible to all; it should be conducted by persons who know the inside of books better than their backs and catalogue numbers. The college should have a theatre for the drama and facilities for hearing and studying music. But above and beyond this it should have a distinct department of adult education calculated to teach its students from the first the art of reading and writing. Most of the students who come to college, white and black all over the United States, do not read and write well. And many who come to our colleges cannot read and write at all. The reason for this does not necessarily involve any individual blame. It is because of the wretched system of public schools where these students have been trained. The system of elementary education in the United States has got to be improved and in the end will be; but in the meantime one or two generations of students will grow-up and will have to know how to read and write and cipher in order to pursue a college course. Each college, therefore, should have provision for the scientific teaching of reading, writing and arithmetic to adult persons. The experience of the army in this war has shown that this is a perfectly feasible program.

Finally a main object of such a college should be vocational guidance. So much nonsense has been taught on this subject that we often fail to realize its real function. It goes back to the old Socratic "know thyself." When a man goes through college he ought to go through a general process of becoming acquainted with his own ability and desires so that by the time he graduates he will have a fairly clear idea of what place he can and ought to occupy in the world.

Not a Professional School

This means that the small college which I have in mind would not be a professional school, would not be an industrial school, would not attempt to teach anybody how to earn a living. Its object would be to teach youth what the world is and what it means; and then after the college course we should learn the technique of earning a living in any way one can and wishes. The main job of such a college course is the unified cultural message. It takes the boy and shows him the world as it is with its customs and habits, its memories and ideals and works from that toward a vision of real life. Above all in our case it shows him our world—the one in which we live and must work.

For this reason the college should be closely integrated with its surrounding social setting. One of the great limitations of the older Negro college was that they came up with the idea of detachment from the town, city and state where they were. In part this was forced upon them by slavery and its consequences but it afterward became a habit; so that an intellectual class was trained which had no organic connection with the community around. In the small college which I have in mind this should no longer be true. The college should be an integral part of the community, of the colored community, of course, first; but also and just as needfully of the white community, so that in all its work and thinking, its government and art expression the community and college should be one and inseparable and at the same time the college could retain its leading function because of its independence and its clear ideals.

Such a college should be under the absolute control of the alumni: they should elect the trustees and hold them to strict account. Of course for such work the alumni themselves would need training: they would have to adopt a self-denying ordinance not to use their power to make jobs for themselves or children and to hold their lower as a sacred trust for the education of a new and redeeming generation of men.

This may be a dream but it is worth considering.

PART SIX

Du Bois, Education and Literature

CHAPTER TWENTY-TWO

The New Education

Du Bois experimented with writing fiction and poetry throughout much of his career. In 1911 he published his first novel, *The Quest of the Silver Fleece.* His most ambitious effort in fiction was the Black Flame Trilogy which was published during the 1950s. These included *The Ordeal of Mansart* (1957), *Mansart Builds a School* (1959) and *Worlds of Color* (1961).

As literature, the Black Flame Trilogy seems rather artificial and stilted. Despite this fact, the work is of considerable interest in terms of understanding Du Bois's feelings about the world. In *Mansart Builds a School*, he includes a chapter entitled "The New Education." This chapter is remarkably interesting in the context of the debate over the Hampton Model, as well as Du Bois's perceptions concerning the outlook and role of wealthy patrons in supporting black higher education.

The dinner which Mrs. Van Rensaeler was induced to give the Chinese ambassador was most interesting. Wu Ting Fang had proven to be a great social attraction in America; his gracious manners; his old world culture and his curiously frank but always intriguing conversation were widely commented on. Then, too, his costumes, that mandarin's gown, with its priceless silk and lovely and intricate embroidery gave an exotic finish to his personality. The ambassador had expressed interest in the problem of Negroes in America. "I have been quite curious to know just how your effort at emancipating slaves turned out. In China, from age to age, either the enslaved died out or became a part of the master class. What's happening here?"

It was determined to have present at the dinner Lyman Abbott, the leading New York protestant minister, and Hamilton Mabie, editor of the widely influential weekly, the *Outlook.* Oswald Villard, grandson of Garrison, the abolitionist, must be there. Not only was he liberal by birth, but his other grandfather represented Big Business. It was significant that this Villard not only had married a Southern girl but was president of the new emancipation movement, the NAACP. Also, he was a close friend of Booker Washington.

"Ah yes, yes, indeed," murmured Wu Ting Fang. "I shall be glad to meet this Mr. Washington."

The dinner took place in the old Fifth Avenue homestead of the hostess. There were a dozen guests and naturally none were colored. Characteristically the guest of honor noted this and remarked upon it. He peered about:

"Am I right," he said, "in assuming that none of you have Negro blood? I had looked at least to meet that friend of yours, Booker Washington." He looked at Mr. Villard.

Mr. Villard explained the social conventions—

"Yes, yes," replied the guest. "But when the NAACP succeeds in its mission will Negroes be asked to dinner?"

"You have put your finger on one of our main difficulties," answered Lyman Abbott.

"I see, I see," responded the guest. "You are not sure how much emancipation you want. Of course, of course, that is natural. I am most interested. Something of the past I know. Your slaves revolted as all slaves eventually do—"

"Oh, no; our slaves were quite docile."

"Indeed; but how about Toussaint and Gabriel; Vesey, Nat Turner, and 200,000 Negro soldiers in the Civil War? But never mind that. Since then, I believe you had high hopes that the Negroes would die out, unable to stand competition of the whites. Are they dying duly?"

"Most certainly not."

"How thoughtless! I note the lower classes are often that way; they seldom do what is expected of them. And then you planned to re-export them back to Africa. That I hear was dropped because you needed their labor. They became serfs, without votes or justice. So to preserve civilization, here is the NAACP. What does it propose to do?"

Hamilton Mabie laid down his fork and leaned forward.

"The fact is, Your Excellency, this second decade of the new century has brought us face to face with decision. The Negro is here to stay. If he remains a second-class citizen, disfranchised and lynched, we cannot maintain our democracy. Therefore he must be raised."

"Or," said the guest, "be allowed to raise himself."

"There lies the trouble," said Villard. "William English Walling, a Kentucky white man, resented a lynching in the birthplace of Abraham Lincoln and called for a second emancipation movement. I joined and promised to raise funds for the movement among my wealthy friends. Mary Ovington, a social worker, urged that we ask the help of Negroes themselves and Henry Moskovitz brought us the views of liberal Jews, and was later joined by Singarns.

"Then came trouble. Dr. Abbott and Mr. Mabie looked on Booker Washington as spokesman for Negroes and I largely agreed. But I was willing to invite to our councils the more radical Negro group. The Boston contingent led by Trotter and Ida Wells Barnett refused to cooperate. A less radical group joined, but to my disgust they came to lead, not to follow, to tell us, not to listen. Through the Crisis, they took over the policy of the NAACP and demanded not only equality before the law for Negroes and the right to vote, but as they brazenly proclaimed, 'every right which belongs to an American citizen.' "

The guest of honor smiled. "This was going too far for you?"

"Not perhaps too far, but certainly too fast."

"It was crazy," interrupted Mabie. "This land naturally must keep law and order. As a democracy it is bound to let those persons vote who reach a certain standard. But Americans simply cannot assimilate Negroes—they just cannot."

"But I am told you have assimilated several million, of whom your Mr. Washington is one."

"That was due to slavery. It has now ceased."

"And to keep it so you refuse to invite Negroes to dinner. And Negroes agree?"

"Wise Negroes do. Others foolishly demand social equality."

"And if and when they rise to equality, won't they continue to insist? Won't they marry those who want to marry them? This, my friend, can be stopped only in one way. Prevent this rise to equality and restore slavery whatever you may call it. Otherwise, face the fact: in a century you'll be octoroons." The diners were silent with disgust, but the suave guest continued unchecked. "You will find before this century dies that stopping the rise of a determined people is a hard job. We Chinese know, and we are still learning." The ambassador leaned back and sampled his champagne again, and belched openly and without apology. He waxed philosophical:

"The fact is you Americans may look forward with a certain complacency to the next two hundred years. Your rather coarse and hard faces will acquire some of the soft curves of Africa and what is more important, your distressing lack of what the Chinese regard as good manners will receive touches of Negro humility and graciousness which I'm sure you all realize is desperately needed.—Yes, of course," and Wu Ting Fung arose courteously with his hostess, and bowing to take her arm, strode majestically toward the drawing room.

The Chinese ambassador was too great a gentleman to pursue further a subject which he saw was proving embarrassing to his hosts. The rest of the evening was devoted to a most interesting examination of the history and deeper meaning of Chinese art. Mrs. Van Rensaeler was deeply gratified.

His Excellency, Wu Ting Fang, was determined to have a heart to heart talk with Booker T. Washington. He began next morning, but learned to his regret that Mr. Washington had just died.

With the death of Booker Washington, the white South began to gather up into its own hands the direction of Negro education. Negroes themselves, except one in the influential position of Washington, could have little educational leadership. Disfranchised, they could not make the Southern states support decent Negro public schools. Philanthropy, chiefly from white Northern churches, still helped. But after the First World War this source of funds began to die away, partly because of the increasing cost and partly because of the call of other causes, but also because the new South stridently promised to assume the burden of Negro schools provided southern advice and direction replaced northern. But for this the South asked a price: northern gifts must be handled by southern whites and white education must take precedence over Negro in time and cost.

This was the educational reasoning behind the Booker Washington "Atlanta Compromise": the white South would direct all schools, black and white; the white South would handle all or most gifts to Negro education and would direct all educational policies. All this planning had not worked out as well as northern philanthropy had hoped.

On the other hand, all the Negro organizations—the NAACP, the Urban League, the great church organizations—continued to stress better Negro education, and this unanimity was a direct descendant of the educational crusade following the Civil War. The public schools were admittedly bad; there were few high schools. Higher education depended still almost entirely on private philanthropy. When the Federal government began to appropriate funds for state colleges, especially in agriculture and industry, the pressure on the South to share these funds equitably with Negroes increased. Most of the Southern States began to establish colored state agricultural and mechanical colleges, but with wretchedly inadequate funds. Negroes, forming over a fourth of the Southern population, got less than a tenth of the appropriations. A dominant Southern white philosophy was that educational facilities should be measured by ownership of property. The rich should have good schools; the poor, bad schools or none. This was heritage from slavery. It was modified after 1880; the whites should have the better schools because they pay most of the taxes and have better brains; Negroes should have schools, but schools suited to their needs and these needs corresponded with the demands of white employers for profit. Here the popular Hampton and Tuskegee philosophy saw eye to eye with

Big Business. But white artisans and the labor movement opposed this kind of Negro education as well as Negro public schools.

Then came the demand from Negroes for equal educational facilities, at least in expenditure of federal funds. The Federal land-grant funds of 1862 went entirely to white schools in the South; but in 1890 a further grant allotted a small share to Negro schools, which necessitated the furnishing of buildings by the states. Several Negro Land-Grant colleges were started, varying widely in efficiency. By the time of the First World War, there were seventeen such colleges and they shared, albeit inequitably, in the Federal funds given thereafter. Under Northern pressure, and because of increasing Negro agitation, these Negro colleges, supported in part by federal funds, had to be improved.

It was considerations like this, added to what he thought were the much greater needs of the white colleges, which moved John Baldwin to undertake Baldwin to undertake a complete reorganization of the educational system of Georgia. John Baldwin never became governor of Georgia. After the First World War there came unexpected developments. Tom Watson, after his fierce anti-Negro campaign which helped bring the Atlanta riot in 1906, had gone into retirement for a decade in disappointment and frustration. But in 1920 he appeared again upon the scene to run for United States senator. He had dropped the Negro, was half-hearted in fighting for white labor, and fulminated against Jews and the Catholic Church. At the same time, the Ku Klux Klan was revived and business began that miraculous upsurge which ended with the crash of 1929.

John Pierce, banker and mouthpiece of Big Business, talked with Baldwin:

"John, I had always pictured you in a successful political career-governor, and senator; perhaps even higher. Now I doubt. In this next state campaign we need a rabble-rouser like Tom Hardwick. He can sweep the state and we can handle him. Meantime, your role is in business; there you'll have more power than any official. We're facing a tremendous era. Power to help guide it will be in your hands."

Baldwin demurred as did his mother and wife. But Pierce prevailed. One matter, however, Baldwin managed to guide, especially since it accorded with the plans of Big Business, and that was the rehabilitation of the state university system. This he could guide from his powerful position in the Legislature.

The old university, once presided over by his father, was well enough on its way, but needed revamping and expansion. It must be made part of a state-wide industrial development which would especially include the Atlanta Institute of Technology and a new liberal arts college in Atlanta with modern professional schools. These new institutions might replace or complement the University at Athens; agriculture and some other branches of science might remain there.

Finally, higher Negro education must somehow be fitted in, if for no other reason than to retain Federal funds for the state. Moreover, there had got under way a Negro demand for trained leadership which could not be stemmed. There was no use today in trying to tell Negroes that all they needed was skilled or half skilled workers. A mass must be led, and Negroes no longer trusted whites as leaders of their race. They did not even trust Negro leaders like Washington, who did what whites wanted done. It was a peculiar complication that at present the Negro private college, Atlanta University, was actually the best college in Atlanta; while a poor state school in Savannah was the state supported Negro institution. The head of this branch was called Principal of the Colored A & M, and spent most of his time distributing among his white trustees and merchants such favors in spending and purchasing as his institution's small income would allow.

Baldwin's first step toward his educational program was to secure ample state funds for the white Institute of Technology in Atlanta, to be supplemented by donations from corporations interested in having gifted young men trained for their factories, mines and business. At the State University in Athens, a new College of Agriculture on a large scale was given appropriations by the Legislature.

After this, Baldwin called in Coypel and rather suddenly offered him a position which would eventually make him Chancellor of a new University of Georgia.

"My dear Coypel, there is one anomaly in our Atlanta educational system, which I am sure has struck you as it has many others, and that is that the only first-class college in the city is the Negro Atlanta University. We need a great college for whites. Such a college can become an integral part of a state system, comprehended under a re-furbished University of Georgia. I am glad to say that at last such a system is in sight. Northern finance has promised us a nest egg of five million to establish a college in this city to be known as Fulton University. This institution, along with the Institute of Technology, Agnes Scott College for Women, and the University at Athens, will be united into a new State University. With these in time will be incorporated all the other higher schools of the state, white and black.

"All of this is for the future. What I want to offer you now is the position of dean of the University of Georgia, and later the presidency of Fulton University when it is started. Meanwhile, I want you to act as head of a powerful and well-financed committee of the proposed

University System. You will also be appointed to the present University Board of Regents and to the trustee boards of most of the colleges of the state. You will have suitable offices, and a home in the suburbs for your family. Your real work will depend on legislative action which will be pushed as rapidly as possible."

Coypel had by this time become thoroughly uncomfortable in his job as Superintendent of Atlanta city schools. This was not the small, precise, well-ordered program which he had been able to carry out in Lanark. It was a big, sprawling mess, and while he had made the schools of Atlanta very considerably better than they had ever been before, it was not yet a good school system and he knew it. With the pulling and hauling in the city, the various special interests, the people who wanted positions for their friends and favors for their enterprises, agitators like Scroggs, and with the over-shadowing industrial empire—well, with all this he could not see his way to a fine, complete educational job. He was especially irked by the small progress made by the Negro schools because of small funds. He was ready for a change.

Baldwin sensed this and he made his offer of a new position attractive. Here, withdrawn from the center of strife in a big, brawling metropolis, was a chance to start a fine educational job and to build practically from the ground up.

Coypel hesitated. It was not a real job but the prospect of a vast one. It was the beginning of a plan yet to be worked out. For assured success it called for a man of wide reputation and proven ability in educational work. Coypel was a small man with only local renown. He had concepts; he was widely read; he felt he might in time measure up to this great opportunity. He knew what a great State University in Georgia might yet mean to America. But could he start this great enterprise? And would Baldwin and the forces supporting him really give him a chance or were they merely pushing him forward as a stopgap, holding on until some great educator was willing to take on the real job, backed by real organization and large funds?

Coypel finally said Yes because there was nothing else to say. He did not want to remain in his present job. He would try this new one. If he failed or if it failed him, he could go back to his flowers in Lanark. He had already made overtures. He even felt a glow at the prospect of failure here. He said:

"But remember, Mr. Baldwin, that I may fail. First of all, my preparation for conducting an educational organization for a great state and indeed of a region is painfully narrow. What the masses of this state are interested in and must be educated for is first earning a decent living."

"Good," said Baldwin, "and that is just what we want."

"Yes, but that is not all we want. We want these people to know just what the life is and can be which they are preparing to live. The Institute of Technology can teach weaving, building electric motors and bridges, but what can a college teach about Life, Love, Tolerance and Dreams? I don't know and I accept this job because I know so few others who know more or as much as I."

"Let it go at that," laughed Baldwin. But Coypel interrupted:

"And now, about the Negroes?"

Baldwin smiled. "I knew you would bring that up," he said. "There again I have plans. What we have now is a mess. The old Booker Washington program has not worked. We can't confine all Negroes to cheap common labor. We can't reserve a well-paid aristocracy of labor for whites. Mass production and Negro colleges have changed all that. Negroes are slipping into skilled labor and white-collar jobs; whites are falling down to common labor. Both will be forced sooner or later into a common labor union movement. Very good; we've got to seek out a new program.

"First as to Negro higher education: it's here to stay. There are four or five private Negro colleges. All depend on philanthropy which is fading away. There are three state colored industrial schools, none of them efficient or getting enough money. We are going to cooperate with Northern philanthropy to consolidate the best private Negro colleges into one university. Meantime, by action of the State Board of Education and legislative appropriations which are already certain, we are uniting all the Negro state schools into one Negro State Agricultural and Mechanical College with new buildings and equipment.

"Our ultimate aim is to unite both private and state higher training for Negroes under single state control; but that we're not yet announcing. What we'll try right off is to increase appropriations for white education to five million a year; and Negro appropriations to a half million. That is not fair, I know full well. But it's three times what the Negroes are getting now and it's all and perhaps more than I can get today. Tomorrow we may do better but never in our day can we expect Georgia to do for blacks what she does for whites. Meantime, we're ready to appoint Manuel Mansart principal of the new State School.

"Now, as I said before, Mr. Coypel, this isn't justice. But it is as much as the state dares to do just now. If the black school does its job, it will be getting a million in ten years while the whites will be getting, well, at least ten million."

"I accept on one condition," said Coypel. "It must be 'President' Mansart, not 'Principal.' "

"Accepted," answered Baldwin after a pause. "But, Mr. Coypel, remember this: whatever the title, it is largely empty; you as representing the white university are going to be the real head of the colored college with Mansart as your assistant and under your orders. On no other terms can we get money for this program. Let Mansart wear whatever title he wishes, the real head of this institution is you."

Coypel was silent. If he had spoken he would have said that Mansart would have complete power so far as he was concerned. But under what other white man likely to succeed him would this be true? He was Mansart's only chance. He said nothing more.

The State Board of Education began the establishment of the new Negro college in Macon by buying a private Negro school which had been run by missionaries of the Northern Baptist church and served as a high school for the colored community. It had a good location with about fifty acres of land and three buildings, once substantial but now needing repair. The governor appointed a Board of Trustees and in a subtle way the New Education began in Georgia.

One of Mansart's first problems was that of preliminary housing for the college. It was too soon to consider a complete building program but a beginning must be made. There was already on the old campus one building which had been used for forty years for recitations, assemblies and administration. It must be largely rebuilt or entirely discarded. There was one old girls' dormitory and a president's home. Mansart and Coypel after careful consideration decided for the present to repair the main building, rebuild the dormitory and make the residence serve as Mansart's home with room for a small number of men students.

Later the whole problem of suitable buildings on a scale suited to the growth of the institution could be faced. There is, of course, no standard of cost for school building and particularly buildings for schools in the South adapted to Negroes. In fact, the only matter that received careful and prolonged attention was usually how much the white contractors could make in profit out of the state appropriation. Such appropriations for colored schools had been very popular in the past and much sought after by white trustees.

Coypel and Mansart had talked over the matter rather carefully, and had decided on two policies: first, the permanent buildings were going to be well planned, and secondly, the contracts were going to be carefully drawn. Before, however, anything had really been decided on or even the size of the legislative appropriation made definite, Mansart had a visit in his office from one of the trustees. He was a local Macon white man, not one of the cotton aristocracy, but he had been expanding in business and making considerable money in various ways.

Mr. Sykes was in a hurry, and greeted the president by his first name. This Manuel had some time ago decided was of little real account. The only difficulty, of course, was in the case of being thus addressed in the presence of students. Perhaps that could later be arranged. He would talk to Coypel about it.

Mr. Sykes brought out a paper which was the contract for an administration building, along with plans. Mansart looked at it with astonishment but gave no sign of what he was thinking. Evidently Mr. Sykes was going to jam through a contract quickly and get his profit settled. Evidently, too, Sykes was insinuating himself into the space between the white president and his colored representative. Mansart was expected to be flattered by this recognition of his authority and once his assent was gained, Coypel could be handled as he did not seem too strong.

Manuel took the paper and began to study it carefully. "Thank you very much, Mr. Sykes," he said. "I will look over this matter and consult about it."

"That isn't necessary at all," said Sykes, "and, er,—I'm in a hurry. I want to get this settled; the lumber business is facing a fluctuating market and we must make our decisions immediately."

"Well, of course, Mr. Sykes, but I would not want to decide anything before I had put it before the trustees and consulted—"

"Listen, Manuel, it isn't necessary for you to consult anybody. You and I are going to settle this thing and settle it right here. Now, let's have a clear understanding. As the best known local member of the Board, I propose to take a leading role in running this institution."

Manuel paused a moment and looked out the window. He made up his mind slowly. Then he said, "Mr. Sykes, I'm afraid you and I are not going to agree."

"We'll either agree, Manuel, or you will lose this job."

"All right," said Manuel, "then I'll lose it."

Sykes stared at him in astonishment. He knew, of course, that he was being a bit high-handed. Coypel and the trustees might object if he pushed this thing through too fast. But he had not expected any opposition on the part of Manuel. He leaned forward.

"Of course, er, you understand, President Mansart, that you're going to get a reasonable cut—"

Manuel pretended not to understand the implication at all.

"Of course, of course," he said, "Mr. Sykes, I shall get my salary, I hope, regularly, but—er—let me be plain. I do not want to appear stubborn or anything of that sort, but this contract is not going to be settled today or any day soon until I have a chance to think it over and consult with the authorities and with my friends."

Sykes sat back in astonishment. Slowly he arose. "All right, boy," he said, "apparently you are making your choice. And let me tell you, you're making the wrong one. Good day."

For some time Mansart heard no more of Sykes. But he knew he would hear. The main building and land-buying program had not yet come up. When it did, there was no doubt but Mr. Sykes would be on hand and a crucial battle would have to be joined.

This was, as of course Manuel knew it would be, only the beginning of a series of encounters. Everything that was done for the school or bought for the school was carried out on the supposition that the smallest possible sum would be paid for materials and work, a large part of the remainder would go to the contractors or the white merchant, and a small amount of graft would be handed to the president. That had long been the rule in state schools, and especially Negro schools.

Word got around. The white merchants now made up their minds that they probably would have to give a little larger share to the president than they had planned. They didn't like it, but after all, these were new times, Mansart was stubborn and they must yield.

Even beyond this it occurred to several of them that perhaps this upstart was proposing to take over the whole of the graft from this new venture for himself, in which case he had better be warned. It was for this reason that the next week one afternoon a small, self-appointed committee called on Mansart representing the grocery firms where the school would buy its food, the bookstore which would furnish textbooks, and the large repair shop which might do a good deal of work for the school. They were quite polite. They addressed Manuel as "President Mansart," and after they were sure that the doors were closed they got right down to business.

"Now, President Mansart, there will be, as you know, large profits in furnishing this school. We can understand that you may want a share more favorable to yourself than is usual. But don't get any ideas. You are not going to be the sole one to profit from the business of this school. Let's have that understood—"

Manuel interrupted. "Gentlemen, you quite mistake me. I not only am not going to be the only one profiting from school business, but no one, so long as I am president here, is going to get anything more than the proper current recompense. That is to go solely to the person who furnishes us the best goods and services. I do not propose to take anything in any way beyond my salary."

The six men each in his own way laughed in Mansart's face, and gave him to understand that it was quite unnecessary for him to rehearse any such fairy tale. There wasn't a single school in the state that was run that way and there wouldn't be and that he was crazy to think that they believed he had any such project.

They talked a long time and the more they talked on the less the participants understood each other until finally the white merchants laid down a pretty clear statement.

"If you try anything smart in this case, Mansart, you are not only going to find yourself out of a job, you might find yourself pretty dead." And they got up and left.

It was not a pleasant project, but in time Mansart's firmness and integrity established certain business methods so that he was able with Coypel's cooperation to get more honest contracts.

On the other hand, in the matter of labor, the question could not be so easily settled. White union labor insisted upon its right to do union work at union wages on buildings put up on the campus. And colored laborers, because they were excluded from the unions, were to be deprived of work on what they regarded as their own school. This was a source of continuing friction, and here Mansart waged his fiercest battles. There were no unions among the colored carpenters, masons and plasterers in Macon. There had been in the past, but these unions had been broken up and put out of business by the new white unions who had united in a city center.

The head of the city center soon came down to warn Mansart concerning the relations of colored people and particularly on the proposed training of his students to work in the building trades. He could have all the so-called industrial education he wanted to, in cooking and house service, but there was to be no training in masonry, carpentry or plastering; not one of his students was to do work of that sort even though the work was for the school, and no colored workmen could be hired on school contracts. That was the decision of the unions and that was going to be carried through. Now, if he wanted to get on in his position he had best understand that.

"But my dear sir," argued Mansart, "one of the reasons for this school, the original reason, was particularly to train Negroes in the trades. You know quite as well as I that most of the work in the building trades in this city used to be done by Negroes."

"Yes, we know, and because we do know, it's going to be stopped. The skilled trades hereafter in the South are going to be confined to white men. No matter what Booker Washington or anyone else said, we are not going to have our wages dragged down by cheap 'niggers.'"

"But," interjected Mansart, "that's just the point. If Negroes receive good training and are admitted to the union they will make just as good union members as white people, and help keep wages up."

"They don't know nothing about unions," answered the men. "They couldn't keep a promise to save their necks. And if they did, and kept wages up, we still don't want them, Nope, they're not going to be admitted to the unions and they ain't going to work."

"It seems to me, gentlemen," retorted Mansart, "that you are going against the whole trend of the times, and that you are attempting an impossible thing. If there is a body of labor fitted for this work and yet not admitted to it, it will become your competitors by underbidding. You are asking for the very thing that you are trying to prevent."

"Listen, Mansart, you needn't keep up this kind of talk. There ain't going to be no Negro skilled workers on any school jobs. Get that into your black head. Good day."

Here was the threat of mob law and aggression from poor whites who envied the colored students the beautiful campus and good buildings which were expected; from the rich who wanted good servants rather than lawyers and doctors would come added opposition. Here Mansart determined to make a fight. He had to; this was an open and conspicuous matter. If colored masons and carpenters were not employed on colored school work, if no Negroes were hired, this would arouse the Negroes of the state. Moreover, here Mansart could get sympathy from both races; from whites who wanted Negroes kept on the job so as to keep wages down; from the Negroes compelled to keep these skilled jobs or sink to the inadequate wage of common labor.

In 1920, Manuel Mansart became the president of the Georgia State Colored Agricultural and Mechanical College at Macon. He held this position from 1920 to 1946, over a quarter of a century. It became his life work. In this era between the first and second world wars, Manuel Mansart developed his theory of life, of what it was and how it should be lived.

Manuel hoped that his sons would unite and help him in his new career. But Douglass preferred remaining in Atlanta at present to help Perry in the insurance business. Eventually, he was still determined to live in Chicago. Meantime, he would come to Macon regularly and see if he could help. Revels was determined never again to live in the South. He was studying law in New York. Bruce was about to enter college. He would go to Macon, but was not sure what eventually he would want to do. Just now, most of his time went to football. Sojourner did not count although she seemed interested in music.

Manuel tried to get some broad grasp of the world about him at this time. He took the *Crisis* and read each word each month. The new emancipation centering in the North was really pointed at this Southern world where Mansart lived and where the results of emancipation must be worked out if at all. Mansart looked around him. In the world of Manuel Mansart of that time there were separate churches and separate schools. On the whole, the neighborhoods were separate, although not completely. The kind of work which the colored people and white people did differed in general—the colored people doing the more subservient kind of labor and service. When it came to the government, the colored people had little to do with it. Their contacts were brusque and formal and consisted of paying taxes and obeying ordinances. The policemen had attitudes toward the colored group which they did not have toward the whites. In white stores, there was a certain separation and subservience in the way in which colored people were waited upon. There were separate seats in the streetcars and buses, the colored people filling up from the back or indeed standing, while the whites filled up from the front or left empty seats which the Negroes dare not occupy. There was, of course, separation in the railway depots and trains; although once in a while a well-to-do colored man would ride on a pullman, usually being assigned one of the end seats. In the depots, the whites were sold tickets at their windows first, and then the agent turned to the window opening into the colored waiting room. Often, there was no time for them to buy tickets and if they did not get them, they had to pay extra on the train.

In public, it was the white people that gave the orders and the colored people that took them. This was not always so; but anything else was regarded as unusual and exceptional. One expected to see colored people as laborers, porters, public servants of various sorts, janitors and scrubwomen; while the whites were merchants, officials, policemen and foremen, and if engaged in labor, working in separate gangs or on separate jobs. Colored and white artisans were usually separated, sometimes by job, sometimes on the job.

There were certain happenings that were of interest to colored people and not to white people, so that a sort of world of colored news and white news and gossip grew up. Usually, the colored people knew more about the general facts and gossip of the white world than the whites did of the colored world, although this was not always true. There were Negro newspapers, usually weekly. The history of the past was separated, there being a history of the colored world written and unwritten, and a general history of the white world which both worlds shared.

The colored world around Manuel tended to be a larger and more complete unity. The neighborhood organized itself for various local purposes like adorning the streets and fixing playgrounds and visiting the schools. There were united protests to the authorities about clearing the streets and garbage removal, and sometimes about the actions of the police or their absence.

Then, in larger matters concerning the city there were Negro agitation for appropriations to their schools, and for the few and bare parks, or perhaps for admission to the public parks. Beyond this came the state and the attitude of Georgia toward its colored people, the work on the legislature, not so much to get it to do things for Negroes as to keep them from various kinds of new oppression. The legislators seemed *continuously* to forget that one-third of the inhabitants of the state were Negroes; that black workers were an asset and not merely a cost and liability.

The attitude and thought of the Negroes of Georgia was illustrated as early as 1899 by their protest to proposed disfranchisement. Twenty-four prominent Negroes wrote:

"We, your petitioners, understanding that there lies before your honorable body, a bill known as the Hardwick bill, designed to change radically the basis of suffrage in this Commonwealth, desire respectfully to lay the following considerations before you.

"It is a solemn moment when a free community proposes to change the fundamental form of its Government, and especially to determine what voice its citizens shall have in the conduct of its affairs. Such changes and decisions, affecting the very root of democratic institutions in this country, ought not to be undertaken and carried through without careful deliberation, wise forethought and a broad and statesmanlike spirit of justice.

"Especially is this true in Georgia today. The future prosperity of our State depends upon the preservation within her borders of peace and security, good government and the impartial administration of law. Whatever tends to excite strife and restlessness, or opens the door to unfair dealing, or spreads the sense of injustice among the masses of the people is unwise and impolitic.

"It has come to be the consensus of opinion in civilized Nations that in the long run government must be based on the consent of the governed. This is the verdict of more than three centuries of strife and bloodshed, and it is a verdict not lightly to be set aside. Nevertheless, the Nineteenth century with its broader outlook and deeper experience has added one modifying clause to this, to which the world now assents, namely: that in order to take part in government, the governed must be intelligent enough to recognize and choose their own best good; that consequently in free governments based on universal manhood suffrage, it is fair and right to impose on voters an educational qualification, so long as the State furnishes free school facilities to all children.

"To these principles, we, as representatives of the Negroes of Georgia, give full assent. We join heartily with the best conscience of the State, of the Nation, and of the civilized world in demanding a pure intelligent ballot, free from bribery, ignorance, fraud and intimidation. And to secure this, we concur in the movement toward imposing fair and impartial qualifications upon voters, whether based on education, or property, or both.

"Nor is this, gentlemen of the Legislature, a light sacrifice on our part. We Negroes are today, in large degree, poor and ignorant through the crime of the Nation. Through no fault of our own, are we here brought into contact with a civilization higher than that of the average of our race. We have not been sparing in our efforts to improve.

"Notwithstanding all this, so far as the Hardwick bill proposes to restrict the right of suffrage to all who, irrespective of race or color, are intelligent enough to vote properly, we heartily endorse it. But there are two features of the proposed law against which we desire hereby to enter solemn and emphatic protest. There are:

"First. The so-called 'Grandfather' clause, which provides 'That no male person who was on January 1st, 1867 or any time prior thereto, entitled to vote under the laws of the State wherein he then resided, and no lineal descendent of such person shall be denied the right to register or vote at any election in this State by reason of his failure to possess the educational qualification provided for in this paragraph.' And

"Secondly. We protest against the clause which restricts the right to vote to those who can read AND UNDERSTAND a clause in the Constitution; and which allows the local election officers to be the final judges of this 'understanding.' We firmly believe that the exceptions in the first mentioned clause are wrong in principle, unfair in application, and in flat contradiction to those very principles of reform upon which the whole proposal is based; while the second clause is a direct invitation to injustice and fraud.

"We know that there are among our white fellow citizens broad-minded men who realize that the prosperity of Georgia is bound up with the prosperity of the Georgia Negro; That no Nation or State can advance faster than its laboring classes, and that whatever hinders, degrades or discourages the Negroes weakens and injures the State. To such Georgians we appeal in this crisis: Race antagonism and hatred have gone too far in this State; let us stop here; let us insist that we go no further; let us countenance no measure or movement calculated to increase that deep and terrible sense of wrong-doing under which so many today labor."

A general thought and action and stream of consciousness coursed through the colored world. It was still remembered what a thrill went through the dark people when Jack Johnson defeated Jim Jeffries; how white mobs broke out here and there, and white newspapers sternly warned Negroes not to be too "uppish." The whites rejoiced and the Negroes were sad when Johnson ran athwart the law. But the Negroes knew this was simply because he had married a white woman. Then came the *Birth of a Nation*, that splendid new effort at moving pictures which unfortunately centered on the race problem and aroused the passions of the mob. Negro audiences shrank at the wild ride of the Ku Klux Klan to rescue the white girl. They knew just what the white world was thinking.

The Pan-American Congresses in Europe in 1919 and after scarcely interested Mansart. There were, however, several persons, ministers and teachers, who took the trip to England, France and Belgium to attend the second, in 1921, largely because of the novelty of traveling abroad, but also because of interest in Africa and the feel of a tie between the American Negroes and their African cousins. When they came back, there were some speeches. One delegate told about the meeting in the largest city in the world, and especially of discussion and dispute in Brussels, where the Belgians were afraid that American Negroes were trying to put radical and rebellious ideas into the minds of the Congolese. It was, however, in Georgia a minor matter and aroused but passing interest.

The matter of taking part in politics always interested Negroes and divided them. There was an incident in Louisville where in order to issue bonds, in this case for school purposes, a majority of all the citizens and not simply of the whites, was required. This made Negroes in several Southern cities realize the power that they had, and in Louisville they proceeded to defeat the bond issue, which kept the city from spending money for public schools. The reason, of course, on the part of the Negroes was because the money was going to be spent almost entirely for white schools. In the future, this political tactic was destined to play considerable part in the South, and Manuel gave attention to it.

Bibliography

General Sources

The starting point for any serious study of Du Bois is the outstanding two-volume biography of him by David Levering Lewis.

Lewis, David Levering. 1993. *W. E. B. Du Bois: Biography of a Race 1868-1919*. New York: Henry Holt.

———. 2000. *W. E. B. Du Bois: The Fight for Equality and the American Century, 1919-1963*. New York: Henry Holt.

General background on Du Bois can be found in his own words in his two autobiographies.

Du Bois, W. E. B. 1940. *Dusk of Dawn: An Essay Toward an Autobiography of a Race Concept*. New York: Harcourt Brace and Company (rep., 1968, New York: Schocken).

———. 1968. *The Autobiography of W. E. B. Du Bois: A Soliloquy on Viewing My Life from the Last Decade of Its First Century*. New York: International Publishers.

The two best general collections of Du Bois's writings are:

Du Bois, W. E. B. 1986. *W. E. B. Du Bois: Writings*. New York: Library of America. This volume includes *The Suppression of the African Slave Trade* (1896), *The Souls of Black Folks* (1903), *Dusk of Dawn* (1940) and selected essays and articles.

Lewis, David Levering, ed. 1995. *W. E. B. Du Bois: A Reader*. New York: Henry Holt.

Philip S. Foner provides excellent compilations of Du Bois's speeches in two volumes.

Philip S. Foner, ed. 1970. *W. E. B. Du Bois Speaks: Speeches and Addresses 1890-1919*. New York: Pathfinder.

————. 1991. *W. E. B. Du Bois Speaks: Speeches and Addresses 1920-1963*. New York: Pathfinder.

Background on Du Bois as a pioneering sociologist can be found in:

Green, Dan S. and Edwin D. Driver, eds. 1978. *W. E. B. DuBois: On Sociology and the Black Community*. Chicago: University of Chicago Press.

The main general bibliography on Du Bois is:

Aptheker, Herbert. 1973. *Annotated Bibliography of the Published Writings of W. E. B. Du Bois*. Millwood, N.Y.: Kraus-Thomson Organization.

There are two particularly valuable publications on Du Bois and education that should be noted.

Alridge, Derrick P. 1999. "Conceptualizing a Du Boisian Philosophy of Education: Toward a Model for African-American Education," *Educational Theory*, 49(3): 359-380.

Aptheker, Herbert, ed. 1973. *The Education of Black People: Ten Critiques 1906-1960*. Amherst: University of Massachusetts Press.

In addition, Gerald Gutek provides an excellent introduction to Du Bois and his educational ideas in the following textbook:

Gutek, Gerald L. 1991. *Cultural Foundations of Education: A Biographical Approach*. New York: Collier McMillian.

James D. Anderson provides the best source available on the debate between Washington and Du Bois and the controversy over the Hampton Model in the following work:

Anderson, James D. 1988. *The Education of Blacks in the South, 1860-1935*. Chapel Hill: University of North Carolina Press.

Other general sources on Du Bois consulted for this study include:

Banks, James A. 1992. "African American Scholarship and the Evolution of Multicultural Education," *Journal of Negro Education*, 61(3): 273-286.

Diggs, Irene. 1976. "Du Bois and Children," *Phylon*, 37(4): 370-399.

Dunn, Frederick. 1993. "The Educational Philosophies of Washington, Du Bois, and Houston: Laying the Foundations for Afrocentrism and Multiculturalism," *Journal of Negro Education*, 62(1): 24-34.

Franklin, Vincent P. 1976. "W. E. B. Du Bois and the Education of Black Folk," *History of Education Quarterly*, 16(1): 11-118.

Gates, Henry Louis, Jr. 2000. "W. E. B. Du Bois and the Encyclopedia Africana, 1909-63," *Annals of the American Academy of Political and Social Science*, 568: 203-219.

Green, Dan S. 1977. "W. E. B. Du Bois's Talented Tenth: A Strategy for Racial Advancement." *Journal of Negro Education*, 46(3): 358-366.

Kilson, Martin. 2000. "The Washington and Du Bois Leadership Paradigms Reconsidered," *Annals of the American Academy of Political and Social Science*, 568: 298-313.

Lacy, L. A. 1970. *Cheer the Lonesome Traveler: The Life of W. E. B. Du Bois*. New York: Dial Press.

Miller, Jan. 1994. "Annotated Bibliography of the Washington-Dubois Controversy," *Journal of Black Studies*, 25(2): 250-272.

Moore, J. B. 1981. *W. E. B. Du Bois*. Boston: Twayne Publishers.

Outlaw, Lucius T., Jr. 2000. "W. E. B. Du Bois on the Study of Social Problems," *Annals of the American Academy of Political and Social Science*, 568: 281-297.

Spiers, Fiona E. 1978. "The Talented Tenth: Leadership Problems and the Afro-American Intellectuals, 1895-1919," *Bulletin of the John Rylands University Library of Manchester*, 61(1): 206-231.

Townsend, Kim. 1996. "'Manhood' At Harvard: W. E. B. Du Bois," *Raritan*, 15(4): 70-82.

Vaughn-Roberson, Courtney and Brenda Hill. 1989. "The Brownies' Book and Ebony Jr.!: Literature as a Mirror of the Afro-American Experience," *Journal of Negro Education*, 58(4): 494-510.

West, Cornel. 1999. "W. E. B. Du Bois: An Interpretation." In Anthony Kwame Appiah and Henry Louis Gates, eds., *Africana: The Encyclopedia of the African American Experience*. New York: Basic Books (1967-1982).

General Works by Du Bois

Below are general works by Du Bois either referred to in, or with relevance to, this book.

Du Bois, W. E. B. 1896. *The Suppression of the African Slave Trade to the United States of America, 1638-1870*. Cambridge, Mass.: Harvard Historical Series Number 1.

————. 1896 (1970). *The Suppression of the African Slave Trade to the United States of America, 1638-1870*. New York: Dover Publications.

————, and I. Eaton. 1899. *The Philadelphia Negro; A Social Study*. Philadelphia: Published for the University of Pennsylvania.

————. 1903. *The Souls of Black Folks*. Chicago: A. C. McClurg.

————. 1909 (1962). *John Brown*. New York: International Publishers.

————. 1911 (1989). *The Quest of the Silver Fleece*. Boston: Northeastern University Press.

————. 1915. *The Negro*. New York: Henry Holt.

————. 1921 (1969). *Darkwater: Voices from within the Veil*. New York: AMS Press.

————. 1924. *The Gift of Black Folk: The Negroes in the Making of America*. Boston: Stratford Co.

————. 1947. *The World and Africa: An Inquiry into the Part Which Africa Has Played in World History, by W. E. Burghardt Du Bois*. New York: Viking Press.

————. 1957 (1976). *The Ordeal of Mansart*. Millwood, N.Y.:Kraus-Thomson Organization.

————. 1959. *Mansart Builds a School*. New York: Mainstream Publishers.

————. 1980. *Selections from the Brownies' Book*. Herbert Aptheker, ed. Millwood, N.Y.: Kraus-Thomson Organization.

Works by W. E. B. Du Bois Dealing with Education

Works preceded by an asterisk (*) are included in this volume. This portion of the bibliography is largely based on the sources provided by Herbert Aptheker in his 1973 book on Du Bois and higher education, The Education of Black People: Ten Critiques 1906-1960 *by W. E. B. Du Bois. Aptheker includes references to newspaper articles dealing with educational issues written by Du Bois which may be of interest to readers, but which are not included in this volume.*

In addition to articles, Du Bois included extensive material about education in many of his books, and for approximately twenty years, beginning in 1896, edited most of the reports for the Atlanta University Conferences. A number of the conferences focused on educational issues, including the "College-bred Negro" in 1900 and the "Negro Common School" in 1901. These reports, while of great value historically, tend to be compilations of statistics and general data, and have not been included in this work because of their length and diffuse content.

*Du Bois, W. E. B. 1898. "Careers Open to College-Bred Negroes." Included in the pamphlet *Two Addresses Delivered by Alumni of Fisk University in Connection with the Anniversary Exercises of Their Alma Mater, June 1898*. Nashville: Fisk University, 1-14.

*———. 1899. "A Negro Schoolmaster in the New South," *Atlantic Monthly*, 83 (January): 99-104. This essay was included in *The Souls of Black Folks*.

———. 1900. *The College-Bred Negro.* Report of a Social Study Made under the Direction of Atlanta University; Together with the Proceedings of the Fifth Conference for the Study of the Negro Problems, Held at Atlanta University, May 29-30, 1900. Atlanta: Atlanta University Press. Pages 10-114 are by Du Bois.

———. 1900. *Memorial to the Legislature of Georgia on Negro Common Schools.* Single-page printed leaflet signed by eight leading Georgia blacks. Herbert Aptheker identifies this document as having been printed in Atlanta in 1900.

———. 1901. Testimony given February 13, 1901, in Washington, D.C., before the Congressionally appointed Industrial Commission. "Immigration and Education." *Hearings on General and Industrial Education.* Volume XV. Washington, D. C.: Government Printing Office, 159-175.

*———.1901. "The Freedman's Bureau," *Atlantic Monthly*, 57 (March): 354-365.

———. 1901. *The Negro Common School.* Report of a Social Study Made under the Direction of Atlanta University; Together with the Proceedings of the Sixth Conference for the Study of the Negro Problems, Held at Atlanta University, on May 28, 1901. Atlanta: Atlanta University Press.

———. 1901. "The Burden of Negro Schooling," *Independent,* 53 (July): 1667-1668.

*———. 1902. "Of the Training of Black Men," *Atlantic Monthly*, 90 (September): 289-297.

———. 1902. "Higher Education of the Negro," *Talladega College Record,* 10 (November): 2.

———. "The Two Sorts of Schooling." 900-word essay included in the Du Bois papers.

*————. 1903. "Of Mr. Booker T. Washington and Others." Chapter III of *The Souls of Black Folks*. Chicago: A. C. McClurg.

*————. 1903. "The Training of Negroes for Social Power," *Outlook* (New York), 75 (October 17): 409-414. This article was reprinted by Atlanta University as a pamphlet in 1903 under the title *The Training of Negroes for Social Reform*.

————. 1903. "Cultured Negro Model for Race." *Chicago Tribune*, June 18: 1.

*————. 1903. "The Talented Tenth." *The Negro Problem: A Series of Articles by Representative American Negroes of Today*. Contributions by Booker T. Washington, W. E. Burghardt Du Bois, Paul Laurence Dunbar, Charles W. Chesnutt and others. New York: James Pott, 33-75.

*————. 1904. *Heredity and the Public Schools*. A Lecture Delivered under the Auspices of the Principals' Association of the Colored Schools of Washington, D.C. Friday March 25, 1904. Washington: R. L. Pendelton.

————. 1904. "The Joy of Living." A speech delivered in 1904 in Washington, D.C. (probably as a high school commencement speech), first published by Herbert Aptheker in *Political Affairs*, 44:2 (February 1965): 35-44.

————. 1904. "The Development of a People," *International Journal of Ethics* (Philadelphia), 14 (April): 292-311.

————. 1904. "What Intellectual Training Is Doing for the Negro," *Missionary Review of the World*, 17 (August): 578-582.

*————. 1905. "Atlanta University." In *From Servitude to Service*. Boston: American Unitarian Association, 155-97.

————. 1906. "The Hampton Idea," *Voice of the Negro*, 3 (September): 332-336.

————. 1906. "St. Francis of Assisi." *Voice of the Negro*, 3 (October): 419-426. Originally delivered as a graduation speech for the Colored High Schools of Washington, D.C., June 15, 1906.

———. 1907. "Sociology and Industry in Southern Education," *Voice of the Negro*, 4 (May): 170-175.

———. 1910. "Negro Education and Evangelization." Signed essay in *The New Schaff-Herzog Religious Encyclopedia*. Samuel M. Jackson, ed. 12 volumes. New York: Funk & Wagnalls, Vol. VIII, 100-108.

———. 1910. *College-Bred Negro Communities: Address of Professor W. E. B. Du Bois at Brookline, Massachusetts*. Atlanta University Leaflet No. 23. Atlanta: Atlanta University Press.

———. 1910. *The College-Bred Negro*. Report of a Social Study Made by Atlanta University under the Patronage of the Trustees of the John F. Slater Fund; with the Proceedings of the 15th Annual Conference for the Study of Negro Problems, held at Atlanta University on May 24, 1910. Atlanta: Atlanta University Press.

———. 1911. *The Common School and the Negro American*. Report of a Social Study Made by Atlanta University under the Patronage of the Trustees of the John F. Slater Fund; with the Proceedings of the 16th Annual Conference for the Study of the Negro Problems held at Atlanta University on May 30, 1911. Atlanta: Atlanta University Press.

———. 1914. *Memorandum in Support of Proposed Amendment to H. R. 7951, Entitled a Bill to Provide for Co-operative Agricultural Extension Work between the Agricultural Colleges in the Several States. . . and the U.S. Department of Agriculture*. A sixteen-page pamphlet issued by the NAACP in 1914. Signed by Chapin Brinsmade as Attorney and by Du Bois as Director of Publicity and Research.

———. 1917. "Hampton," *The Crisis*, 15 (November): 10-12.

———. 1918. "Negro Education" (review of book by Thomas Jesse Jones), *The Crisis*, 15 (February): 173-178.

———. 1921. "Colored Teachers in Charleston (S.C.) Schools," *The Crisis*, 22 (June): 57-60.

———. 1923. "The Negro and the Northern Public Schools," *The Crisis*, 25 (March and April): 205-208, 262-265.

———. 1923. "The Tragedy of Jim Crow," *The Crisis*, 26 (August): 169-172.

———. 1923. "To American Students," *New Student*, 3 (December 1): 1.

———. 1924. "Diuturni Silenti," *Fisk Herald*, 33: i-xii.

———. 1924. "Fisk" *The Crisis*, 28 (October): 251-252.

———. 1925. "Missouri Shows Us," *The Crisis*, 30 (September): 226-227. Unsigned article deals with developments at Lincoln University in Missouri.

———. 1926. "Education in Africa," *The Crisis*, 33 (June): 86-89. Review of two-volume report on the subject by Thomas Jesse Jones.

*———. 1926. "Negroes in College," *Nation*, 122 (March 13): 228-230.

———. 1927. "The Hampton Strike," *Nation*, 125 (November 2): 471-472.

———. 1929. "Postscript," *The Crisis*, 36 (September): 313-314, 317. Regular department dealing with segregated education.

*———. 1931. "Education and Work," *Howard University Bulletin*, 9 (January): 1-22; and republished with minor changes in the *Journal of Negro Education*, 1 (April 1932): 60-74.

———. 1933. *The Field and Function of a Negro College*. Nashville: Fisk University Press. Republished with minor changes as "The Negro College" (see below).

*———. 1933. "The Negro College," *The Crisis*, 40 (August): 175-177.

*———. 1935. "Does the Negro Need Separate Schools?" *Journal of Negro Education*, 4 (July): 328-335.

———. 1937. Testimony before the Committee on Education, House of Representatives, 75th Cong., 1st Sess., Hearings on Federal Aid for the Support of Public Schools, April 2. Washington, D.C.: Government Printing Office: 284-295.

*———. 1938. "How Negroes Have Taken Advantage of Educational Opportunities Offered by Friends," *Journal of Negro Education*, 7 (April): 124-131.

———. 1938. "The Revelation of Saint Orgne the Dammed," *Fisk News*, 9 (November-December): 3-9.

———. 1940. "Review of Horace Mann Bond. *Negro Education in Alabama. A Study in Cotton and Steel*," *American Historical Review*, 45 (April): 669-670.

*———. 1940. "The Future of Wilberforce University," *Journal of Negro Education*. 9 (October): 553-570.

———. 1941. "The Future of the Negro State University," *Wilberforce University Quarterly*, 2 (April): 53-60.

———. 1941. "A Program for the Land-Grant Colleges." *Proceedings of the Nineteenth Annual Conference of the Presidents of Negro Land Grant Colleges*, November 11-13, 1941, Chicago (n.p., n.d.): 42-56.

———. 1942. "The Cultural Missions of Atlanta University," *Phylon*, 3(2): 105-115.

———. 1943. Report of the First Conference of Negro Land-Grant Colleges for Coordinating a Program of Cooperative Social Studies. Twenty-Sixth Atlanta University Conference to Study the Negro Problems, No. 22. Atlanta: Atlanta University Publications.

———. 1943. "Reading, Writing, and Real Estate," *Negro Digest*, October.

*———. 1946. "The Future and Function of the Private Negro College," *The Crisis*, 53 (August): 234-236, 253-254.

———. 1949. "The Nature of Intellectual Freedom," in Daniel S. Gillmo, ed., *Speaking of Peace: An Edited Report of the Cultural and Scientific Conference for World Peace, New York, March 25-27, 1949, under the Auspices of the National Council of the Arts, Sciences and Professions*, 78.

———. 1949. "The Freedom to Learn," *Midwest Journal*, 2: 9-11.

*———. 1956. "Two Hundred Years of Segregated Schools," *Jewish Life Anthology, 1946-1956*: 201-206.

———. 1956. "Review of Samuel R. Spencer, *Booker T. Washington and the Negro's Place in American Life*," *Science & Society*, 20 (Spring): 183-185.

*———. 1960. "A Negro Student at Harvard at the End of the 19th Century," *Massachusetts Review*, 1 (May): 439-458.

Index

abolition, 78-79, 87, 147-
54, 165,
289
Adams, Charles Francis, 33
Adams, John Quincy, 33
Addams, Jane, 112
administrators, 238-39
Africa, history, 281
African Church, 166
African Methodist Church, 148,
239, 260
African Methodist Episcopal
Church, 253, 262, 265, 267,
270, 272
African-American studies, 134, 253
Agassiz, Alexander, 33
agriculture, 207, 218
Aldridge, Ira, 78
Allen, Richard, 147-48
Alridge, Derrick P., 1, 15-17
ambition, 54, 80, 170-72, 221-23,
246
American Anti-Slavery Society, 79
American Freedmen's Union, 97
American Historical Association,
47
American Historical Society, 45
American Mercury, The, 13
American Missionary Association,
97, 164, 219, 222
American Missionary Society, 151
Amherst College, 135
Anderson, James, 6-7
apathy, 80, 186
apprenticeship, 68
Aptheker, Herbert, 10, 157, 179,
235, 243
aristocracy, 207, 248
Aristophanes, 36
Armstrong, Samuel Chapman, 6,
105
art, 142, 177, 211, 248-50, 281-83
assimilation, 166-67

Associated Press, 170
Atlanta Compromise, 7-8, 164,
170, 292
Atlanta Constitution, 216
Atlanta Institute of Technology,
293, 296
Atlanta University, 2, 57, 67, 82,
92, 105, 128, 142-43;
curriculum, 225-26, 277-78;
facilities, 225-26; funding, 130,
238, 270; purpose, 72;
standards, 237-38; student
statistics, 229-30; success, 223,
229, 259; teacher training, 227,
230
Atlantic Monthly, 21, 51, 95, 145
Attucks, Crispus, 141, 166

Baker, Bessie, 37
Banneker, Benjamin, 77, 142, 149,
166
Baptist Church, 153, 228
Benezet, Anthony, 147, 149, 157
Berlin Conference, 41
Bethel Church, 151
Bettle, Edward, 150
Birds, The, 36
Birth of a Nation, 305
Black Flame Trilogy, 289
Black History Week, 134
Black Power, 134
Board of Review of the
Commission on Higher Education,
273
Bogle, Robert, 153
Boston Herald, 44, 46
Boston Latin School, 223
Boston University, 225
bounties, 104, 107
Bowdoin College, 82
Boylston Prize, 38-39
brain measurements, 119
Bray Associates, 146

Bray, Thomas, 157
British Empire, 194
British Society for the Propagation of the Gospel, 157
Brooks, Phillips, 33
"Brother in Black," 221
Brown vs. Topeka, 157
Brown, John, 152, 167
Brown, William Wells, 151
Brownies' Book, The, 15
Bureau for Freedmen, 99
Bureau of Education, 69
Bureau of Emancipation, 98
Bureau of Refugees, Freedmen, and Abandoned Lands, 99
business, 183-87, 189, 191-193, 208, 218

Cambridge University, 151
capital, 185, 188-89, 208, 247
capitalism, 147, 190, 279
Carlon, Sam, 29
Carnegie Corporation, 12
Carnegie, Andrew, 8, 222
caste system, 66, 187-90, 196, 233, 249
Catholicism, 146-47, 240, 279, 293
Channing, Edward, 33
Chapman, Maria Weston, 79
character, 56, 67-72, 104, 138, 239
charity, 208-10, 234
Chavis, John, 157
Child, Francis, 31, 33
Christianity, 78, 169, 210, 220-21
Church of Christ, 170
Church of England, 146
church property, 208
civic rights, 79, 88, 163, 173, 177
Civil Rights march (1963), 3
Civil Rights movement, 76
Civil War, 6, 153, 158, 271-77, 290
class discrimination, 75
college graduates, 83-84
"College-Bred Community, The," 11
College-Bred Negro, The, 215, 232

colleges, 133, 191, 193, 240; administration, 240, 283; as communities, 228, 283; curriculum, 283; facilities, 283; funding, 278, 292; land grant, 160, 184, 189, 265; Negro, 73, 125, 182-86, 209, 280; success, 188, 190, 282-85
colonization, 166
color line, 95, 110, 133-35, 217, 251
color prejudice, 52, 165
Columbia University, 136, 140, 225
commerce, 185, 209
communal education, 16
communism, 2
Communist Party, 2
community, 56, 88
Conference at Atlanta University, 58
Conference for Southern Education, 227
Congo Free State, 41
Congregationalists, 153
consumer power, 274
Cook, George William, 236
Coolidge, Calvin, 37
Cope, Alfred, 154
corruption, 298-301
Cotton States Exposition, 7
Courant, The, 37
courtesy, 213
courts, 106-07, 109
Coxey's Army, 40
Crandall, Prudence, 152, 158
Cravath, Erastus, 105
Cravath, Paul, 13
Crawford, George, 179
creation, 113-14, 118
credit, 185, 189
crime, 61, 71-73, 107-10, 190, 219, 231
Crime Among Negroes, 215, 232
Crisis, The, 13-15, 123, 145, 175-79, 233

Croly, Herbert, 38
Crothers, Samuel M., 219
Crummel, Alexander, 79, 157, 167
Cuffe, Paul, 77, 149
culture, 213, 218, 230-31, 281-82;
    in education, 191, 201-202,
    244-45
Cuney, Maud, 37-38
curriculum, 82, 124
Curry, Jabez L. M., 8, 219, 225

Dartmouth College, 230
Darusmont, Fannie Wright, 150
Darwin, Charles, 114, 118-19, 204
Davis, J. E., 175
Davis, Jefferson, 32, 41, 164
Day, Carolyn Bond, 142
DeForest Medal, 225
democracy, 141, 153, 205, 250,
    291, 303
Derham, Dr. James, 77
desegregation, 15, 134
Detroit College, 240
Dewey, John, 16-17, 112
Dial, The, 232
"Dilemma of the Negro, The," 13
discipline, 67-68, 231, 235, 239
discrimination, 3, 22, 139, 163-69
disease, 148
"Diuturni Silenti," 235
"Does The Negro Need Separate
Schools?," 15
Dorsey, George, 38
Douglass, Frederick, 79, 142, 149
Dowell, Fanny, 25
Dowell, Josie, 22-23
Dowell, Martha, 25
Du Bois, John, 254
Du Bois, Nina Gomer. *See* Nina
    Gomer
Du Bois, Shirley Graham. *See*
    Shirley Graham
Du Bois, Yolande, 12, 235
Dunbar, Paul Laurence, 254
Dunn, James, 142
Durkee, J. Stanley, 236

Dusk of Dawn, 3, 17, 21, 32, 216

Eastman, George, 8
economy, 54, 69, 71, 141
education, 76, 86, 152;
    administration, 67, 90, 159,
    250; advanced, 56, 123-26,
    172-76, 262; common, 53, 55,
    73, 171-72; elementary, 14,
    126, 153; funding, 68-69, 123,
    139-42, 159, 278; industrial, 73,
    86-88, 170-75, 193, 300;
    liberal, 201-203, 239; mixed,
    15, 134-35, 137, 143, 158;
    Negro, 88-89, 109, 159, 187,
    210, 236, 277; private, 127,
    158; public, 53, 68-69, 134-37,
    244, 293; secondary, 14, 68-69,
    153, 158; separate, 134, 143,
    159; State, 129, 159; systems,
    5, 81, 126, 169-70; of teachers,
    67, 85-86
*Education of Black People: Ten
Critiques 1906-1960*, 10
Edward Waters College, 270
Eliot, Charles William, 8, 31, 33
elitism, 75
emancipation, 70-71, 149-53, 181,
    277, 302
Emancipation Proclamation, 79, 95,
    98
Encyclopedia Africana, 2
Episcopalian Church, 147-48
equality, civic, 9, 164; social, 135,
    150, 240, 291
ethics, 192, 197
evolution, 114-19
"Exhibit of the Georgia Negro," 95
extra-curricular activities, 135

family, 186, 197, 207, 227, 248
fatalism, 118
Ferguson, Katy, 157
Fifteenth Amendment, 103, 109
Fisk Herald, 13
Fisk University, 1-4, 23-27, 70-75,

123-28, 225; administration, 235-36; funding, 235-36, 270
Flexner, Abraham, 243-44
Florida A. and M. College, 258
Folks, Homer, 38
Forbes, George, 37
Foreign Agents Registration Act, 2
Fordham College, 240
Forten, James, 149
Fortress Monroe, 96
Fourteenth Amendment, 103
Fox, George, 146, 154
Frank, Kuno, 46
Franklin, Benjamin, 147
Franklin, Vincent P., 14
fraternities, 240
fraud, 106-108, 130
Frederic Wilhelm University, 1-2
Free African Society, 148
Freedmen's Aid Societies, 96-98
Freedmen's Bureau, 53, 100, 145, 158, 220
French Black Code, 146
French Revolution, 157
Frissell, Hollis Burke, 175
From Servitude to Service, 215
Furber, Dr. D. L., 222

"Galileo Galilei," 235
Garfield, James A., 8
Garnett, Highland, 79
Garrison, William Lloyd, 152-53
General Education Board (GEB), 11-14, 129-31, 238, 259
George, Henry, 40
Ghana, 1-3
Gibbs, Jonathan E., 159
"Gifts and Education," 13
Gomer, Nina, 2, 253
Graham, Shirley, 2
Grandfather clause, 304
Grant, Ulysses S., 8
Great Depression, 249
Guardian, The, 37

Haitian Revolution, 149, 166

Hall, Charles Cuthbert, 219
"Hampton Idea, The," 10
Hampton Institute, 6-7, 56-57, 105, 175-76, 238
Hampton model, 6-8, 10, 179, 289
"Hampton Model," 163
Hampton-Tuskegee model, 7-8, 292
Hand, Augustus, 38
Hapgood, Norman, 38
Hardwick bill, 303
Harris, Joel Chandler, 216
Hart, Albert Bushnell, 33-34, 41, 44
Harvard Historical Studies, 145
Harvard University, 1-4, 55-58, 135-36, 230; Business School, 140; and Negroes, 225, 240-41
Hasty Pudding Club, 33
Hayes, Rutherford B., 8, 32, 46-47
Haygood, Atticus G., 47, 89, 219-21
Haynes, Lemuel, 77
Henson, Josiah, 152
Heredity, physical, 111-13, 117-20, 122, 142; social, 117-18, 120-21
Heredity and the Public Schools, 111
heroism, 222
Herrick, Robert, 38
Hill, Leslie P., 271
Holmes, Oliver Wendell, 31, 33
Homestead strike, 40
Hopkins, Mark, 87, 269
Hose, Sam, 216
Hosmer, Frank, 3
Howard University, 82, 105, 179, 247; administration, 236-37; funding, 233, 270; purpose, 259
Howard Welfare League, 236
Howard, Oliver O., 100, 103, 107
Howell, Clark, 8
Humphries, Richard, 152, 207
identity, 280

ignorance, 4, 66-70, 148, 266, 304
illiteracy, 4, 68
immigration, 150, 166
imperialism, 54
independence, 192, 285
Independent, The, 8, 232
Indiana University, 265
individualism, 43, 62, 138
Industrial North, 39
industrial revolution, 53-54, 147, 191
industrial schools, 54, 69, 125, 186-89, 208; Negro, 70, 190
industrialism, 39, 87, 295
industry, 127, 183-85, 192-93, 218, 280; development, 183; model, 180; ideal, 195, 206
inferiority complex, 35, 143
Institute for Colored Youth, 152, 271
integration, 36
intelligence, 70
Interfraternity Council, 240
intermarriage, 61

James, Steven, 151
James, William, 2, 31-34, 41, 44, 114
Jefferson, Thomas, 77, 149
Jeffries, Jim, 305
Jesuits, 146
Jesus Christ, 212
Jim Crow, 30, 38, 159, 245
Johns Hopkins University, 46-47, 241
Johnson, Jack, 305
Jones, Absalom, 147-49
Jones, Thomas E., 243
Journal of Negro Education, 133, 145, 253

Kant, Immanuel, 41
Kate Field's Washington, 44
Keith, George, 146
King, Martin Luther, Jr., 3
knowledge, 196

Ku Klux Klan, 293, 305
labor, 97, 183-85, 247, 274; free, 104, 107, 109; movement, 190-91, 293; Negro, 133, 182, 249, 300-301; skilled, 207, 296; white, 130, 233, 300
land-grant funds, 293
law, 209
Lay, Benjamin, 147
leadership, 71-72, 80, 185-86, 192, 216; educational, 253, 292; skilled, 87, 154; white, 75, 163
League of Europe, 194
League of Nations, 194
Lebanon Teacher Institute, 21
Lee, Benjamin, 260
legal protection, 59
Lewis, David Levering, 15, 21-22, 179
Lewis, William H., 37
liberal arts, 180, 201, 213, 224
liberalism, 239
"Liberator," 79
Lincoln Institute, 258
Lincoln University, 158, 237, 239
Lincoln, Abraham, 98, 103, 142, 212, 290
literacy, 231. *See also* illiteracy
literature, 177, 211, 248-49, 281
Livingstone, David, 204
Lodge, Henry Cabot, 33
London Times, 232
Lowell, James Russell, 31, 33

Manchester Guardian, The, 232
Mansart Builds a School, 289
Marx, Karl, 34, 40
mass production, 188
materialism, 54
Matseliger, Jan, 142
McCoy, Elijah, 142
McKenzie, Fayette A., 12-14, 235
McMillan, R. C., 21
medicine, 209
meritocracy, 6
Merrill, James G., 235

Methodist Church, 147-48, 153, 158, 228, 270
Methodist Episcopal Church, 221
Methods and Results of Ten Years' Study, 215, 232
Middlebury College, 77
Midsummer Night's Dream, 257
migration, 152, 166, 274
military, 102, 106
Miller, Kelly, 236
missionaries, 8, 55, 146, 158
Mitchell, John, 260
Mitchell, Samuel T., 261-64
mob law, 245, 251, 301
modernity, 127, 182, 188, 194, 197, 208
moral teaching, 221, 228
morals, 68-69, 205-207, 210, 260
Morgan, Clement, 38, 46
Morgan, Thomas J., 8
Morris Brown College, 270
Mortality among Negroes in Cities, 215, 232
Muensterberg, Hugo, 46
music, 142, 177

Nation, The, 232, 235
National Association for the Advancement of Colored People (NAACP), 2-3, 212-13, 215, 289-91
National Convention of Negroes, 152
National Freedmen's Relief Association, 97
National Survey of Higher Education of Negroes, 282
natural selection, 115
Negro Artisan, The, 215, 232
Negro Church, The, 215, 232
Negro College, The, 151
Negro Common School, The, 215, 232
Negro convention (1831), 78
Negro Health Week, 141
Negro History Week, 141

Negro in Business, The, 213, 232
Negro Problem, The, 5, 51, 75
Negro property, 105, 127, 227, 231
Negro State Agricultural and Mechanical College, 296
Nell, William C., 151, 158
"New Education, The," 289
New England Conservatory of Music, 38
New South, 39
New York Independent, The, 45
Niagara movement, 37
Nkrumah, Kwame, 2
North Central Association of Colleges and Secondary Schools, 273
Norton, Charles Eliot, 31, 33
Norwich Free Academy, 219

"Of Mr. Booker T. Washington and Others," 9
"Of the Meaning of Progress," 21
"Of the Training of Black Men," 65
Ogden parties, 227
Ohio State University, 253, 256, 272
oligarchy, 280
Ordeal of Mansart, The, 289
orthodoxy, 239
Outlook, The, 65, 232

Page, Thomas Nelson, 171
Palmer, George, 33, 41
Pan-Africanism, 16-17
Pan-American Congress, 305
Paris 1900 International Exposition, 95
particularism, 262
partisan politics, 258, 263
patriotism, 171
Payne, Daniel, 167, 260, 263
Peabody, Francis, 33-34
Peace Information Center, 2
Penn, William, 146
Pennsylvania Hall, 151
Phelps Stokes Fund, 14, 123, 130,

233-34
Phi Beta Kappa, 33, 236
Philadelphia Yearly Meeting, 147
philanthropic agencies, 131, 238
philanthropy, 68, 123, 128-30, 153,
    278-80; Northern, 129, 182,
    233, 292; white, 177, 239
Pindell, Deenie, 37
Pleasants, Robert, 146
Populist movement, 40
Port Royal plan, 97
poverty, 22, 66-70, 176, 249, 304
Prairie View College, 270
Presbyterian Church, 153, 158,
    237, 270
Princeton University, 135-36, 240
Principal's Association of the
Colored Schools, 111
professional class, 209, 249
progress, 55, 75, 168, 249, 266
public opinion, 130, 136, 143, 165,
    176
public property, 102

Quakers, 145-50, 152-54, 271
Queen's Jubilee, 40
Quest of the Silver Fleece, The, 289

racism, 51, 54, 171-72, 183, 252-56
radicalism, 238
railway strikes, 40
Reason, Charles L., 151-52
Reconstruction, 141, 167, 192, 218
Reconstruction Governments, 153,
    158
Reform Convention, 151
religion, 72, 85, 196, 211, 250;
    Negro, 59, 81, 210
revolt, 61, 150, 157, 165-66
Revolution of 1876, 167
Revolutionary War, 146-47
Ricardo, David, 40
Riis, Jacob, 112
riots, 150-51
Rockefeller Foundation, 14, 233
Rockefeller, John D., Jr., 8

Rogers, Henry Bromfield, 45
Roosevelt, Theodore, 8
Rosenwald, Julius, 8
Royce, Josiah, 33, 41, 44
Ruffin, Josephine St. Pierre, 36-37

sacrifice, 196, 203-205, 219-23,
    283
Saint George's Methodist Church,
    148
Saint Peter, 212
Santayana, George, 2, 31, 33, 41-44
Scarborough, William Sander, 253
scholarship, 62, 203, 224, 258-60
science, 206, 211, 247-49. 283
Scott, James Brown, 38
segregation, 35-36, 55, 109, 160,
    244; and education, 133-37,
    139-42, 158, 250-51, 302
self-realization, 75, 163, 165, 205
self-reliance, 107, 203, 208, 256,
    274
self-respect, 128, 140, 143, 168-69,
    177
"Seven Critiques of Negro
Education, 1908-1938," 10
Shakespeare, William, 257
Shaler, Nathan, 33, 41
Shelter for Colored Orphans, 151
Sherman Act, 39
Shorter, J. P., 264
Sidney, Thomas, 147
Sixth Atlanta Conference (1901),
    88
Slater Fund, 32, 46-47
slaves, slavery, 103, 106, 109, 150,
    172, 228
Smith, Dr. James McCune, 151
social advancement, 62, 155
*Social and Physical Condition of
Negroes in Cities*, 215, 232
social change, 171, 231
social reform, 71, 101, 118
social regeneration, 66, 73, 103
socialism, 2, 62, 141
Society for the Propagation of the

Gospel in Foreign Parts, 146
sociology, 45
Socrates, 204
Some Efforts of Negroes for Social Betterment, 215, 232
Souls of Black Folks, The, 21, 51, 95, 277
South Carolina Act, 158
Southern Education Board, 159
Southern Educational Association, 127
Southern University of Louisiana, 27
Spanish-American War, 165
Spectator, The, 232
Spelman Seminary, 56
Spence, Adam K., 124-125
Stanley, Henry, 40
Storrs' School, 221
Streator, George, 235
suffrage, 108-109, 167-70, 172, 291, 303-304
Sumner, Charles, 99
superstition, 148, 239
Suppression of the African Slave Trade in America, 2, 32

Taft, William Howard, 8
talent, 177, 229
talented tenth, 5, 10-12, 60
"Talented Tenth, The," 5, 51, 201
tariff policy, 40
Taussig, Frank, 33-34
Tawawa Springs, 257
taxation, 69, 88, 109, 128, 282-83
teachers, 229, 266; education of, 194, 225; Negro, 90, 126, 133-38, 185, 238
Tempelhofer Feld, 41
Texas Colored State College, 259
textbooks, 142, 158
The Philadelphia Negro, 2
Thirteenth Amendment, 102-103
thrift, 69-70, 72, 169, 172
Tillman, Ben, 171
Total Abstinence Club, 37

trade schools. *See* industrial schools
"Tragedy of Jim Crow, The," 14
"Training of Negroes for Social Power, The," 4
Triple Alliance, 41
Trotter, Monroe, 37
Trowbridge, John, 31, 33
Truth, Sojourner, 79, 149
Tubman, Harriet, 152
Turner, Nat, 166
Turner, T. W., 236
Tuskegee Institute, 7, 164-65, 172, 189; funding, 184, 279
Tuskegee Machine, 179
"Tuskegee Machine," 8, 163

Underground Railroad, 152
Union Station, 245
Union Theological Seminary, 219, 228
unions, 190, 296, 300-301. *See also* labor
United States Office of Education, 282
universities, 80-81, 246; Negro, 80, 153, 223, 244
University at Athens, 293
University of Berlin, 32-33, 154
University of Chicago, 46, 136, 140, 230, 253-56
University of Glasgow, 151
University of Illinois, 265
University of Michigan, 230, 240, 265
University of Pennsylvania, 2, 271
University of Pennsylvania Medical School, 230
University of Pittsburgh, 271
University of Wisconsin, 265
Urban League, 292

Vanderbilt University, 245
Vassar College, 37, 240
Vesey, Denmark, 150, 166
Virginia State College, 259, 270

Wages-fund, 40
Walker, David, 78, 150
war, 181, 256
War of 1812, 150
Ward, Samuel, 151
Ward, William Hayes, 8
Ware, Edmund T., 219-23, 225,
    238, 289-92
Washington, Booker T., 5-9, 92,
    179, 183; and Du Bois, 163,
    171-72
Wayland Seminary, 7
Weber, Max, 2
Wells, Nelson, 149
Wendell, Barrett, 33, 41
Wesley, Charles, 266
West Virginia State College, 256
West, Cornel, 3, 75
Western Freedmen's Aid
Commission, 97
Wheatley, Phillis, 77
white supremacy, 160
Whitefield, George, 146
Whitney, Eli, 78
Wilberforce University, 82, 158,
    239, 254-58; administration,
    165, 270, 273, 279; and
    Christianity, 267-69; and
    politics, 264, 268
Wilberforce University Quarterly,
    256
Wilkins, Roy, 3
Williams College, 219
Williams, W. T. B., 130
Willis, Nathaniel P., 223
Wilson Tariff, 39
Wilson, Woodrow, 8
Winsor, Justin, 31, 33
Wood, Fernando, 108
Woodson, Carter G., 236, 243
Worcester Polytechnic, 225
work, 72, 166, 205, 208, 231
working class, 182-83, 196, 204
World War I, 292-93
Worlds of Color, 289
Yale University, 58, 135-36, 154,
    225
Young, Charles, 254
Young, Nathan, 239

Zane, Jonathan, 152

About the Editor

Eugene F. Provenzo Jr. is a professor in the School of Education at the University of Miami. The author of a wide range of books on education, history and cultural studies, he is currently at work on a book that reconstructs the Exhibit of American Negroes at the Paris 1900 International Exposition.